WS2

The Pursuit of Mind

THE PURSUIT OF MIND

EDITED BY
RAYMOND TALLIS AND HOWARD ROBINSON

CARCANET

First published in 1991 by
Carcanet Press Limited
208–212 Corn Exchange Buildings
Manchester M4 3BQ

British Library Cataloguing in Publication Data
The pursuit of mind.
  I. Tallis, Raymond   II. Robinson, Howard
616.8

  ISBN 0 85635 918 1

The publisher acknowledges financial assistance
from the Arts Council of Great Britain

Set in 10/11½ Plantin by Paragon Photoset, Aylesbury
Printed and bound in England by SRP Ltd, Exeter

Contents

List of Contributors

RICHARD P. BENTALL
  Lecturer in Clinical Psychology, University of Liverpool

ANDREW CLARK
  Lecturer, School of Cognitive Sciences,
  University of Sussex

STEPHEN R. F. CLARK
  Professor of Philosophy, University of Liverpool

J. RICHARD HANLEY
  Lecturer in Psychology, University of Liverpool

PAMELA HUBY
  Reader in Philosophy (retired), Honorary Senior Fellow,
  University of Liverpool

RICHARD LATTO
  Head of Department of Psychology, University of Liverpool

HOWARD ROBINSON
  Senior Lecturer in Philosophy, University of Liverpool

JAMES RUSSELL
  Lecturer in Experimental Psychology, University of Cambridge

MARK SACKS
  Lecturer in Philosophy, University of Liverpool

RAYMOND TALLIS
  Professor of Geriatric Medicine, University of Manchester

Preface

Academics in general and philosophers in particular may find themselves bound by conflicting obligations. First, there is the need to maintain a proper professional rigour; secondly, there is the obligation to contribute to a general understanding of the world in which everyone can share. The attempt to be rigorous is likely also to make one technical and hence incomprehensible to the layman. On the other hand trying to excite the interest of a more general audience can reduce intellectual discourse to affected café-talk. This, in the view of many Anglo-Saxon philosophers, characterizes much continental philosophy. More recently there has emerged a brand of philosophizing, widely cultivated by non-philosophers, which combines the worst of both worlds. Post-Saussurean 'theory' has the opacity of some technical philosophy while lacking its rigour. Its popularity gives support to Bertrand Russell's complaint that the philosophers who have the greatest influence on non-philosophers have been, in general, bad philosophers.

Nevertheless, some subjects are important in a way that demands a general audience. This is plainly true of certain problems in ethics, but not only of these. There are few issues in which the general reader has a more legitimate interest than the debate on the nature of the human mind. It reaches right to the heart of everyone's sense of self-understanding and self-image. It is also currently an area of intense academic activity. The philosophy of mind is replacing the philosophy of language as the central concern of professional philosophers. The various attempts to develop artificial intelligence and to create computers that may behave like 'stand-alone minds' have brought issues in the philosophy of mind to the fore in cognitive psychology. Advances in brain science have encouraged what has been called the 'neurophilosophical' approach to mind. Although philosophy, computer science, psychology and neurology may all in their different ways be highly technical, professionals working within them are now increasingly obliged to communicate across disciplinary boundaries, and such interdisciplinary discussion is at least half-way towards being accessible to a non-professional audience.

The essays in this volume exemplify a variety of approaches to the mind. The authors come from quite disparate disciplines and they have widely differing – and often conflicting – philosophical orientations. The work of clinical and experimental psychologists is represented alongside that of the cognitive scientist and the pure philosopher. Some of the contributors are firmly materialist, whilst others are either sceptical about, or determinedly reject, the materialist reduction of the mind to a function of the body or the brain. All are in agreement that various disciplines can throw light on the nature of the mind and that the mutual sympathy and understanding which interdisciplinary work requires forces us to express ourselves in ways which can be understood by readers outside of our specialities. This is a lesson that most of our contributors have learned through being, at some time, members of a particular interdisciplinary group based in the University of Liverpool, which has been meeting regularly for several years and discussing papers rather like those in this volume.

These essays present a wide, synoptic view of the mind and of approaches to studying it, and it should be valuable reading for anyone interested in the mind. Olaf Stapledon, in his philosophical novel *First and Last Men* claimed that, by the end of time, the mind-body problem would be the only philosophical problem still unsolved. It would be rash, therefore, to pretend that those who set out in *the pursuit of mind* are likely to catch it. We believe, however, that with this volume they should be well-equipped for the chase.

Raymond Tallis
Howard Robinson

1

The Flight From Mind

HOWARD ROBINSON

There is an account of the mind-body problem which could, with some oversimplification, be described as the currently fashionable one. According to this account, the mind-body distinction as we know it was invented by Descartes. He it was who conceived the idea of identifying mind with consciousness and of claiming that consciousness and its contents are radically different sorts of things from bodies and their properties. The mind is a sort of arena in which private objects are viewed: all our experience is, ultimately, confined to this arena. Descartes, so the story goes, reached this conception because, unlike his predecessors, the Aristotelians, he was obsessed by epistemological questions – that is, questions about what we can know and how we can know it. He thought that the only things of which we could be really certain were things of which we were directly aware, that is, things in our own minds. The empiricists, although they may not have taken up Descartes' idea that the mind is an immaterial substance, followed him in treating the contents of mind as objects private and internal to the individual and different from physical objects.

This conception of the mind is now almost universally regarded as disastrously wrong, for two reasons: first, because it creates a dualism of mind and body and second, because it is held to create insuperable sceptical problems. The dualism is deemed disastrous because it prevents us from having a unified conception of the world built around the natural sciences, and because it leaves the relationship between the mental and the physical an insoluble mystery. The scepticism follows because if we are confined in experience to the contents of our own minds alone, it would seem to be impossible that we should ever come to know anything about – or even come intelligibly to think about – things outside our own minds. The programme of many modern philosophers, therefore, has been to develop a conception of man and his mind which either disposes of or downgrades the inner, private arena, making the function of mind essentially a part of the public and physical world. Once this is achieved – and this, it is held, can be done by some sort of physicalist theory of mind with strong behaviourist elements – then most of the insoluble problems of early modern philosophy disappear.

I want to defend a radically different picture, which takes a much broader historical perspective. This alternative picture involves denying that there is a coherent materialist alternative to the Cartesian 'private theatre' view of the mind; but it also involves placing the attack on the Cartesian picture in a wider context. From the point of view of those who have a high doctrine of the mind, the Cartesian developments of the seventeenth century were ambiguous. The concentration on the subjective nature of experience made clear the logical privacy, and hence non-physicality, of sense experience in a way in which it was never made clear within the classical and scholastic traditions. The earlier traditions had focused not on experience as the key element in mind, but on intellect and thought; it was this that made mind special and different from anything physical. As I shall explain in the next section, this earlier privileging of intellect was intimately connected with resistance to nominalism, and, in the seventeenth century nominalism triumphed. The emphasis on the mentality and immateriality of sense experience was associated with the denial that there was anything special about intellect. Even whilst developing the modern im-materialist notion of consciousness, the eighteenth-century empiricists and others were attacking the dignity of intellect and assimilating it to sensory activity by treating thoughts as mere images. As well as being a defence of mind, therefore, the early modern philosophy, through its nominalism, was also an attack on it. And, in certain important respects, the general form of this attack is preserved in contemporary physicalist theories. Like the physicalist attacks on the privacy of subjective experience, these attacks on intellect are self-defeating, in that they end up denying the very realities they are trying to explain. What I hope to show is that the attacks on the reality and irreducibility of both subjective experience and thought leave one with no contentful conception of the world. The flight from mind in respect either of its intellectual or sensational aspects would be disastrous, but the cur-rently fashionable flight from both leaves us with no world at all.

II

In the *Phaedo*, Socrates praises Anaxagoras for saying that the world must be explained by reference to mind, and then criticizes him for not acting on the principle that he recommends. Most pre-Socratic philosophy had been a form of primitive natural science, explaining everything in terms of the physical elements. By contrast, the metaphysical question of what the preconditions are for the world's being accessible to thought was uppermost for Plato and Aristotle. This is explained via the role of *form* in the world.

The important thing about form, in either the Platonic or

Aristotelian senses, is that forms are the sort of things that can be thought, or apprehended intellectually. There is, in common sense, something close to a paradox which generates the problem of universals. This problem dominated philosophy from Plato until the seventeenth century. On the one hand, it is natural to think of the world outside mind as consisting solely of particulars: the only things that could be general would be ideas. But if ideas are to fit the world there must be something which answers to that generality. According to Plato, that generality is found in a pure way in the Forms, and derivatively in particular physical objects because they participate imperfectly in the Forms. For Aristotle, forms are in objects and are themselves particular, though they are by their nature potentially universal, becoming actually so when they are apprehended by the intellect.

The disturbing thought that motivates both theories is that, if the world is to be intelligible, it must be mind-like, in the sense that generality – the feature of thought, concepts and meanings – must in some way, run through the world itself. A world that was, *per impossibile*, purely particular, in the sense of not allowing forms or universals to be an essential component or determinant of it, would have nothing which intellect could grasp. The reason for this is straightforward. Human thought is something essentially expressible in language, and language is possible only if there are predicates as well as names. But predicates are essentially general. Consider the sentence 'John is tall'. For this sentence to express something, 'John' must refer to a unique individual, but 'tall' must express a feature that is general, that is, that many different things might possess. If this were not so, and all statements simply joined names that referred to individuals, nothing would be said *about* those individuals. But if a statement such as 'John is tall' is to be true, then the predicate 'is tall' must latch on to the world, just as 'John' does. So there has to be something in the world answering to the general predicate, just as there is something answering to the name. This thought casts the world in a profoundly different light from common sense in its materialistic moment; and much of metaphysics can be seen as a response to it.

Aristotle was the first to try to naturalize the veins of generality that must structure any intelligible world, by saying that forms in things were individuals, not universals. The controversy surrounding the interpretation of Aristotle's conception of form is unending, but, on all interpretations, his objective is to give forms as great an affinity with particulars as is possible, consistent with their retaining a sort of generality which is, so to speak, released in the intellect when they are thought. Something that was not form, but was only matter, could not become general in this way and could not answer to the generality of the concepts with which we think. The naturalistic instinct has been to claim that mind somehow creates generality in a sense stronger than that which Aristotle allows; it does not merely release generality from its potential state in matter, but fabricates it. The mind puts together certain things and deems them to be of the same kind. The medium in which the mind fabricates generality is language. This vision lies behind nominalism, which claims that it is the mind's capacity for creating general *words* that creates the illusion of generality in the world itself.

But the problem of generality has two locations. The first, about which I have mainly been talking so far, is the generality, or potential for generality, of things in the world. The reductive instinct is to explain this by reference to the generalizing capacity of the mind. This leaves generality as a real capacity of the mind. Philosophers have often been content to assign to the mind features that they are unwilling to ascribe to the physical world. Most empiricists, for example, have been prepared to do this with secondary qualities, such as colours, sounds and smells, which, they believe, science could not allow to the external world. In so doing, they claim that it is not just secondary qualities that are confined to the mind, but, with them, the whole vivid force of the world-as-we-perceive-it, – what some philosophers call the *manifest image* of the world – which is intrinsically bound up with the secondary qualities. David Hume went further, transferring causal power from the world of objects to the mind, making of it a tendency of the mind to pass from the thing we call 'the cause' to the one we call 'the effect'.

But someone committed to a thorough-going naturalism is no more prepared to allow to the mind mysterious properties than he is prepared to allow them to matter: for the thorough-going naturalist, after all, mind is no more than a manifestation of matter. The nominalist impulse, therefore, which originates from the attempt to make generality in the world a creation of mind – thus allowing the extra-mental world to consist only of particulars – eventually leads to trying to explain the powers of the mind entirely in terms of the work of particulars. This move from nominalism about the extra-mental to nominalism about mental acts can be seen in the development from Descartes to Locke and Berkeley, or, perhaps, in the contrast between such continental rationalists as Descartes, Malebranche and Leibnitz on the one hand, and British philosophers from Bacon and Hobbes on the other. Descartes believed firmly that universals were formed in the mind and that ideas possessed 'objective' and 'formal' reality; that is, that it was an irreducible feature of ideas that they were able to be *about* a class of objects.

Descartes is true to his radical dualism: everything that is a mark of mind is withdrawn into the mind, leaving the external world in atomistic darkness. But mind remains truly special. The materialist Hobbes, by contrast, denies that universality is really found even in the mind:

> This word *universal* is never the name of anything existent in nature, *nor of any idea or phantasm found in the mind* [my italics], but always the name of some word or name; so that when a *living creature, a stone, a spirit*, or any other thing, is said to be *universal*, it is not to be understood that any man, stone etc., ever was or can be universal, but only that the words, living creature, stone, etc., are *universal names*, that is, names common to many things; and *the conceptions answering them in the mind are the images and phantasms of several living creatures or other things.* (*Concerning Body*, Molesworth's *English Works of Thomas Hobbes*, vol. 1, p. 74; my italics)

But, by a tragic irony, it is not a materialist who most influentially encapsulated nominalism about the mind; it was the idealist Bishop Berkeley. Hume described Berkeley's attack on abstract ideas as 'the most important development of late in the republic of letters'. The purport of that attack was to prove that generality could never be an intrinsic property of a mental content. Berkeley's reason for thinking this was that he believed mental contents to be mental images, and there cannot be a general image. It never seemed to occur to him that a general idea might be an entirely different sort of thing from an image.

Ideas, according to Berkeley, are particulars whose significance is explained by saying that they *stand for* the things they represent. This naturally prompts the question what it is for one purely particular object to *stand for* another. Specifiedly general objects, such as forms and universals, by their very nature stand for the many things which are instances of them: a single particular may be in a variety of relations – most obviously causal, spatial or temporal – to others, but the nature of a 'standing for' relation is obscure. At first sight this might not seem to be a serious problem; one thing stands for others if it is *used* or *taken as representing* them. But this only restates the problem. *Using* or *taking as representing* is a mental act, and it presupposes that the mind has the power of seeing generality in things, by seeing the class (or form) in the particular. It is exactly this power that the nominalist is trying to analyse and explain. If one is to avoid this simple circularity, then

one must explain *standing for* in terms of some natural relation
between particulars.

Berkeley's theory gave rise to the development of modern *externalist*
theories of mental content. By 'externalist' in this context I mean any
theory which denies that a mental episode has any meaning-content
intrinsically, and affirms that its content consists in some external
relation to other things. The first expression of this was associationist
psychology. At its simplest, associationism is the theory that a mental
content has the meaning it does because of the things that tend to
follow, or precede, it into the mind. So the word 'red' means red
because thought of the word tends to be succeeded by a mental image
of the colour, or *vice versa*. This can be expressed in Hume's terms
of the *tendency of the mind to pass* from one to the other, but one
must be careful how one interprets such a tendency. It is tempting
to think of it as a *felt* tendency, so that one is somehow aware of
where the mind is going. This will not do, for it is no different from
saying that when one experiences 'red' one thinks or conceives of
the colour, whereas the point of the theory was to explain what such
thinking, or conceiving, is. It is similarly tempting to think of the
colour image as hovering in the background, somehow anticipated
by the mind; but this is a metaphor, for the image either is or is
not in consciousness. And, contrary to Hume's contention, being
very dimly in consciousness is not the same as being thought of.
The tendency of the mind to move from one thing to another has
to consist in the straightforward fact that one thing usually follows,
or is caused by, the other; the tendency or association cannot be
thought of as some *experienced* feature of the situation without
reviving the original situation of having an unanalysed conception
of the mind's ability to reach out and apprehend things. So the
meaning of a sign consists in the bare fact that it stands in an
external causal relation to that which we say it signifies. From the
point of view of the experiencing subject, the meaningfulness is not
something of which he is conscious; all he experiences is, first the
word 'red', then a mental image: there is nothing that could count
as his internally and introspectably associating them which does not
reintroduce the mysterious generality of thought. It does not help the
associationist to press the concept of resemblance to his aid. It might
seem that it would, because it might seem very natural to think that
one red thing or image might be taken as standing for red things in
general because of its natural resemblance to the other members of
the class, this constituting the most fundamental sort of association.
But resemblance cannot explain how a thinker could experience one
object as standing for another; for how could the fact that a particular

datum is similar to other things mean anything to a thinker unless he experienced it *as* being like many others – that is, unless he grasped it, not just as a particular but *as* an instance of a kind? But this is the very ability for which we are trying to account.

If we are to abide by a pure nominalism or particularism, we are forced into externalism, and this is vicious. It is vicious because, as I have just argued, the external relation that constitutes the meaning of the mental content is not something that the subject himself can apprehend: it can only be constructed from a third-person perspective. The reality of meaning therefore, would only be accessible to some idealized third person who was able to observe the relation between the particulars. But there never could be such an observer – at least not if his thought-processes were to be analysed in the same way as ours – because his thoughts about the relations of the particulars would themselves be just a succession of particulars whose relations, which give them meaning, were not directly accessible to him.

Associationism is long dead as a theory of thought, but externalism remains as a feature of most of its naturalistic successors, because, by virtue of their naturalism, they can find no space for intrinsic generality of mental contents. The problem for the associationalist is exactly mirrored in those theories of thought and mind inspired by computers and artificial intelligence. The human mind – which, from this viewpoint, is the brain – is said to work on the same plan as a computer, with operations being carried out on physical symbols. The question is, 'what gives these symbols meaning?' The answer is that, as with associationism, their meaning comes from their relations to things external to themselves. Their relations to one another determine the syntax (that is, the grammar) of the language they constitute, and their causal relations to the external world determine their semantics (that is, what they are about or refer to). These causal relations are essential to what they mean: without semantics a language is an uninterpreted formal language. But if we think of the conscious subject as located within, or identical to, the brain, then external relations are beyond his gaze. John Searle has compared the computational view of mind to an Englishman who has no understanding of Chinese processing Chinese symbols according to rules which correspond to the grammar of Chinese: what he deals with may be meaningful Chinese sentences, but he is none the wiser. Only an idealized observer could see both the inner processing *and* the causal relations of the symbols to outside objects that give them meaning: no one could actually be that idealized observer, because each observer is confined to operating on the symbols that are within his computational machinery, and this excludes their external causal relations.

There is a tendency of protagonists of the computational theory of mind to boast that they are restoring the Aristotelian emphasis on cognition and thought, and unseating Descartes' modernist emphasis on consciousness. One such protagonist has recently gone so far as to claim that Aristotle's *phantasmata* – the mental images that are involved in most or all mental activities – are identical with the symbols on which computational procedures are carried out. This approach sees classical and ultra-modern theories as constituting a sound tradition from which the Cartesian emphasis on consciousness constitutes an unfortunate aberration. I have tried to sketch in outline why I think this to be wrong. Far from being of a piece with classical theories, computational theories share with early modern ones the nominalism that made them oblivious of what was important in the classical tradition: namely the irreducibility of thought and universals.

III

The problem that consciousness sets for the materialist is well known. Imagine a scientist in the distant future who knows everything about the mechanism and neurology of vision, but who is blind from birth. That there is something he does not know is shown by the fact that if he were to gain his sight, he would come to know something that he previously had not known. This might be characterized as 'what it is like to see' or 'what things look like' or, most especially, 'what colours are like' (that is, what they look like – there is no difference in their case). No amount of unsighted knowledge of neuronal activity or light wave-lengths could amount to this.

The same point can be made in a slightly different way. Call our blind super-scientist 'BS' and an ordinary sighted subject 'V'. BS is supposed to have complete scientific knowledge of V and his physical environment when V sees: yet BS does not know what it is like for V to see, what colours look like, etcetera. As BS knows everything relevant about the physical state of affairs, the things that he does not know about are not physical states of affairs. Since these states of affairs are of the essence of human perceptual consciousness and, therefore, of the human mind, it must follow that there are non-physical states of affairs essential to the human mind. So a materialist theory of the mind is false.

The most primitive physicalist response to this argument is to deny the claim that there is anything about the mind that BS does not know. All that BS lacks is an ability to respond directly to stimuli of certain sorts: V knows no more than BS, he can simply do something BS cannot. BS is like a man who knows all about swimming, even to the point of being able to train the Olympic team, but who cannot swim himself, and V is the man with the normal talent for swimming. I think that it would be true to say that, nowadays, most materialists want to avoid theories that are as nakedly behaviouristic as this, and want to accommodate the common-sense intuition that something inner and introspectible is missing in the blind or deaf, for example, in addition to their lost capacity to respond. On the other hand, materialists seem to be prevented by their materialism from allowing that there is any relevant fact that BS does not know. The way that most materialists try to reconcile their flight from behaviourism with their materialist world picture is to say that when V sees something, and BS observes V's brain, BS knows everything about V's mental states that V himself knows, but that he *knows about it in a different way*. It is this *difference of way* which constitutes the difference of 'feel' in their experience.

This reply sounds very plausible, until one reflects on it; and then a serious difficulty emerges. For a physicalist, a mode of access is just a physical process, so any mode of access V enjoys should, if physicalism be true, be available to BS. Differentiating modes of access seems relevant only because of the covert assumption that different ways of knowing *feel* different - that is, what it is like to have those experiences is different. But this brings us back to the initial problem, which was precisely to explain how materialism could accommodate such a 'feel'. We cannot, therefore, leave it as an irreducible fact about different physical processes that they 'feel' different.

In fact, the 'mode of access' argument is ambiguous. It might be interpreted as saying that V has a mode of access to his own brain different from any modes of access to V's brain available to BS; or that V has a different mode of access to the external world, and that this constitutes the difference between him and BS. It is impossible to deny that V has a different mode of access to the external world from BS, for V can see and BS cannot. But the question is how this constitutes a subjective difference. One can then choose to say either that it constitutes the difference *by virtue of* having a particular internal 'feel' associated with it, or that it is itself the difference, *simpliciter*. The former simply reinstates the problem of the inner 'feel'. Within the 'mode of knowledge' framework, the 'feel' will be explained by the special mode of access to one's own brain. That this will not do is what I have just argued. The second response, that the difference consists solely and simply in a mode of knowledge of the external world, without invoking any internal and introspectible 'feel', requires one to explain perceptual experiences with different modes of access without reference to a subjective component. As far as I can see, the only way to do this is to adopt a behaviouristic approach to this knowledge and characterize it as an ability to discriminate visual objects. To take this road is to resort to what I earlier described as the 'most primitive physicalist response' to the problem, which involves denying that there is anything about the nature of experience that BS does not know.

Michael Tye, in his recent book *The Metaphysics of Mind* (Cambridge, 1989), has a way of dealing with the difficulty which, if it worked, would solve the materialist's problem. He combines the view that *what it is like to see, for example colour* is something BS would come to know on gaining his sight, with the view that *what it is like to see, for example, colour* is not a further *fact* in addition to the physical facts about the brain (p. 146f). So it is something further, without being a further *fact*. At first sight this looks like an uninteresting stipulation about how to use the word 'fact' – uninteresting because the anti-materialist could as well state his case using some such term as 'feature' or 'aspect', and it is difficult to see how, once having allowed that there is something called 'what it is like to see' which one only learns by seeing, one could refuse to describe this as a feature or aspect of mental life. (Tye does compare this learning to learning to balance a pencil on your nose, but if that comparison is made to do any work, Tye's theory will simply be a behaviouristic one, and he usually seems to want it to be more than this.) Tye, however, does have an argument for his conclusion that what is extra is not 'really' something extra. I think the argument is that if we call the nature of the experience 'R', and if we concede the materialist claim that R is a brain state, then in knowing the brain state the blind scientist knows R, though not what R is like. Because BS knows all the facts about the brain state, and the experience just *is* the brain state, then *what the experience is like* must be something other than a fact about the experience.

The argument transposes, however. Since merely knowing the brain state does not reveal what the experience is like, and since *what the experience is like*, if it is a reality at all (which Tye does not dispute), must be a fact about the experience (or a feature or aspect of the experience, which will do just as well), it follows that the experience is not a brain state.

There is one well-known materialist account of different modes of knowledge that might seem to be useful here in preserving the 'mode of knowledge' approach against the need for the more drastic behaviouristic alternative. Physicalists of the 1950s and 1960s were worried by the following problem. Experiences, they argued, are identical with brain states; but when someone is conscious of his experiences he is not conscious of his brain as such: it takes modern science to tell us that consciousness is a state of the brain. They therefore concluded that in consciousness itself we are aware of the brain *topic-neutrally*; that is, not *as* the brain, but in some way that is neutral about the nature of the object of our consciousness. Thus, one might characterize one's grasp on the experience of seeming to see a red object as *something is going on in me (I don't know what it is) which is like what goes on when a red object is acting on my eyes;* or . . . *like what goes on in me to make me behave in a red-object-appropriate way.* It takes science to come along and tell us that *what is going on* under these circumstances is a brain process, let alone to tell us which brain process it is. All consciousness does in its own right is to tell us that it is *something* internal which fulfils a certain role.

But even if treating our awareness of our own mental states as topic-neutral plausibly explains why we are not aware of our brains as such when we are aware of our mental states, it does not explain why knowing fully about the brain does not include knowledge of the nature of experience. Topic-neutral knowledge is weaker than, and hence is entailed by, full knowledge, though it does not entail it. So, if the blind scientist BS knows that V is in brain state B and that B is the state usually brought about by experience of a red object, then he knows that V is in *some state or other* of the sort usually brought about by red objects. So, if he abstracts from his knowledge of what the brain state actually is, he can form the same conception of experience as that had by the subject of the experience. In brief, topic neutrality was invoked to explain why, within the materialist scheme, consciousness of our mental states is not sufficient for knowledge of them *as* brain states: what it cannot do is explain why knowledge of brain states is not sufficient for knowledge of their nature as conscious states.

A rather similar, and equally mistaken, line of thought which might appeal is as follows. It might be thought that the subject's apprehension of his own brain is more *immediate* and more *holistic* than any external knowledge, however complete, and that this explains the experiential difference between the two kinds of knowledge. The scientist has essentially separate pieces of information, whereas the subject has a sort of *Gestalt*.

Once again, this explanation shows a failure to grasp the radicalness of the physicalist perspective. A *Gestalt* is a mode of perception of a group of objects – say of the dots in a printed picture – so that they are seen as one thing. It would make no sense to say that the dots in the picture had a *Gestalt* of themselves, but to apply this model to the brain and experience would be just like that; for, if the experience just *is* a state of the brain, then there is no way in which the character of the experience can be explained as the result of *some perspective on* the brain. Nor, more abstractedly, could it be the result of a perspective on the informational content of the brain; for, in either case, the perspective would have to be the occurrence of some further brain or informational state and to both of these the scientist has complete access, and the problem reoccurs.

If what I said above is correct, failure of the 'mode of access' argument forces the materialist to deny that BS lacks any knowledge and to adopt a behaviourist theory.

When a behaviourist approach is employed, it is not applied only to perception, but to all cognitive states. Remembering that philosophers of the seventeenth and eighteenth century had already assimilated thought to perception, this is not surprising. But this historical reason is not the only one, for, if the project is to develop a materialist theory of the mind in general, thought requires a materialist analysis as much as perception. It is in its form as a general theory of cognition that the behaviouristic approach is most clearly refutable, but from the general refutation we can refute its application to perception.

The behaviourist theory of knowledge says that for someone, S, to know or believe that some proposition p is true is for S to be disposed to *behave* in some way which is supposed to be appropriate to the world's being as p says. The problem with any general behaviouristic account of knowledge is that it is impossible to make sense of any behavioural description without being able to make sense independently of statements about how the world is. So, for example, it is impossible to make sense of a statement that S is disposed to behave in a certain way unless one already understands the concepts required to understand the content of the relevant behaviour. As this content will involve the movement of bodies through space and time in relation to other bodies, an understanding of 'behaviour' presupposes a general grasp on the layout and nature of the physical world. The experimental context in which the behavioural understanding of cognition developed involved such a presupposition: we understand the rat's or the pigeon's behavioural repertoire because we see it in the context of a physical layout that we take as given. If I had no grasp on the shape of the maze, that is, at least its basic spatial properties, I could not understand any ascription of behaviour to the rat. This leads to problems when I try to conceive of my own knowing, believing or thinking in behaviourist terms. I cannot think of my own knowledge of the physical world in terms of my dispositions to behave, but only as my dispositions, *construed as operating in the world of which I conceive without reference to my dispositions*. I cannot understand my conception of the world in terms of, or reduce it to, some account of my dispositions, as it seems plausible one might for the rat's (or any third person's) conception of the world and its dispositions. In my case at least, therefore, thought, belief or knowledge concerning the world cannot be analysed simply in terms of dispositions to behave.

There are two responses that defenders of the behavioural approach might make to this argument. First, an objector might try to press the fashionable distaste for the first-person perspective and say that the fact that I cannot apply the theory to myself shows nothing except that one should not approach the philosophy of mind via the first person. A philosophical theory is essentially a reflection on a practice, and the first-person perspective expresses engagement in the practice: to apply the theory first-personally is to confuse levels.

This is a spurious argument. A philosophical account gives the necessary and sufficient conditions (at least in outline form) for the application of a concept, and it should, therefore, apply in principle to anything that is a case of that concept. If it really is the case that all I am doing when I have beliefs about the world is to have dispositions to behave, then it ought to make sense for me to think of my believing in those terms. But no such general reduction can be carried out. There cannot be a genuine perspective from which a true analysis does not apply.

The behaviourist's second line of defence is to distinguish between knowing and what is known, and say that the behavioural reduction applies only to the former. So when S knows that p, it is his *knowing* that is his disposition, not *what he knows*. This line of defence is no better than the first. The dispositional analysis is meant to cover the whole of the relevant mental state, not just part of it, and that mental state must include its content, otherwise *what is thought* will not be the content of the psychological act of my thinking. There is no way that the content of my thought can both be something that the subject really thinks, apprehends or is conscious of, and yet fall outside the scope of an analysis of the act of thinking.

All behaviouristic theories of cognition are viciously third-personal, where that expression signifies, first, that they cannot be applied to the first-person perspective and, second that our ability to apply them to the third person really rests on our bringing to bear first-person knowledge: as with rats in mazes, where *my* plain and unreduced apprehension of the rat's environment enables me to see *its* grasp of that environment in terms of its behaviour within it.

Our general topic of discussion is perceptual consciousness and the problem that it constitutes for physicalism. In showing that cognition as a whole cannot be treated behaviouristically, I have not thereby shown that a behaviouristic treatment of sense-experience is false. So perhaps my overkill misses the target: perhaps the behaviourist analysis of perception is sound, even though a general behaviourism is not, and what BS lacks is not knowledge of the nature of certain mental states, but only the ability to respond spontaneously to visual stimuli, that is, to respond as a result of actually seeing them. Reflection on the nature of the argument against behaviourism in general, however, reveals that the argument refutes the behaviourist treatment of perception in particular. That argument showed that knowledge of the external world cannot be reduced to behavioural dispositions, for the very idea of a disposition functions only in the context of an unreduced grasp on the physical world. But there is nowhere else that we might get our conception of the physical world from, other than perception. It is the content specifically of sense-perception that must be taken non-reductively, if the contrast required by our concept of disposition is to be maintained.

Some philosophers might suspect that I have not considered the behaviouristic theories in their most sophisticated form. Would it not make a difference if one identified experience, not with some disposition to overt behaviour, but with the 'behaviour' of the brain as it 'discriminates' the various sorts of stimuli within the nervous system? This is a version of the supposedly *post*-behaviourist theory called 'functionalism', which treats mental states as responding to other internal and mental states as well as to external stimuli.

The first thing to notice about functionalism is that it does not fare any better than behaviourism in providing an account of what it is that V knows and BS does not, for BS could know all about V's functional or covertly behavioural states; so there is no lack of knowledge that his deficit could consist in. It can reside only in his inability to do certain things spontaneously. The situation would be different from this only if the internal discriminations carried with them some experiential 'feel' that was not to be identified with some physical process of which BS could know. But this is just what the physicalist cannot allow. The second and more important point is that the general argument against behaviouristic theories does take in functionalism and is not merely directed against traditional behaviourism: it works against any theory that analyses one's conception of the world simply in terms of the way one *functions* – that is, *behaves* – in the world. The addition of internal discriminations within the nervous system adds nothing relevant to this, unless the internal discriminations really possessed semantic properties, so that they somehow contained in themselves a real description of the world. But it is accepted by physicalists of all kinds that the *meaning* or *semantic value* of internal states must be analysed in terms of their causal relations to stimulus and response, just as it is for the behaviourist's dispositions, and is not something they possess in their own right, or of themselves.

IV

I have considered the flight from mind in two major aspects: first in the flight from the generality of form and universality, both in the world and thought; second, in the flight from consciousness. There has not been space to say much about the flight from generality in the world outside mind, but I have tried to show how the attempts to flee generality within the mind and to abandon or reduce consciousness must both fail. I promised at the outset, however, to show that reductive treatment of these features of the mind leads to an incoherent conception of the world, quite independently of the inadequacies of the reductions themselves: that is, even if the reduction of consciousness and thought were not independently flawed, the picture of the world that emerges is incoherent.

The physicist's picture of the world is extremely formal. I mean by this not merely that it can be represented mathematically, but that, such is its concern with the *quantative* aspects of reality that it consigns all the *qualitative content* in our conception of the world to the realm of conscious experience. Science tells us about the structural and relational properties of objects, while consciousness tells us what they are *qualitatively like*. This qualitativeness – the 'manifest image of the world' – is irreducibly connected with what experience is subjectively like, and it is part of what is lost if consciousness is analysed away or otherwise abandoned. It is not surprising, therefore, to observe a tendency amongst materialists to treat *all* properties as if they were purely relational.

The historical progression that has led to this can, at the price of great oversimplification, be seen as follows. Aristotelian physics was not essentially mathematical. The physical world is composed of the elements, earth, fire, air and water which are characterized by the qualities hotness, coldness, dryness and wetness. These qualities are perceptible but the nature of their interactions is never talked of as if they could be quantified. In contrast, the atomistic physics which was revived in the seventeenth century concentrated on quantifiable properties. Secondary qualities, such as colour and hardness, were confined to the senses, and were marginalized. When this picture was fully developed, even space was represented not as being qualitatively the way it is in vision, but as a structural isomorph of visual and tactile space. By this point, every knowable quality was confined to the mind. But the modern behaviourist and functionalist analyses of mind treat mental states as mere powers to produce behaviour: that is, they abolish the intrinsic qualitative content of mental states, replacing it by causal, hence relational, properties. We have then reached the absurd position that nothing in the world possesses a knowable intrinsic or qualitative nature, for all properties are essentially relational. This predicament arises out of the demise of consciousness, when only consciousness, understood in a traditional way, can bring us face to face with, and hence give us any grasp on, the qualitative, as opposed to relational, properties.

So the flight from consciousness is the flight from any grasp on the intrinsic nature of any properties – not merely, as with Russell, of properties in the external world, but also of the features in our experience. This is not merely a very bare conception of the world, but argument supports intuition in pronouncing it an incoherent one. It reduces language to an uninterpreted formal system. All we know about As, for example, is that they have relation to R to Bs, relation R' to Cs, relation R'' to Ds, etc; and similarly for our understanding of Bs, Cs and Ds, and the variety of Rs. What any of these things is like in itself, even the qualitative nature of the spatial medium of the relations, remains unknown. It is not surprising that reductive treatment of consciousness should have this effect. In consciousness alone is it possible to confront at least some empirical properties and apprehend them directly, and if consciousness is analysed in terms of some purely non-mental notion this grasp is lost; just as, in the analysis of thought, if the irreducible generality of thought is analysed away, our ability to think and refer is wished away with it.

V

If, as I have argued, thought and consciousness irreducibly escape the net of physicalist interpretation, and if, as I have suggested, the external world must possess the mind-like property of generality if it is to be conceivable, then we can see that Socrates' assertion in the *Phaedo*, that the world must be explained by reference to mind, was essentially correct. In metaphysics, the understanding of everything begins with mind, not with natural science, and modern philosophy's flight from mind is a flight from reality.

Bibliography

Berkeley's attack on abstract ideas is to be found in the introduction to his *Principles of Human Knowledge*, of which there are many editions. The best discussion of the problem of universals is D. A. Armstrong, *A Theory of Universals*, vol. I (Cambridge University Press, 1978). The best statement of materialism is also by Armstrong, *A Materialist Theory of the Mind* (London: Routledge & Kegan Paul, 1968). A lucid introduction to contemporary theories of mind – mainly materialist – is P. M. Churchland, *Matter and Consciousness* (Cambridge University Press, 2nd edn, 1988). There is an attack on a variety of materialist positions in Howard Robinson, *Matter and Sense* (Cambridge University Press, 1982).

2

'In the Beginning Was the Deed': Mental Development and the Philosophy of Mind

JAMES RUSSELL

> *'Tis writ, 'In the beginning was the Word.'*
> *I pause, to wonder what is here inferred.*
> *The Word I cannot set supremely high:*
> *A new translation I will try.*
> *I read, if by the spirit I am taught,*
> *This sense: 'In the beginning was the Thought.'*
> *This opening I need to weigh again,*
> *Or sense may suffer from a hasty pen.*
> *Does Thought create, and work, and rule the hour?*
> *'Twere best: 'In the beginning was the Power.'*
> *Yet, while the pen is urged with willing fingers,*
> *A sense of doubt and hesitancy lingers.*
> *The spirit comes to guide me in my need,*
> *I write, 'In the beginning was the Deed.'*

> Goethe, *Faust*
> I, 1224–37
> (tr. Philip Wayne)

It would seem that, for the foreseeable future at least, we are stuck with the 'mind-body problem'. How anything physical – a brain – should be able to support a mental life is beyond the reach not only of our science but of our imagination. There is, of course, a school of thought which says that a bit of straight thinking, a kind of conceptual analysis-cum-psychotherapy, will sweep this puzzlement away. I do not take this view, but I do think that there are certain deep assumptions about how the mind-body problem should be addressed which increase its difficulty. These two assumptions are: that our main questions should be about how *individual* mental states relate to *individual* neural events; and that we should view the mind primarily as something which *represents* reality. I want to look at the consequences of replacing these assumptions by two others: that we should concentrate on how mind might *develop* out of matter; and that we should view the mind primarily as something which enables *action*.

My first task will be to say why the focus upon mental representation has muddied the waters. This will lead on to a discussion of an action-based theory of mentality, the theory developed by the Swiss developmental psychologist and philosopher Jean Piaget, and then to some discussion of mental development itself. By the end of it all the mind-body problem will loom large – but this *may* be because we are now a little closer to it.

Thinking and representing: the representational theory of mind

It would seem to be a truism that the mind is a representing device. What else *could* it be? Evolution must surely have seen to it that a good proportion of our thoughts are true of the world, and so in some simple sense the mind must perform computations which record the world and direct our behaviour appropriately. This does not mean that the mind just responds to information in the way in which a thermostat, for instance, transduces information about temperature and performs switching operations. We act upon reality as we represent it to ourselves, not as it physically is. Thus, Oedipus married Jocasta and knew he did; he also married his mother and did not know he did. His representation of Jocasta was, as are all representations, incomplete; and his behaviour was driven by this representation of the woman not by some physical fact about the world. This is one of the things that philosophers mean when they say that our mental representations are 'opaque': thoughts are (necessarily partial) representations of reality and therefore we can have one thought about a referent without having any access to another ('lover'/'mother'). Considerations such as these would seem to lead inevitably towards what is often called a 'representational theory of the mind'.

So what can we say about these 'representations'? Doesn't the term suggest something like 'mental pictures'? Much of our thinking would seem to have a more-or-less pictorial character, after all. There are, though, a host of reasons for resisting any kind of equation between mental representations and mental pictures; and all of these derive from one fundamental reason. Any mental picture will require interpretation, and this interpretation will be another mental operation, which, on the view that thinking is having mental pictures, will be another picture, which itself will require interpretation, and so on and so on. This may look like an easy knock-down argument against a silly theory which nobody has ever seriously held: but what is true of mental pictures would seem to be true of *any* kind of mental representing process which encodes sensations in some determinate form. In other words, the argument works equally against the view that we think in a kind of mental language, that mental sentences rather than mental pictures are the stuff of thought. Sentences and words also require interpretation – indeed they would seem to require this more obviously than pictures – and so we're back on the circle of infinite regress.

This was the kind of dilemma which the American philosopher Jerry Fodor faced up to in his important book *The Language of Thought*. Very roughly, Fodor argued that this kind of blanket objection to representational theories of mind does not work against the mental-sentence kind of theory for the simple reason that we know just what it would be like for a system to work on the mental-sentence principle. Digital computers work on this principle. Computers have a machine-code into which instructions on the program are translated, a code which is a kind of computational 'bottom line' – a language that does not require a further interpretive step because it comes complete with its own interpretation. It drives the machine; with the 'interpretation' being the action, or output, of the machine. We can have, then, an analogy between the natural languages that we think in (English, Swahili . . .) and the programming language, on the one hand, and the machine code and our 'language of thought', on the other hand. So long as we adopt a broadly 'functionalist' philosophy of mind – in which mental states are defined in terms of their causal relations to sensory inputs, motor outputs and to one another – this 'computational theory of the mind' is a very satisfying general account of the mind-body relationship. It implies, of course, that as long as they have the right kind of causal relations, other machines, apart from brains, can possess mentality; and it also implies that the study of artificial intelligence and computational modelling is the royal road to understanding mentality. The *Language of Thought*, is, for my money, the major text of the 'cognitive science' movement.

I would say that there are two major problems with the mental-sentence thesis which both lead – one ultimately, the other directly – to the kind of developmental questions I shall be raising shortly.

The first problem arises once we admit that in order for a 'system' (I shall use this neutral term) to think, its thoughts must have *reference*: that is to say, they must refer to things regarded by the system as existing and enduring independently of itself. In short, thinking implies something that we can call 'a theory of the external world'. Now the machine-code analogy works well only so long as we forget that all a computer program has to do is *run*. The machine does not need to know anything: it has to perform a task. (For the functionalist, I should interject, knowledge is decomposable into tasks.) Robot arms driven by digital computers can carry out instructions to, say, 'put a pyramid on the big block' even if successful completion of the instructions means first removing a small block from the big one. This is a very sophisticated procedure, but only in the most metaphorical sense would we want to say that the computer has a theory of the external world. (John Searle, the Reith Lecturer in 1984, built up a critique of computational psychology around considerations such as these.)

Well how do I *know* that this computer does not have a theory of the external world? I have no argument, an objector would say, just a prejudice. Well, I think that there is an argument of sorts for saying that a computer of the kind described does not have a theory of the external world, does not have mental states which refer, and does not therefore have thoughts in any significant sense. There is representation in a language but no knowledge, and therefore no thought in the human sense.

We should attend to the fact that knowledge of the external world means representing a lot of facts at once, so many facts that we lose hold of the idea of 'representation'. The computer which can move blocks around to instructions represents, in contrast, a few facts and does what it can with them. I will try to illustrate this by example.

I am thinking about my spectacles lying on the desk before me as I write. Maybe the thought is 'They need cleaning'. In fact, it doesn't matter what the thought is, what predicate I ascribe to them, just that they are the object of some kind of thought. To put it simply: I can never have just *one* thought about the spectacles, and if it could be truly said that I was only able to entertain, say, two or ten thoughts about them – if my thinking consisted of discrete, countable thoughts – then they would not be thoughts at all. For example, the thought 'They are on my left' does not 'succeed' as a thought unless I can also have other thoughts such as 'If I move to my left they will move to my right', 'They are substantial' (that is, not a chimera), 'They are reachable/not reachable', 'They are supported by something', 'A large opaque object coming between me and them would render them invisible to me' . . . Any of us could fill this chapter with similar thoughts. And these are just thoughts about the spectacles *qua* physical objects of a certain size and weight. If we also consider thoughts about them *qua spectacles*, then we would say that I have not succeeded in thinking about them unless I am thinking about artefacts, thinking about items that can be worn on the nose, that aid vision, that are more-or-less breakable, that did not exist a thousand years ago, that this pair existed yesterday but did not exist in 1983, and so on. Moreover, these potential thoughts do not just lie there like strands of spaghetti on a plate: each must have a certain kind of relation to the others. Thoughts about how the spectacles would appear to me if I moved towards them leftwards must be related in the correct way to thoughts about how they would look if I moved above them to the right; thoughts about their being artefacts must be related to thoughts about their not existing before a certain time or not coming into existence in the kitchen as the kettle boils. The phrase *the holism of the mental* is used in a number of ways; but I hope the reader now understands what I intend by it. One thought succeeds only because of the relations that it has to innumerable other potential thoughts.

But isn't there something artificial in my references to bunches of individual thoughts? Certainly, the idea that when I look at my spectacles and think 'So that's where I put them' I am having thousands of other little thoughts at the same time is a silly idea; and some would say that the doctrine of the holism of the mental *is* just a silly idea. But this silliness does not derive from what I claimed about what it means to have successful thoughts: it derives from our habit of regarding individual thoughts as if they were like sentences. It looks silly from the perspective of our so-called 'folk psychology' of thinking. For, paradoxically enough, it is the 'language of thought' thesis which is closer to the layman's intuitions about thinking. We have a way of talking, and thus a way of thinking, about thoughts as if they were sentences in the head; and it is worth noting that Fodor (for example in *Psychosemantics*) regards folk psychology as providing a rough but reliable account of mental life and behaviour. The doctrine of holism, by contrast, challenges our folk psychology of thought (see Note 1).

How, then, might a supporter of the mental sentence view try to deal with the holism of the mental? Well, he might say that one mental sentence is, as it were, 'upfront' (for example 'The spectacles are broken!'), but that this sentence has a network of connections to other sentences in the mental architecture ('They are made of glass', 'They were purchased', 'They are not unique'). This kind of view is, in fact, quite a familiar one in artificial intelligence-influenced cognitive modelling. But really it is just a *reductio ad absurdum* of the mental sentence view. Each of the 'sentences' in the network only has meaning in terms of its relations to other sentences, and each of these sentences only has meaning in relation to others, and so on.[1] In which case they have no independent meaning or function at all. To put the point another way: proponents of the mental-sentence view – being functionalists – typically see the meaning of mental sentences (or mental 'states') in terms of their causal role *vis-à-vis* other such sentences. But how can a sentence have a causal role in relation to other sentences if the second sentence's causal role is defined in terms of its relation to the first sentence? Where does the meaning come in? It can only come in as some kind of 'emergent property' of all these causal interactions. Well if that is the case, then this is just another way of expressing the holism of the mental.

Now for the second difficulty with the mental-sentence view, taking this view, remember, as the most sophisticated expression to date of the representational theory of the mind. It is about the possibility of *learning*. I don't mean learning facts like 'Lemur is the capital of Peru' or that 'St Tracy is the patron saint of the dormer window' (we can learn things that are false: learning is not mere information pick-up), but acquiring concepts such as what is to count as a 'chair', that weight is conserved through transformations of shape, that the earth is a heavenly body circling a larger heavenly body.

It is self-evident that learning something entails a prior capacity to learn it. How are we going to understand this 'prior capacity' on the mental-sentence view? There is only one way: in terms of symbolic representations of the predicates, as in 'X is a chair and only if it is a portable seat for one person'. This means that a child acquiring language who does not yet know what *chair* means but will acquire the knowledge must already have represented in his 'language of thought' a predicate of the kind 'is a portable seat for one'. Or to put it another way: on the representational theory of mind, all learning is the testing of hypotheses which are already represented in the mind in some form (for instance as sentences). This means, in turn, that the initial state of the learner must be as a possessor of vast battalions of hypotheses which are selected out as the child bumps up against the physical world and the human conceptual system. This is a way of thinking derived from Chomsky (and ultimately from Plato), and it is one with which Fodor is quite happy. He writes – perhaps *pour épater les empiricistes* – that 'all concepts are innate'.

But this is a fairly repugnant conclusion to most of us. Do we really want to say that all we ever learn we knew before – even if we *are* saying this in some technical 'computational' sense? How about a more modest version of the argument which says that only certain 'primitive' concepts are innate (about three-dimensionality, causal relations, etcetera), and that the more sophisticated concepts develop out of these through the time-honoured processes of *differentiating* finer concepts from global ones and *integrating* the results into complex, structured concepts. This is not much help because (a) later-developing concepts must still *on the representational theory of the mind* be present in these primitive concepts (there are no merely *potential competences* such as my potential but non-existing competence to know Portuguese); and (b) how and where do we draw the line between the primitive concepts and the developed ones?

Predictably, perhaps, I regard this argument not as a demonstration that the acquisition of new concepts is impossible, but as another *reductio ad absurdum* of the representational theory of the mind. The holism of the mental should make us suspicious, I have argued, of the mental-sentence view. Well, if a thesis that it is difficult to make sense of allows a conclusion that is repugnant, then the rational course would seem to be to take this as another reason for distrusting the thesis: not as a reason for admitting the repugnant conclusion.

Methodological dualism

The reader cannot have failed to notice that J. A. Fodor is fast emerging here as the *bête noire*, in that he both presents the strongest case for the representational theory of the mind and champions the conclusion which flows from it about the impossibility of concept-learning. Well, now I want to introduce another of Fodor's theses which, for my money, is as correct as the other two are false. Fodor has written in *The Modularity of Mind* that the consequence of accepting the representational theory of mind in cognitive psychology is a kind of 'methodological solipsism' (that is, we deal with representations, not the with relations between organisms and real objects out there). I like to think of this next Fodorian thesis as a kind of 'methodological *dualism*'.

Recall that at the beginning of this piece I briefly discussed what the representational theory of the mind has got right: that thoughts are not simple responses, reactions or reverberations to environmental stimulation – contrasting this with the case of the thermostat which automatically switches on and off at pre-set temperatures. Thinking involves taking perspectives on reality, rather as drawing does. Let us now consider the class of mental processes which are not perspective-takings of this kind, which *are*, in some sense, directly caused by proximal stimuli. A reflex would be the paradigm case here. To take Fodor's nice example, imagine that you are chatting to an old friend. That this person should harbour aggressive feelings towards you is unimaginable, but then suddenly, she goes to poke you in the eye – and *you blink*. The blinking was a reflex which could equally well have been set off by a puff of wind or a flash of light. The causal chain between stimulus and response had a kind of inevitability, an independence from processes which we would normally regard as mental: it by-passed our knowledge of the friend's personality, history, and basic assumptions about human motivation, the orderliness of conduct, and so forth. Now if the reflexive processes were *not* autonomous in just this way, if they were determined 'top down' by our thoughts then we would *not* have blinked.

This much is not controversial. But Fodor goes on to argue that much of what can be said about reflexes can also be said about processes which we would normally regard as 'cognitive' rather than 'neurological' or 'behavioural': the parsing of heard sentences, for example.[2] There is something reflexive rather than rational, automatic rather than deliberative, circumscribed and autonomous rather than holistic about parsing a sentence such as 'She met John before Mary arrived at the airport' in the way we do (with the pronoun *she* not referring to Mary but to some other female). We have, as it were, no *choice* but to parse sentences in a particular way. *Believing* sentences and slotting the information that they convey into our knowledge base (for instance, what we used to think about the referent of *she*) is another story. That is, it is open to us to *deliberate* about the light that this fact throws on the person's character; but deliberation is not open to us when it comes to parsing the sentence.

From facts such as this, Fodor argues that the parsing mechanism constitutes one independent cognitive *module* among others, which can be studied in terms of representations that are built from the raw input of the speech stream 'bottom up'. We can ignore the influence of higher-level systems. There are a large number of psycholinguists who would say that Fodor is overstating his case here and that parsing is indeed canalized by so-called 'real world knowledge'. However even these workers opt for something that they call 'interactionism', in which there is a clearly modular, autonomous element which can be studied in isolation from the knowledge systems.

Vision is a better example of a modular processing system. Not only does seeing a chair as a three-dimensional object have this character, but so does seeing one line as longer in the Muller-Lyer illusion (in which two lines of equal length look unequal when differently slanting lines are drawn at the tips) despite our knowing that the two lines are really the same length. Visual illusions are an excellent illustration, in fact, of the division between a specialized and autonomous mechanism for seeing and the cognitive system which determines whether we should believe what we see, as Helmholtz pointed out over a century ago. We can disbelieve the evidences of our senses, we can suspend disbelief, as well as believing the world is such-and-such with no sensory evidence at all.

So, to introduce Fodor's terminology, the mechanisms for delivering up packaged information about the world (a parsed sentence, a representation of a three-dimensional object . . .) he calls *the input systems*. What I have been referring to vaguely as the knowledge system, Fodor calls *the central systems*. Unsurprisingly, Fodor characterizes the central systems as holistic – though he prefers the term 'global'.[3] But somewhat surprisingly (given that the representational theory of the mind is supposed to be a theory of thinking, not of how we handle inputs) he concludes that a psychology of the central systems is beyond our reach: the more global a mental process is the less we are likely to understand about it. *This* is what I mean, then, by 'methodological dualism'.

I think we should see this pessimism as a direct result of adopting the representational theory of the mind. The *last* thing that a representational theorist really wants to have to explain is the global nature of thinking; and I suppose we can regard Fodor's pessimism as an implicit kind of owning up to this. But when we turn to the input systems there would seem to be no choice *but* to use the language of 'representations'. Psychologists of vision, for example, have to think in terms of levels of representation that the nervous system computes[4] and not to do so would be to render unintelligible the processes that occur between the transducing of light-rays into electrical impulses at the retina and the cortex recording the object as (say) a rigid cylinder rotating at such and such a distance from the viewing point. The alternatives would be to theorize exclusively in terms of neuronal processes (impossibly fine-grained) or in terms of drawing inferences from 'cues' (inappropriately rational). In the first case we need a level 'above' physiology and in the second we need a level 'below' reasoning.

Much the same can be said about sentence parsing. Although, as I mentioned before, rival groups of psycholinguists dispute the question of whether, when, and how the central systems exert a top-down influence upon the parsing processes, contemporary psycholinguistics proceeds on the assumption that levels of linguistic representation (phoneme, morpheme, noun phrase, clause, etcetera) are 'psychologically real' in the sense of referring to processes in the nervous system which take a certain time, which happen in a particular order, and which have determinate causal relations to similar processes. Why? Because these representations refer to computational achievements within systems which are *by definition* (Fodor's definition) *not holistic*. The same kind of representational language could be used to refer to the working of a television set or indeed a thermostat. In short, a representational theory of the input systems would seem to be a necessity, whereas a representational theory of the central systems would seem to be a non-starter. This is not just a point I am making in passing. The input/central distinction is something on which I shall be heavily reliant when I come to my positive thesis. This is now due.

Constructivism and development

The constructivist theory of mind regards thinking on an analogy with action; just as the representation theory takes an analogy with drawing and writing. Moreover, to the same extent that the representational theory is non-developmental (recall the Fodor's argument against learning), the constructivist theory is developmental. I would not say that the developmental view is a consequence of the thought-action analogy exactly, because there could be constructivist theories that do not mention development. It is certain, though, that the constructivism that has received the most attention in psychology and philosophy has been the developmental theory of Jean Piaget.[5]

Although, as I say, constructivism and the developmental view are separable, constructivism invites a developmental perspective on thinking in the following sense. On the representational theory nothing can be prior to a mental representation – the bedrock of thought is representational. On the constructivist view, by contrast, actions exist before central systems exist – before thoughts, beliefs, hypotheses, justifications, notions of truth. Obviously enough, action is not all that is required for thought. We need input systems. In other words, the representations which exist before cognitive 'representations' (in the 'representational theory of mind' sense) are of the input system variety. That is to say, the infant must convert stimulation from light rays, sound waves, from the speech stream into the appropriate representational grist if it is to get the kind of information that it requires from the world; but this gleaning of information does not constitute thought.

The next claim which constructivism makes is that central-system thinking emerges out of the organism's interaction with the environment, an interaction that is initially a literal inter-*action* but which is later carried out internally, at least in the human case. Thoughts are – as the slogan has it – 'internalized actions'.

Before passing on, I will introduce a piece of terminology of my own and call central-system thinking 'cognisance', a term chosen so as to give the flavour of knowledge, rationality, and accessibility to consciousness. Thoughts will be referred to as 'cognisant acts'. The simplest and most fundamental aspect of cognisance (fundamental philosophically and developmentally) is what is usually referred to as 'self-world dualism': the knowledge that there is a physical world out there of which I am an experiencer and that is distinct from me. Mental development, on the constructivist view, consists in the elaboration of this knowledge; so that if there is one central difference between the mental processes of the baby, the child, and of the adult it is in terms of how self-world dualism is manifest in (and to) the subject.

The representational theory of mind treats the explanation of mental life as a kind of engineering problem; it starts from the *inside*, from the representational state, and asks how mental states interact with one another to produce something that we would call 'knowledge'; the representational theorist proceeds like a sceptical philosopher who thinks that what figures in our mental life is not reality but our mental representations of it (recall my saying the Fodor described his position as 'methodological solipsism'). The constructivist starting-point could not be more different, and might be said to be 'biological' where the representational theory is 'engineering' – or 'machinological'. Constructivists do not admit such scepticism: the existence of an external world is one of the factors which make cognisance possible. With its existence thus assumed it is *knowledge* of the external world which has to be explained.[6] In constructivism we view the organism-environment dyad from the *outside* and ask how it might be possible that an organism which has input systems and which is active could ever come to know that the environment exists.

Consider then, an organism in a world of inanimate objects. (There is a lot to be said about the role of other persons too, but I am leaving that out for the time being.) There are three crucial differences between the organism and the objects. (1) It can move itself and has biological needs (not just for food and warmth and the like, but the need to use its faculties – *Functionlust* as it was once called by a German psychologist). (2) It has input systems. (3) It is designed so that the interaction between (1) and (2) and other objects in the world will result in cognisance. To put it epigramatically, the bridge between information pick-up and knowledge is action. And this means that the task of a constructivist developmental psychology of cognisance is to describe how this bridge comes to be built.

When introducing the notion of mental holism earlier, I said that thoughts must have *reference* and I implied that only holistic systems could achieve this reference. Constructivism is designed to deal with reference and holism. First, we assume that the neonate's input systems deliver up more-or-less true information about the external world, telling a six-week-old, say, that although the 'retinal' image of a square piece of cardboard changes to a trapezium when it or the baby moves sideways, the shape really remains square, and enabling it to discriminate between changes in angle and changes in orientation. These systems also enable neonates to discriminate between different facial expressions of emotion (for example, smiling versus frowning) and, sometimes, to imitate these expressions as well as non-emotional ones (for example, mouth-widening, tongue protrusion). The reader only has to glance at a good modern textbook of infant development (say, Bremner's *Infancy*) to get the main message: very young humans are prodigiously skilled at picking up geometric and social information, and this can be seen both informally (a neonate turning to a voice) and in the laboratory.[7] None of this implies of course that babies *know* anything about the external world at all. It is a matter of their input systems being tuned to the contours of this physical and this social reality.

Now it is frequently said that the development of skilled movement 'lags' a long way behind that of skilled perception, and in one sense this is certainly true: young babies have excellent visual acuity as revealed by their behavioural discrimination of, and neural responsivity, to gratings and chequerboards – but we don't see them playing darts! The *presence* of movement is one of our main criteria for being alive, and yet infant movements appear at least to be random, reflexive and undirected. Moreover, we know that people who are born with severe motor impairments develop normal and sometimes supra-normal intelligence. They may indeed, as in the case of Christy Nolan, win the Whitbread Prize for literature. So why not say, then, that in development perception 'teaches' action, that as the information delivered up by the input systems becomes progressively 'richer' the infant becomes better able to direct his own movements, rather than saying that cognisance develops out of action?

My answer to this point will be more philosophical than empirical. It will rely upon an argument from Kant. In the *Critique of Pure Reason*, Kant's aim was to show how objective experience is possible, to set out the conditions necessary for this; whilst Piaget's aim was to show, given certain Kantian assumptions, how objective experience actually develops. One of the conditions for ascribing to oneself experiences of a mind-independent reality, Kant argued, was that we should be capable of distinguishing between those sequences of perceptions (if you like, 'representations delivered up by the input systems') which are determined by the movement of objects and those which are determined by our own movements.[8] In the former category we have, to take Kant's example, watching a ship sailing upstream: here an object moves against a more-or-less stable background from (say) left to right. We have no option but to see it as movement from left to right. To describe self-governed perceptual sequences, Kant gave the example of scanning the front elevation of a building; in doing which *we* determine what we see and the order in which we see it – roof, front-door, top-left-hand window, and so forth. Obviously, each kind of experience necessarily contains elements of the other. Thus, there is some degree of self-determination in the ship case because we are free to shut our eyes, to cross the river and see it move from right to left, free to jump into the water and watch it coming towards us, free to determine the speed with which it passes across our visual field by moving our eyes with or against its movement. In the house example, we can choose the order in which we see the parts of the building but we surely cannot see occluded portions, and we surely cannot look up to see a thatched roof – because that's the kind of roof we want to see – when the roof is tiled. In fact, in every microsecond of perceptual experience there is a tension between the real as refractory[9], as something we cannot choose or will, and the subjective as chosen and willed. This may sound a somewhat highfalutin' way of making an obvious point; but the obvious points are often the important ones: in this tension we find the *limits* of experience, beyond which we locate an objective universe and within which we locate subjectivity. (One caveat: I am not saying that this is the *only* necessary experiential condition for objectivity: it is, though, the one which highlights the importance of action most clearly in differentiating the objective from the subjective within the stream of experience.)

Without the possibility, then, of altering one's perceptual inputs at will it is difficult to see how the information provided by the input systems could ever be centered upon a self, a self that is not just a repository of information, but something which addresses itself to reality and for whom reality is centred upon itself. I will give just one reason for this. If there were no refractoriness (no *failures* to experience X when trying to have an X-experience) there could be no basis on which to draw a distinction between appearance and reality, and without this distinction there can be no possibility of thinking about reality. There would be no distinction between the thinker and the reality he was thinking about. You may say, against this, that there can surely be some form of appearance/reality distinction so long as the input systems can deliver up information about such objective facts as *occlusion*. In this case, the reality of (say) of an orange being behind the breadboard is different from the appearance – which is that of a breadboard leaning against the kitchen wall. And what of the unseen portions of the wall behind the board? The 'appearance' is of the wall stopping just as it reaches the board; but do not the input systems deliver up the information that the wall continues behind the occluder? Indeed, as I mentioned above, there *is* plenty of evidence from research with the very young infants that their input systems allow them to make appearance-reality distinctions (for example, apparent versus real shape) at so young an age that the possibility that they have to rely upon records of their actions to do this is just not worth considering.

I think that this kind of objection rests upon a false way of thinking about the information that the input system provides. I shall have more to say about occlusion a little later, but for now: grasping the fact of occlusion in the sense of grasping the fact that if something were removed then something behind it would be perceived *because the something behind was there all along* is an achievement of the central systems. It means that we can think about things that are not present. Sure enough, we would expect the input systems to ensure that the right kinds of distinctions are drawn – between contour changes that define occlusion and those which define disappearance, for example – but this surely does not mean that the possessor of these input systems is capable of thinking about unperceived entities.

What this adds up to, then, is the claim that if there existed an organism which either could not act or whose actions made no difference to its perceptions then not only would that organism not be cognisant, it could never become cognisant. (It is not clear to me whether this is some kind of philosophical claim or an hypothesis. You may say that it is *refutable* and so it is empirical; but then – see below – our criteria for cognisance are so much bound up with what the subject can do that it is difficult to see how we could assess the cognisance of a totally passive creature.)

Perhaps the reader is now in a position to understand what Piaget intended when he said that infants 'construct' reality through action. They surely do not 'construct' it in the sense of making it up! They construct it in the sense of developing a conception of the real as being the refractory limit of their own actions. But does this not leave babies with an awful lot to do *for themselves*? And does it not have the ludicrous implication that a two-month-old only knows more than the two-week-old because he is more active? What is more, we still have to answer the objection that intellectual development can be normal in people with very severe motor impairments. If we find cognisance flourishing where there is a set of actions as restricted as those of Christy Nolan's, then how can reality be something that we posit as the limits of action: in this case a poor actor should have a correspondingly poor grasp of the real.

The answer is that by 'action' the constructivist intends something much broader than 'motor behaviour'. The term is supposed to encompass *any intentional change in the perceptual input*. There need be no movement. Thus, *attention* – listening to one voice rather than another for example – is non-overt action. Obviously, if the infant were deaf, blind, without tactile sensations, and totally immobile then the prospects for cognisance would not be very rosy; but in this case the input systems would fail to function as well, so both constructivists and nativists (those who believe in innate mental structures) would predict failure. (Even the radical nativist has to admit that information has to impinge upon the organism.) Indeed action would seem to be necessary for the input systems to function properly: the role of eye-movements in vision being the most obvious case.

So far we have been discussing the role of activity in the development of referential thinking, the development of the knowledge that 'there is a world out there'. What of the claim that I made earlier that no such conception could ever exist without the mental system being holistic? How does the necessity for action relate to the necessity for mental holism?

According to the kind of constructivism that I am espousing, the holism of the mental is logically and developmentally dependent upon the holism of directed action. That is to say, a system could not be cognisant unless it appreciated how intentional changes in its perceptions were constrained by reality. Among other things, this means that we should look for the origins of cognisance, as did Piaget, in infancy (babyhood). Initially, the infant perceives and the infant acts, but nothing suggests that the infant understands the relation between these perceptions and these actions. Take the example of following an object by eye-movements (so-called 'tracking'). As Piaget observed, very young infants will do this, but that if the object (mother, say) leaves the visual field it will not be followed. Why not? Because there exists no distinction between causing the experience by acting and the maintenance of the experience requiring action, and so no conception of acting in order to experience a *something* in the external world. How could infants develop towards such a conception? Not, the constructivist argues, by the enrichment of perceptual input (in any case the evidence tells us that this is already rich): only through action itself. Specifically, in Piaget's theory the infant's central systems develop by 'assimilating' perceptual data (data implying 'graspable'/'suckable'/'trackable'/whatever) to actions whilst 'accommodating' (that is changing in a goal-driven way) the actions taken in terms of the outcome (changing the grasp, the suck, or the head movement in terms of the size, contour, or the trajectory of the datum). So the basic assumption is that the developmental process is failure-driven: actions are continually failing to fulfil the assimilatory intention (recall the term *Functionlust* that I used earlier) and must therefore be modified. The infant's brain records the results of this modification and gradually 'constructs' a model of reality on that basis.

It must be said, however, that despite the beautiful detail of Piaget's behavioural descriptions, his picture of the mental reorganizations underlying behavioural change was painted with a very broad brush (by present-day standards); and indeed the assimilation-accommodation model is little more than a description of what has to be explained, awaiting, what we now call, a 'computational model'. My own view is that connectionism (see Chapter 7) is well placed to provide such a computational account of sensorimotor development; but that is not the issue here.

Here is Piaget's most well-known demonstration of the infant's failure to relate actions to experiences. At about seven months of age the average baby is quite skilled at removing obstacles to prehension; is well able, for example, to pull a cushion away to reach a rattle behind it. However, if the rattle slips down so far that it is no longer visible, the infant will at once lose interest and behave as if the rattle had also slipped out of existence. By about eight months of age most infants are capable of retrieving completely hidden objects; but between eight and twelve months they show another intriguing pattern of errors. There are now two occluders, A and B, side-by-side before the infant. The infant retrieves, or witnesses the retrieval of an object from behind A (say) three times, after which he watches as the experimenter moves it to place B. On seeing it vanish at B he will go straight back to A. Although the back-to-A error is more likely to be made the longer the delay between hiding at B and allowing search, this is not a memory problem in any simple sense because the infant will return to A even if the object remains *visible* at B. We find a particularly clear demonstration of this kind of 'perseveration' in an experiment by Paul Harris in which there were two transparent, lockable boxes as the A and the B location. After the object (a toy car) had been put at B, the boxes were locked; with the result that most of the infants went straight to B, could not get in, and returned to A and tried to gain entry to a box which they could see (whatever 'see' means here exactly) was empty. A minority of them never went to B at all, but went straight to A and searched, like the others, at a visibly empty space. Until about eighteen months or so they will typically be unable to search for objects which have been displaced invisibly (by transposing containers, for example).

We need fine-grain theories of why the performance breaks down, theories about memory development (a sophisticated memory-failure account is still in the running), about the ability to inhibit actions, about the development of the frontal cortex. But from the perspective of constructivism – which is a general theory of how cognisance is possible and how it develops – the immediate 'information-processing' shortcomings that lead to the failure to relate one's actions to objects is not relevant. *That* infants fail to search in these situations – although they clearly have the motor skills to do so – is one of the empirical bolsters to the view that *what develops* is the ability to relate actions to experiences 'of' them (again: whatever 'of' means in this context!). As Piaget said himself when reporting his original data, it is just not possible to explain the seven-month-old's failure to search in terms of memory failure (that is the baby knows that objects exist unperceived but keeps forgetting that this object went behind there) because if an organism had a memory *this bad* it would *ipso facto* lack object permanence. Moreover, we know that infant memory is remarkably good in other contexts. In fact, cognitive psychologists are nowadays more sympathetic to the Piagetian view that memory is the *result* of cognitive activity, not a passive receptacle in the mind which grows, rather as the body grows. (Note how in-house debates in experimental psychology criss-cross with epistemological issues in this area.)

Before passing on I want to raise a problem with all this. It may have occurred to some readers already. Isn't there something suspicious about making the performance of intentional actions the acid test of objective knowledge when it is quite possible that young babies have a very rich knowledge about the unseen existence of objects but that they lack the capacity to co-ordinate this knowledge with their motor skills at object removal? Constructivism seems to make this a logical impossibility, which of course means that no data could ever disprove the constructivist claims about what develops in infancy: any evidence that object knowledge (the 'object concept' or 'object permanence') exists without reaching behaviour will not be judged to be evidence for object permanence – as a point of logic. I will say two things about this issue.

First, we have evidence from Renée Baillargeon (see the Bremner volume referred to above) that babies as young as three or four months are able to 'represent', in *some* sense, the continuing existence of an invisible object behind a screen because they show 'surprise' when this out-of-sight object does *not* resist the backwards movement of the screen.[10] They do not show surprise when the fall of the screen *is* resisted by the out-of-sight object. Now such infants are too young even to organize a so-called visually-guided reach (that is, reaching for what they can see). The constructivist answer might be that this is behaviour guided by the input systems, with the added assumption that the behavioural expectation of resistance does not entail knowledge of continuing existence – of a continuing object of thought.

Second point: *is* the constructivist's fundamental assumption not justified if *knowledge* is our subject of study rather than successful behaviour? What sense does it make to say that somebody *knows* that there is, for example, a beer in the fridge, *wants* a beer, is *able* to open the fridge door but *doesn't* open it? Something has got to give: all these italicized attributions cannot be true of the same person at once. In our 'folk psychology' of knowledge, the relation between action and knowledge is that secure. Surprise (in the sense studied in Baillargeon's experiment – passive capture of visual attention) is not an action so it cannot tell us about central system function. (Recall Fodor's example of blinking when a good friend goes to poke us in the eye.) If surprise were a central system function then we would *not*, indeed, blink because the blink would be controlled by our knowledge of a friend's good nature. Thus: surprise cannot tell us about the development of the central systems. Needless to say, this is not going to be the last word in the debate between the constructivists and the nativists.

Cognisance after infancy

Piaget's claim that thinking is a kind of internalized action, exemplified in the assimilation-accommodation theory of infant learning mentioned above, is really a global assumption in search of some refined, detailed and testable expression. One way of stating this global assumption is this: what the child has to acquire is the ability to *direct, inhibit, and co-ordinate his thoughts, as he earlier had to direct, inhibit and co-ordinate his actions.*

This is, I would argue, a powerful idea which makes the phenomena of mental development more intelligible to us. What I shall do now is try to back up this last statement by sketching some of the characteristics of childish thought, showing how they can be explained in constructivist terms. They all concern, in different ways, the appearance-reality distinction, because cognisance must be understood in terms of our drawing this distinction in every area of our mental life.

An infant at eight months who retrieves a completely-occluded object has made a major advance in understanding the appearance-reality distinction, at least on the plane of action, because he now knows that, although the perceptual input at one time tells him that there is no rattle in his reachable space, really there is. This also means that the infant can now understand a kind of ambiguity: the rattle is both 'absent' and 'present' at the same time. Piaget's claim is that the cognitive difficulties which infants come to resolve 'on the plane of action' in infancy reappear, in childhood, 'on the plane of [verbal] concepts' and have to receive the same kind of solution – by way of the direction, inhibition and co-ordination of cognitive acts.

John Flavell (see *Cognitive Development*) did the following experiment with pre-school children. In one condition he showed them a series of objects which had been bought from a joke shop: a piece of rubber cheese, a chicken's egg made of stone, and so forth. Even the youngest children, who were three years old, were well aware of the *fact* that appearance and reality were conflicting, but how did this knowledge reveal itself in their *judgements* about the distinction? To put it another way: how did they think they could share their thoughts about the trick objects with another person? When they were asked what the (say) 'egg' was '*really, really*' the three-year-olds answered correctly that it was a stone, but when asked what the object '*looks like to your eyes*' they also said 'stone'. (There are a number of control questions that I am omitting here.) This tendency to give a realist answer when we request a phenomenalist (appearance-based) answer – which Piaget called 'intellectual realism' – is also very easy to see in children's drawings. That is to say, young children frequently draw not how a scene looks from their point of view but a good, revealing representation of it – something which further experiments have shown is *not* explicable by simple graphic incompetence.

This does not mean, however, that young children are realists 'across the board'. Consider another of Flavell's conditions. He also showed the children other kinds of illusion in which object's perceptual properties were altered: a white index card behind a blue light-filter for example. When three-year-olds were asked what colour the card was really they typically said 'blue'. Flavell accounts for this paradox in terms of, what he calls, *cognitive salience*, which amounts to the claim that the thought of the three-year-old is determined by whatever is 'up front in consciousness' at any given moment. So when they see an apparent egg that is really a stone, the fact of its being a *stone* (not that they have found a stone on the beach, say, which happens to look just like an egg) swamps their judgement; similarly when they see a white card changing colour – the blueness is salient not the fact that it started white. And so one may say, in more directly Piagetian terms, that the child's thinking fails, by our lights, in so far as one thought is not balanced ('in equilibrium with' in Piaget's jargon) by another. The child's cognisant acts have the character of perceptions: if an act is done it cannot be undone ('reversed' in the jargon) and so there is no going back and taking another perspective on the question or practical problem. So children are not little realists or little phenomenalists, nor does it really make sense to say that they 'waver' between the two. We should say that their thoughts are captured by salient information where they should be centrally directed, inhibited and co-ordinated.

In a somewhat more subtle form, these tendencies continue into later childhood. Martin Braine found that if children between five and six years of age are shown a standard visual illusion – such as a stick in water appearing to be broken, by light refraction – they will distinguish correctly between 'looks?' and 'really?' questions, but that if they are asked the neutral question 'Is the stick straight or broken?' they will say that it is broken. The neutral question is interpreted phenomenally, where an older child (around seven years) interprets it in a realist fashion. Maybe the reader's first thought here is that 'they are just misinterpreting the question'. However, an experiment of my own showed that this is not misinterpretation in any simple sense. We tested children in pairs so that each child in the pair observed visual illusions from different angles such that one child saw one kind of illusory view and the partner saw an opposite but equally conflicting view. For example both children knew that bricks A and B were the same size, but, when viewed through portholes in a box, A looked bigger to one child and B looked bigger to the partner. They were free to look over the top of the box to see what size the bricks really were, and they were quite aware that their own view was distorted because one of the portholes contained a magnifying lens. The instructions were to agree one answer to this question 'Are these two bricks the same size, or is one of them bigger than the other?' We also gave them colour, length, and brightness illusions. In another experiment one of the pair had a non-illusory view; for example he or she had portholes of plane glass. In control conditions children worked alone, either seeing one view only or walking round the table with the experimenter to see both. The point of the experiments was this: strong *social pressure* was being put on these children to agree to a realist answer (they were not allowed out of the room until they had an answer!) and if their usual tendency to interpret questions phenomenally is a trivial and weak effect then this social pressure should obliterate it. The result was that the social pressure had no effect at all. In children between four and eight years of age there was absolutely no difference between the number of realist answers produced by the pairs and by the control, solo children. They knew the realist option but did not take it as a way out of a social impasse, because, I would argue, the phenomenalist tendency of thought is too strong. What dominated their judgements was the salience of the illusion – *that* was 'most up front in consciousness'.

Many readers who know nothing else about Piaget's work will know of his experiments on 'conservation'. These simple but extremely robust observations concern children's knowledge that although a substance or display is changed perceptually – in other words, that the appearance of an object may change – properties such as length, area, volume, weight, number do not change. Here is perhaps the simplest and most dramatic example: the non-conservation of length by children below about seven years of age. We give the child two pencils of equal length side-by-side, and he correctly judges them to be the 'same size'. We then move one of the pencils upwards on the table, by about an inch or so, and ask again about the relative length of the pencils. It's safe to say that every child in every culture will go through a period of saying that the pencil which has been moved up is now longer or bigger or big now. Why is it longer: 'because it's higher up'. It is pretty certain that, in term of what adults mean by 'longer' the children do not *really* think that the pencil is longer; but why do they say this? They are, in one sense, interpreting the question differently from the way we do; but why do they do it? As Piaget said when he reported the original finding, trying to explain the children's behaviour away by saying that they 'misinterpret the question' is circular: *of course* they are misinterpreting the question and the next question is about cognitive determinants of this misinterpretation – this 'non-conservation'.

Although it is tempting to do so, non-conservation cannot be assimilated to the phenomenalist tendency shown up in Martin

Braine's experiment. For a start, the higher pencil does not *look* longer. Moreover, we showed, in a small study, that non-conservers of length will say that a one-inch and a ten-inch stick are the same length so long as their tips are on a level. Clearly, they do not look the same length; and clearly the child's thought is focused on the tips ('centrated on' in the jargon).

Viewed in constructivist terms, the non-conserver is failing to exert central control (lack of 'direction, inhibition, and co-ordination') over his cognisant acts. The tips of the pencils are 'cognitively salient', and what is seen of their relation determines the child's communicated beliefs about length. What if we simply draw their attention to the trailing ends? I have tested literally hundreds of children on conservation tasks over a period of twenty years and have confirmed (to my own satisfaction at least) that fundamentally – in terms of the central systems – one does not succeed in drawing their attention to non-salient features. The child sees them and talks about them; but this does not affect his beliefs. The judgement of basic physical and geometric phenomena have then – descending still further into metaphor – a perceptually-determined, evoked character, rather like the actions of younger infants.

I will turn finally to experiments on what is now called the 'child's developing theory of mind' (see Astington, Harris and Olson, 1988). By this is meant young children's explicit knowledge that they and others have mental states which are only 'in the running for truth', that beliefs held by people can be false and yet these false beliefs can determine their thought and behaviour. The phenomena studied in theory-of-mind research, I will argue, fill out the Piaget-Flavell picture of the child as a victim of cognitive salience. Here is one of the standard procedures that is used to test whether a child has an adult-like appreciation of false belief. John and Mary (the two experimenters) show a child of three years of age a red box and a blue box and a pound coin. John gives Mary the coin, she hides it in the red box for safe-keeping and departs. Meanwhile John tells the child that he is going to play a trick on Mary and transfers the coin into the blue box. Where will Mary look for the coin when she comes back in? And once Mary has returned, where will she 'think' the coin is? Typically, three-year-olds, but not four-year-olds, say that Mary will look for the coin where it really is – in the blue box. Does the child regard mind and reality as existing in a state of perfect correspondence? That's surely putting it too high. But there is a salience problem here. Recall that it was three-year-olds who had difficulty with Flavell's appearance-versus-reality problems; and indeed further experiments have shown that there is a strong statistical correlation between performance on the appearance-reality and on the false belief task. Where is the salience effect? I would say that the child is capable – more or less – of recognizing that other people have mental states different to his own. Indeed it would be difficult to imagine how children were able to use language to communicate if *no* such conception were present. Moreover in other kinds of false belief experiment (by Henry Wellman) where three-year-olds watch a puppet make a mistake in searching, the children are quite capable of explaining the failure in terms of what the puppet is wrongly thinking. But competing with the conception of the other person's thoughts is the child's *own* knowledge of the location of the coin. This is 'up front in consciousness' and it is this which determines his answer, in the absence of central control.

We recently did a simple experiment which happens to illustrate how children's knowledge of where an object is determines their behaviour. It shows quite dramatically how difficult young children find the inhibition of reference to a salient object. Children played a game against a second experimenter for chocolate. For fifteen trials, two closed boxes were placed between child and experimenter. We told the child that there was a chocolate in one of the boxes and that he had to point to one of them – guessing of course – to tell the experimenter where to look for the chocolate. If the experimenter found it then he kept it, and if he did not find it the child got the chocolate. In this way the child learnt that it was in his own interest for the experimenter to go to the empty box. Then the boxes were changed. This time there were windows facing the child (invisible to the competitor) so the child could see where the chocolate was on each trial. Where will the child now point? If he points to the empty box then it is probably fair to regard this as deliberate misinforming, as the 'implanting' of a false belief in another's mind. In fact we did find a clear difference between the three- and the four-year-olds: the younger ones typically pointed to the box with the chocolate and the older children to the empty box. But what was striking about the three-year-old's behaviour here was that they did this *for twenty trials*. They could see that the competitor's pile of chocolate growing ever higher and that they were winning nothing, and yet they were powerless to do anything about it! If we told them to point to the empty box they would do so; but would revert to pointing to the baited box again on the next trial.

I did not mention before that theory-of-mind tasks are also typically failed by autistic children who are otherwise quite able. That is to say, they behave like three-year-olds on false belief tasks even if their mental ages are, by other criteria, well above three years. This is not the case in *non*-autistic mentally handicapped children, who do well on false belief tasks so long as their mental age, by other criteria, is above three years. We also tested a sample of autistic children in the chocolate-finding task and found that they were again behaving just like the three-year-olds: going to the baited box for twenty trials, despite wanting to win chocolates and occasionally trying to filch them from the experimenter's bag. This suggests the hypothesis that one of the features of autism is a lack of central control of thinking similar to that found in very young normal children. Their input systems function adequately, but their thinking lacks the full, holistic character of normal thought. Uta Frith, in her recent book *Autism*, argues something similar. (Non-autistic mentally-retarded children would appear to have a different kind of problem.) Autism is a very profound cognitive deficit indeed, and everything that I have said up to now entails that a person whose thinking significantly lacks an holistic character, and lacks the related qualities of directedness, inhibition and co-ordination, will be profoundly affected.

Coda

We have covered a lot of ground, and maybe the path through the undergrowth of arguments and data is not a very straight or a very clear one. I certainly would not want to attempt a summary of the route we have taken all the way from the mind-body problem to children trying to win chocolates; but I do need to make some concluding comments to justify the bold claim in the first paragraph that constructivism makes the mind-body problem less intractable.

I argued that the representational theory of mind, with its assumption that thinking is the possession of determinate 'mental states' which are in some sense encodings (pictorial, syntactic) of actual or possible states of affairs, contributes to the difficulty of the mind-body problem. We have mainly been concerned with the modern 'computational' version of the representational theory of mind; but, as I shall mention again later, the more traditional views of mental life are no less representational – phenomenology, for example, is a representational theory of mind.[11] How might such states be both mental and physical at the same time? We do not want to say that one kind of state causes the other kind, but neither does it make much sense to say that they are 'parallel' or 'identical'. There are arguments for all possible positions, but none of them convinces us for long (see chapters 1 and 5).

Recall that constructivism refers only to mental representations at the level of the input systems, as entities which can be translated, more or less directly, into the language of neuropsychology. (It refuses to take seriously the claim that central-system processes – thinking – are explicable in terms of the causal interplay of representations.) Thinking – cognisance – is, however, not a matter of being in one mental state or another, or of flashing through a sequence of mental states: it is having conception of oneself as an experiencer of an external world, an experiencer who has the freedom to perform cognisant acts. Thinking is a capacity to refer at will, whose nature is made more mysterious if we try to chop it up into mental episodes with particular epistemic content or causal power. Inadequate thinking, as I hope to have shown in my section on mental development, can be regarded as the inadequate control of mental attention, and, like inadequate action, fails through misdirection, disinhibition, and unco-ordination. An adequate thought is an achievement made possible through the co-operation of the whole cognitive system: it's not a well-formed encoding of something else.

As I said, it is not only the modern, computational form of representational theory which is, from the point of view of constructivism, mistaken. Throughout the philosophy of mind and certainly amongst both lay and professional psychologists there is the view that basically two kinds of fact exist: physical facts about the brain and the external world, on the one hand, and facts 'about how it is with us', on the other. This may seem harmless enough, but problems arise once we try to describe the latter kind of fact. When trying to describe these facts, we find ourselves being sucked into the language of phenomenology with its core assumption that our experience consists of shifting mosaics of raw experiential data – colours, feelings of pain, desires, glimpsed movements . . . These experiences are at once ineffable and a psychological bedrock beneath which we cannot penetrate. And this conception leads inexorably to the view that experience is like a kind of screen, something which could perhaps be painted if only we had the skill and reflective capacity, or something which could be captured by language or music. Or we might talk in terms of an 'inner world', the world of mental tableaux accessible only to ourselves. How could this phenomenal screen or these phenomenal tableaux also *be* brain activity?

A constructivist would deny the existence of anything that corresponds to this conception of a phenomenal screen. To think there is such an entity is to confuse two kinds of process, processes that correspond roughly to the input and the central systems. (I admit

I am suggesting that we replace one kind of dualism with another!) In accordance with this latter kind of dualism, we have on the one hand our computational successes in recording (the psychologist James Gibson used the useful phrase 'resonating to . . .') information in the external world. On the other hand, we have mental activity which enables us, second-by-second, to conceive of ourselves as mental entities. Without cognisant acts there can be no beliefs about phenomenology: no phenomenology without self-ascription, and no self-ascription without mental actions. Does this conception make the mind-body problem easier for us? Perhaps it does in the following modest sense. At the first, input-process level, we do not encounter philosophical problems in the classic sense: these are problems of mental engineering, of 'cognitive science' – in the current jargon. However, the problem at the cognisance level is to describe how a history of activity (that is, intentional changes in informational content) results in the conceptions which we have about our mental life. It hardly needs saying that how this story is told will depend upon philosophical argument.

But surely, you may say, consciousness *does* consist of determinate mental episodes. I think of eating an omelette or walking by the sea and these thoughts have a determinate 'qualitative' or 'phenomenal' content. And is not the thought of, say, blue different from the thought of green in some way which we may one day be in a position to describe, just as we are now able to describe the causal conditions for the *experience* green which is different from the experience of blue? Why do we have to say that these thoughts are like mental actions? Surely the determinate content of thoughts is not captured by constructivism. At best constructivism is a developmental theory about what kinds of organism-environment interaction are necessary for certain kind of understanding. That is quite a lot; but why be more ambitious and say that it makes the place of mind in Nature more intelligible to us?

Answer: nobody is denying that thoughts have qualitative content. (And why shouldn't the kind of holism that I am espousing not *help* to make processes such as mental imagery more intelligible to us – Piaget published a number of experiments on the development of imagery.) What is being attacked by constructivism is the assumption that these mental contents *are*, in some way, 'consciousness', 'mental life' – whatever term we wish to use. It was primarily David Hume who highlighted the problem of understanding how a coherent, ego-based mental life could emerge from bundles of 'impressions' and 'ideas'. It cannot, and that is the reason, above all others, that classical 'associationism' failed. Paradoxically, associationism is anathema

to representational theorists like Fodor; and Fodor criticizes connectionism (see Chapter 7) for inheriting all the problems of
associationism. But a picture of the mind as consisting of atomic
mental states causally interacting is not a million miles from the
Humean view – a view of which Hume himself was the most insightful
critic. On a more phenomenological level, if we wanted some visual
analogue to the associationist view of mental life we could not do
much better than think of one of those 'psychedelic' slide-shows
popular in the late 1960s, in which lights were projected through oil,
producing coloured globs which met, merged and repelled in a series
of kaleidoscopic patterns. Every emerging pattern was explicable in
terms of principles of local association.

From the standpoint of constructivism, the reason why asso-
ciationist-representational theories so spectacularly fail to capture the
essence of thought is that they ignore the fact that every thought, like
every action, has, at some level, a purpose. The fact that we often feel
that our thoughts come unheralded by 'intentions', that the content
of our mental life is unwilled, just demonstrates how thin is the layer
of consciousness. This is a familiar point to those who know anything
of Freudian theory.

But there is, perhaps, one crucial objection to the constructivist's
claim that moving the focus away from mental representations and
towards mental actions will make the mind-body problem appear
to us as less of a problem. It is this: saying that the character of
'mental representations' (beliefs and imaginings, for example) can
be understood only in terms of a history of activity, or that it is
the subject's conception of himself as active in relation to the world
which gives these 'representations' their 'content' or 'semantics' (I
hope to have shown something like this) is simply *irrelevant* to the
mind-body problem. This is the problem of how mentality – call it
'mental representations' or 'cognisant acts' – relates to its physical
realization in the brain. The constructivist thesis, it is argued, is
not relevant because mental representations have not been defined
away and replaced by talk of actions: we still have to say how mental
life as we know it to be, with the representational character that we
naturally give to it, relates to neuronal life. The only interesting
claim that the constructivist *can* make here, the objection runs, is
that there *is* a prospect of translating all representational language
into action language – with a host of adverbs, perhaps? If *that* is what
is intended, the objector would say, then constructivism is nothing
more than a kind of behaviourism (another attempt to replace the
mental by the behavioural); or perhaps we might lump it together
with Marxist attempts to 'resolve' the mind-body problem in terms

of 'praxis'. That is hardly a solution: it merely changes the subject from the mental/physical relationship to the behavioural/physical relationship. What can I say in answer to this charge of irrelevance?

I will take the example of an experience about whose veridicality a subject is undecided. I do this simply to bracket off questions about how experiences relate to the world and thus to concentrate on the question of subjectivity. Here is the example. Having just been reading a bright-red leaflet we glance up to a plain, white wall – at which instant we see a green patch. For a second or so we are undecided about whether the patch is an after-image or a spot of mildew on the wall. What we do know, however, is that we are seeing a green patch, and our experience has a particular, qualitative – indeed paintable – character. How is a 'cognisant episode' such as this going to be analysed away into the language of activity?

Well clearly it is *not* going to yield to any such analysis, and to believe that it will is to deny the reality of subjective life and to side with the behaviourists. What I can say, however, is that the constructivist position allows a distinctive analysis of the 'mental' when we speak of a '*mental* representation of a green patch': it helps us to understand the difference between mental representations and the non-mental variety (a photograph for example).

At the time of looking up we ascribe an experience of greenness to ourselves; we consider the experience as something being undergone by us before any decision is taken about its veridicality. Such an ascription is a cognisant act involving, at the very least, a conception of a one's self, a conception of experience, and a conception of veridicality. As I argued, given the holism of the mental, we are not going to succeed in analysing these conceptions in terms of some complex causal interplay between determinate representations. We can, however, make some attempt at understanding the cognisant act on the model of a physical act. And that is – I am afraid – as far as it goes. The constructivist says that we should regard the problem of how it is possible to act at will as the best philosophical and psychological road to the problem of mentality. This problem is difficult enough; but starting from the nature of mental representations, considered as entities poised somewhere between subject and object, guarantees failure. I admit that this constructivist way of thinking hardly 'solves' the mind-body problem. But I doubt that it is irrelevant to it.

References

Astington, J., Harris, P. L. and Olson, D. R. (1988) *Developing Theories of Mind*. Cambridge: Cambridge University Press.
Boden, M. (1978) *Piaget*. Fontana Modern Masters.
Bremner, J. G. (1988) *Infancy*. Oxford: Basil Blackwell.
Flavell, J. H. (1985) *Cognitive Development*. Englewood Cliffs, New Jersey: Prentice-Hall.
Frith, U. (1989) *Autism: Explaining the Enigma*. Oxford: Basil Blackwell.
Fodor, J. A. (1975) *The Language of Thought*. Brighton: Harvester Press.
Fodor, J. A. (1983) *The Modularity of Mind*. Cambridge Mass.: MIT Press (Bradford Books).
Fodor, J. A. (1987) *Psychosemantics*. Cambridge Mass.: MIT Press (Bradford Books).
Johnson, M. (1987) *The Body in the Mind: The Bodily Basis of Meaning, Imagination and Reason*. London: University of Chicago Press.
Marr, D. (1982) *Vision*. San Francisco: Freeman.
Piaget, J. (1955) *The Child's Construction of Reality*. London: Routledge and Kegan Paul.
Piaget, J. and Inhelder, B. (1969) *The Psychology of the Child*. London: Routledge and Kegan Paul.
Russell, J. (1978) *The Acquisition of Knowledge*. London: Macmillan.
Stitch, S. P. (1983) *From Folk Psychology to Cognitive Science: the Case against Belief*. Cambridge Mass.: MIT Press (Bradford Books).

Notes

1. Stephen Stich (1983) presents a case for a syntactic theory of mind which is more radical than Fodor's. He argues that the language of folk psychology (talk about 'beliefs', 'desires' and the like) may float free of the kind of mental states that actually do the computational work: these are defined solely by their syntax and causal role, not by their reference. He spends a lot of time saying why this way of regarding syntactic mental states does *not* encounter the problem of the holism of the mental.

2. This means the process of assigning syntactic roles to elements of a sentence: noun phrase, prepositional phrase, adverb, etc. In the dedication of his book, Fodor says that the following remark by the psycholinguist Merrill Garrett had a strong influence on his thesis:

'What you have to remember about parsing is that basically it's a reflex'.

3. The more precise terms that he uses are 'isotropic' and 'Quinean' (after the philosopher W. V. O. Quine). The former means that anything in the domain of belief is potentially relevant to what is being considered; the latter means that the falsification or verification of propositions is done relative to their status in a scientific theory (and, by extension, in a belief system).

4. The main influence on thinking in this area is the work of the late David Marr (e.g. in *Vision*). He described three levels of representation in the process of vision and three levels of explanation.

5. Perhaps the best place to begin reading Piaget in the original is Piaget and Inhelder, *The Psychology of the Child*. Piaget's *The Child's Construction of Reality* (1955) is probably the best source of the constructivist thesis. Boden has written an excellent short introduction to the theory. Piaget is not the only constructivist. The philosopher Mark Johnson has recently produced what can only be called a constructivist account of linguistic meaning and reasoning.

6. This presents the problem for the constructivist of how to regard *beliefs*. To be consistent with holism the constructivist has to say that individual 'beliefs' – mental states that are only in the running for truth – do not correspond to anything in the mind. This is then, in Fodor's (1987) terms, not a 'realist' theory of belief. Paradoxically, constructivism would side with Stich (see note 1) about the unreality of belief.

7. The principal technique for testing babies' perceptual and cognitive capacities is the 'habituation-dishabituation' technique. (This does not, unlike the Piagetian methods, rely on the baby doing anything intentionally – such as reaching. It allows the psychologist to determine whether the subject has detected a change in a stimulus or can discriminate between two stimuli.) Initially the subject will attend to a new stimulus but will then gradually lose interest and start to look away (habituation); if the stimulus is then changed in some way and if this causes a re-awakening of interest (dishabituation) then we can assume that the baby has detected the change. Another technique is 'preferential looking'. If the subject prefers to look at one stimulus rather than another we can assume that he has detected a difference between them.

8. This idea had a great influence upon the thinking of Schopenhauer who followed up its implications more thoroughly than did Kant.

9. The term 'refractory' is taken from the theorist James Mark Baldwin. He had a considerable influence upon the thinking of

Piaget. See Russell, *The Acquisition of Knowledge*, for a comparison of the two.

10. Baillargeon used the habituation-dishabituation technique – see note 7.

11. Phenomenology is the method of enquiry developed by the philosophers Brentano and, later, Husserl. In this, all assumptions about external reality are suspended ('bracketed') and the theorist focuses entirely upon his field of immediate experience. It is not a million miles away from Fodor's 'methodological solipsism' – though phenomenologists have little interest in the causal interplay between the mental states thus identified.

3

The Mind in the Laboratory

RICHARD LATTO

1 *We have the technology*

The increasing power and sophistication of computers is advancing
the brain sciences in two ways. It has improved our ability to
model cognitive processes, both as a spin-off from the computations
necessary to create artificial intelligences and through the computing
metaphors used in cognitive psychology. (See the discussions of these
developments elsewhere in this book, particularly Chapters 4 and
7.) And it has led to the introduction of new technologies for the
direct investigation of the relationships between brain, behaviour
and external events, the subject of the present chapter.

Most current procedures for recording the electrical activity of the
brain, or producing radiographic images of the living human brain,
or investigating the accuracy and timing of behaviour are dependent
on computing capacity which was not available twenty years ago.
But many of the techniques which computers are enabling us to
exploit are not new. By 1875, the Liverpool physiologist Richard
Caton had detected tiny fluctuations in voltages present on the
surface of the brains or scalps of monkeys, cats and rabbits. More
significantly, he also realized that this electrical activity was affected
by external stimuli falling on the sense organs. Fifty-five years
later, Hans Berger, a psychiatrist working in Jena, reported similar
fluctuations in humans and discovered that, in a resting subject,
this electroencephalogram (EEG) oscillated at a regular eight cycles
a second, a pattern he called the alpha rhythm. This disappeared
if the subject was alerted by a noise or touch. Edgar Adrian, in
Cambridge, subsequently demonstrated the importance of the visual
cortex at the back of the brain in generating alpha waves and the
particular effectiveness of visual stimuli in blocking them. In one
especially striking experiment, the alpha waves disappeared when
the subject *imagined* a visual scene. It began to seem a possibility
that an external observer would be able to predict whether or not an
apparently relaxed subject was forming visual images.

Another exciting window on the mind seemed to open up in
Chicago in the 1950s when Nathaniel Kleitman and Bill Dement

began using the techniques of electroencephalography to investigate sleep. Sleep could be divided into a number of different phases which recurred at regular intervals throughout the night. One of these phases was known as paradoxical or rapid eye-movement (REM) sleep. It was paradoxical because although the subject was very deeply asleep, being completely relaxed and more difficult to wake than at any other time during the night, the EEG pattern was that of alert wakefulness. At the same time there were bursts of rapid eye-movements and muscular twitches in other parts of the body. Dement's discovery was that when subjects were woken during REM sleep they nearly always reported that they were dreaming. Later research has shown that dreaming is not unique to this phase of sleep, but REM dreams are typically much more colourful and rich in imagery than non-REM dreams. So again, laboratory techiques were affording scientists a glimpse of their subjects' mental lives.

The brain is not only an electrical machine, it also has a physical and chemical structure and these too are now being monitored in the living brain. By using computers to integrate the information from a large number of different viewpoints round the skull, it is possible to visualize the appearance of a slice through the brain and build up a full three-dimensional image. The viewing medium can be X-rays, as in computerized tomographic (CT) scans; magnetic resonance of atomic nuclei, as in nuclear magnetic resonance (NMR) scans; or emission from radioactively labelled substances incorporated into the structure of nerve cells as in positron emission tomographic (PET) scans. These obviously have considerable clinical value for localizing and identifying areas of brain abnormality, but they also enable areas of activity in the normally functioning brain to be pictured. The resolution of these pictures is still relatively coarse and they produce only a stationary image at a single moment in time. Nevertheless, they have demonstrated activity in the visual areas during an imaging task, in the language areas during a verbal task and even, on one occasion, in the higher visual areas of a schizophrenic patient who subsequently reported that he had been hallucinating. Remarkable as these observations are, they are currently only confirming what was known already about localization within the brain.

All these EEG and scanning techniques are, so far, giving us only very rough correlations between brain structure and function and mental processes. More important, the mental processes being studied are still only crudely defined. A different and apparently much more specific line of research, however, developed from another of Adrian's electrophysiological experiments. While studying the relationship between visual stimuli and the EEG, Adrian found that if a regular series of bright flashes was presented to the subject's eyes there was an equally regular series of blips in the EEG recorded from electrodes on the scalp over the visual areas at the back of the skull. These little potential shifts, known as either evoked potentials (EPs) or event related potentials (ERPs), are normally buried in the random background activity of the EEG. They can be reliably dug out again only by averaging over many presentations so that the random background fluctuations cancel each other out, leaving just the potential shifts that are linked in time to the triggering event. Averaging of this kind was first done at the National Hospital in London in the 1940s by George Dawson, initially using a technique of photographic superimposition and then later a system of addition using banks of condensers, but it was the electronic processing and computing power of the 1960s and 1970s which made the accurate timing of these averaged potentials possible, resulting in a rapid expansion in ERP research. Since then, correlations have been reported between potential shifts and a wide variety of different events, ranging from simple and complex sensory stimuli to whole sequences of behaviour or even internally generated mental events.

It is now being claimed that the ERP allows the objective monitoring of well specified mental activities. As Fergus Campbell has suggested, if the ERP can tell us whether or not the subject has seen a light, it takes the psycho out of psychophysics. It enables the scientist to say something about the internal experiences of others without the tedium of having to ask the subjects themselves. The central consideration of this chapter is the validity of these claims and their significance for our understanding of the mind-body relationship.

2 We know what you're thinking

2.1 Are you ready?

Benjamin Libet of the University of California at San Francisco has been responsible for two sets of experiments which are often cited as crucial evidence in the debate about the relationship between brain and mind. In 1979 he published a paper showing that the perception evoked by stimulating the skin or the neural pathway between the skin and the cortex was *reported* by the subject as occurring a few hundred milliseconds before the cortical ERP was sufficiently complete to generate that perception. In earlier work, he and others had established that the cortical-evoked potential, and also direct cortical stimulation, had to persist for several hundred milliseconds before subjects reported feeling anything. Then in the 1979 paper he found that subjects placed the time of occurrence of this sensation only a few milliseconds after the peripheral stimulus which evoked it. So although the ERP had to persist for several hundred milliseconds before the subject felt anything, they nevertheless *reported* that the sensation had occurred at the moment when the ERP was beginning. Libet concluded from this that the subjective experience was occurring before the neural events which bought it about. This apparently backward causality, if true, would cause problems for identity theories of mind and has been used by dualists like John Eccles to support their position, with the backward step in time made by a non-physical mind.

Libet's second set of experiments, described in 1985, is even more striking. About a second before a subject moves a part of his body, a slow negative shift in the electrical potential generated by the brain begins. This effect, which is strongest over the frontal lobes, was first observed in 1964 by Grey Walter, who called it the Contingent Negative Variation. More recently, and perhaps begging the question of its mental significance, it has come to be known as the Readiness Potential (RP). In Libet's experiment, subjects were asked to move their hands at random times of their own choosing. Averaging the EEG over forty such self-initiated movements, Libet found that there was indeed a time-locked negative shift beginning about 550 msec before the movement. Whatever the particular significance of these RPs in terms of information processing, it is reasonable to conclude with Libet that 550 msec is the minimum interval by which neural activity precedes a self-initiated, and therefore presumably voluntary, movement. At the same time, Libet set up a procedure for allowing subjects to report the time at which they first experienced the conscious intention to act. This was done by asking them to report the position of a dot moving round an oscilloscope screen at the moment of the experience. Knowing the time the dot was in any particular position, Libet was able to calculate that on average the experience of the conscious intention to act was reported as beginning about 200 msec before the movement began. Subtracting these 200 msec from the 550 msec by which the RP preceded the movement, Libet concluded that the neural activity associated with an apparently voluntary act began some 350 msec *before* the first moment at which the subject was aware of his intention to act. So, he argued, the 'cerebral initiation of a spontaneous voluntary act begins unconsciously' (Libet, 1985). If accepted, this somewhat paradoxical suggestion leaves the problem of finding a role for consciousness in voluntary acts. Libet speculates that it may 'function in a permissive fashion, either to permit or prevent the motor implementation of the intention to act that arises unconsciously.' The marginalization of consciousness in this way would certainly make life simpler for those attempting to understand our cognitive processes, but unfortunately Libet's conclusions do not follow from his data.

The problem with the conclusions in both sets of experiments is that they are based on the assumption that we can infer when an experience occurs from a subject's verbal report. In each case, the subject was reporting which other event a particular experience was synchronous with. But, and this is Libet's error, what the subject was actually comparing was the time at which two *experiences* were occurring. We have no way of knowing exactly when these experiences took place. All we can reasonably conclude is that they happened at the same time. A much more likely explanation of Libet's findings is simply that all experiences are delayed relative to the stimulus causing them, so that synchronous external events produce synchronous experiences. (Another useful illusion is that of the instantaneity of experience. We have to view a stimulus for a finite time before it generates a perception, but that perception appears to us to occur instantaneously rather than fading into view like the Cheshire cat.) But there is no way we can test for this hypothetical delay. Subjects are always limited to making judgements about experiences; experimenters are stuck with observing physical events like evoked potentials, verbal reports and button presses. There is no way in which the time of occurrence of an experience can be related to the time of occurrence of a physical event without assuming answers to the questions Libet is asking. (One, untestable, assumption which most reductionists would make is that conscious experiences cannot precede the neural events underlying them.) So Libet's experiments tell us something interesting about the information processing going on in the subject's brain but they tell us nothing about the temporal relationship between physical events – either inside or outside the brain – and conscious experiences.

There is another, apparently much more fundamental although philosophically less interesting, criticism of Libet's work. Perhaps the particular potentials he is recording are not causally linked with the conscious experiences he is investigating? Given that there are good correlations between the two, this would imply that they are both being caused by a third, unidentified event. This event would presumably precede the potentials being recorded and it could provide an explanation for the apparent referral back in time in the first set of experiments, although it does seem electrophysiologically unlikely that there could be a neural change happening sufficiently early after the triggering stimulus. But in the second set of experiments, a neural event preceding the RP would only serve to make the effect Libet is claiming even more striking and alternative explanations still need to be sought.

2.2   Get set

Libet was investigating the processes underlying a decision to move; that is, the ERP that precedes a movement. But most human electrophysiological work has been concerned with the processing of incoming events, that is the ERP that follows the presentation of a stimulus. When, for example, a subject fitted with scalp electrodes over the auditory cortex is played a series of brief clicks through headphones and the EEG following each click is averaged so that random fluctuations cancel each other out, what is left is a systematic but complex pattern of electrical waves which is caused by the click in the same way that the waves on the surface of a pond are caused by dropping a pebble into it. The first fifty or so milliseconds of these waves are the most consistent for any particular stimulus and it is thought that they are almost entirely generated by the incoming stimulus, irrespective of any mental activity on the part of the subject. These early components of the ERP are therefore usually called exogenous. After fifty milliseconds the waves are more labile. Some of them are still exogenous and can be modified only by varying the stimulus, but some of them now seem to depend mainly on the way the subject is processing the stimulus. It is these internally generated or endogenous components, lasting sometimes as long as a second after the triggering stimulus, which offer the most potential for investigating mental activities.

ERPs are very slippery customers. Even those who most strongly advocate their use as research tools would admit that we do not know exactly what neural processes generate them and that any particular fluctuation will be the result of a multiplicity of different kinds of changes occurring in several different and possibly independent systems. Some of these changes will be related to neural processes that have little psychological relevance. Nor is there any reason to suppose that the peaks and valleys of the fluctuations have greater neural or psychological significance than any other intermediate point. So sorting out what is going on in an ERP is like untangling a complex bundle of many different strands of similar wool with one hand tied behind the back. Given this, the progress that has been made is remarkable, particularly in relating components of the ERP to attentional processes.

Whether or not we perceive an event in the world around us

depends on three things. First, it has to fall within our viewing window: we have to have the right apparatus to receive and process the information signalling the event. Thus, we can perceive the sound emitted by a piccolo but not that from a dog whistle. Second, we have to be sufficiently alert: the apparatus has to be switched on. If we are drowsy we may not hear either the piccolo or the dog whistle. Third, in certain circumstances, we have to be attending to the stimulus: the apparatus has to be tuned in correctly. In a complex orchestral passage, we shall probably not be aware of the piccolo unless we are specifically listening out for it. This facility for selective attention increases the processing power of our brains enormously by enabling us to direct our limited processing capacity where it is most needed. It is clearly under voluntary control: we can decide who to listen to in a crowded room and who to shut out. And it is extremely sophisticated: we can pick out our chosen voice from an overlapping background of very similar sounds. From William James at the end of the last century to the present day, psychologists have speculated and experimented to discover how this is done.

A stimulus will generate an ERP only if it falls within our sensory window and the size and form of that ERP will vary according to our general state of alertness, of which alpha blocking is one important indicator. Even more strikingly, the ERP will vary according to whether or not we are selectively attending to it. As early as 1957, Michel Jouvet in Lyons had reported that the size of the ERP generated by a visual stimulus from the occipital cortex at the back of the brain, a primarily visual area, decreased when the subject was asked to attend to an auditory stimulus. Working with Raúl Hernández -Peón, he also showed that the auditory ERPs generated in the neurons in the cat's ear almost disappeared when a salient visual stimulus, for example a mouse, was brought into the cat's field of view. So this damping down of the sensory input when attention moves elsewhere can occur very early in the pathway from the sense organ to the brain. These early experiments were sometimes difficult to interpret, but the general finding that the form of the ERP is affected by shifts in attention has proved very reliable.

Recent experiments on the psychophysiology of selective attention by, for example, Steven Hillyard at San Diego and Emanuel Donchin at Illinois have successfully related different endogenous components in the ERP to different stages in the process of selective attention. Suppose a subject is listening to different sequences of sounds played independently to each ear through a pair of headphones in order to pick out and respond to a particular target sound. If the subject is instructed to attend to one ear and ignore the sounds coming into the other ear, all the sounds in the attended ear will produce an enhanced N100 component in the ERP. (The name N100 indicates a systematically occurring negative shift in the ERP which peaks about 100 msec after the stimulus.) This enhancement is thought to be associated with the extraction of additional information about the stimuli in the attended ear. A more subtle distinction affects a later component, the P300 (a positive shift peaking 300 msec after the stimulus). For while all stimuli in the attended ear give an enhanced N100, only those sounds which the subject, correctly or incorrectly, identifies as the target stimulus will result in an enhanced P300. So the P300 is thought to be associated with the completion of stimulus identification and classification in preparation for a cognitive or motor response.

Late waves like the P300 and the more recently identified N400 are by far the most cognitively interesting of the ERP components. The P300 was first described in 1965 by Sutton. It is generally elicited only by stimuli that are both infrequent (or improbable) and significant in the sense that they require some kind of response by the subject. Its purely endogenous nature is well illustrated by the facts that it can be evoked by the *absence* of a stimulus such as a gap in a long sequence of evenly spaced tones and that the actual probability and significance of the stimulus is less important in determining whether or not the P300 will occur than the subject's perception of its probability and significance. The most cognitively complex association with an ERP was found in 1980 by Kutas and Hillyard for the N400 wave. This is elicited, after the very long delay of 400 msec, by the visual presentation of a semantically improbable word (for example, the word 'socks' in 'He spread the warm bread with socks'). Meaning seems to be the crucial factor, since the presentation of a grammatically inappropriate word or an appropriate word in a new and unexpected typeface does not evoke an N400 wave. And the finding that it takes 400 msec to generate the electrical activity associated with the meaning of visually presented words suggests that this is one of the most complex activities our perceptual systems are asked to perform.

These experiments tell us a great deal about certain aspects of cognitive processes, particularly their relative timing or sequencing. They also provide circumstantial evidence for a close relationship between mind and brain. They have shown that mental processes can be correlated with specific neural changes. This is a necessary condition for a reductionist view of the mind but, particularly given the absence of any effective demonstration of a causal connection between the mental and the neural, it is certainly not a sufficient condition. (The many demonstrations, in neuropsychological experiments of the kind discussed in Chapter 4, of the loss of mental processes caused by the loss of neural processes are more powerful here.) But the electrophysiological examples I have described go some way to countering Wittgenstein's negative assertion: 'No supposition seems to me more natural than that there is no process in the brain correlated with associating or with thinking; so that it would be impossible to read off thought-processes from brain-processes' (Zettel, paragraph 608, Anscombe's translation, 1967). There may of course be some mental processes for which no neural activity exists, but such an awe-inspiring negative could not be proved until we knew the place and function of every least sub-atomic particle in the human brain. And the more links that are discovered between mental and neural processes, the smaller the dualist gap becomes.

3 What have we found?

It is an act of faith of most brain scientists, including, as must be obvious by now, this one, that an understanding of the brain will lead to an understanding of behaviour and of the processes that control and underpin behaviour, some of which are conscious and some unconscious, but which taken together correspond to the folk-psychological term 'mind'. Indeed brain-mind identity is more than a belief, it is a hypothesis which seems to be the simplest explanation of the mind-brain problem, if it is a problem, and therefore one which parsimony requires us to accept. Further, although this hypothesis has not yet resulted in an account incorporating consciousness, it has been remarkably successful in explaining many other mental phenomena which earlier generations saw as necessarily mysterious and as evidence for some kind of duality. Joan of Arc's hallucinations were not so much the voice of God as the voice of some aberrant neurons in her temporal lobes.

Electrophysiology allows us to correlate one set of observable physical events (electrical activity in the brain) with another (the behaviour, including the behaviour of reporting experiences, of the subject being recorded from). It is important to remember that the linguistic utterances of others are just as much externally observed behaviour as walking down stairs or pressing a button in a psychophysics laboratory although, because of the high information content of linguistic behaviour, we are prone to endow it with some mystical quality which opens a special window on to the mind of the person generating it. We must approach observations of linguistic

behaviour with the same careful attitude as we approach other kinds
of behaviour or indeed as we approach our electrophysiological
observations.

It is also worth noting that correlations between ERPs and
behaviour are never perfect, perhaps because of masking of some
of the ERPs by random fluctuations of the background EEG.
An individual event which normally gives a particular ERP may
sometimes yield nothing and the ERP may sometimes occur in the
absence of the evoking event. It is always the case that averaging
over tens of trials is necessary to give consistent results, particularly
with endogenous ERPs. So it is not yet possible to say with absolute
certainty, using evoked potentials that are correlated with reports
of conscious mental events, whether or not an individual external
event has resulted in a particular mental event. Further, the need
for averaging obviously favours repetitive responses to repetitive
stimuli and neural events that do not correlate in a consistent time-
locked way with external stimuli will necessarily be overlooked. This
weakness must become more severe as we move from investigating
relatively simple sensory and motor processes to the study of high
level cognitive processes.

All of these observations of correlations between ERPs and
different kinds of behaviour, including phenomenological reports,
may tell us something about mental representations and the cognitive
processes generating them, but they can tell us nothing about whether
these representations and processes are conscious or unconscious. It
is the essential but usually overlooked fact that in any psychophysical
experiment when, for example, subjects are asked whether or not they
perceive a stimulus, their responses, verbal or otherwise, cannot be
relied on as accurate accounts of their conscious experiences. So,
in a near-threshold task the subject may be accurately identifying
the presence of a stimulus which tells the experimenter that there
is some kind of mental representation of the stimulus, but there is
no way the experimenter can decide whether or not the subject is
consciously aware of the stimulus. Indeed, it is a common observation
in experiments of this kind that subjects themselves often express
confusion about what they are conscious of.

The problem arises whenever we try to use conscious awareness as
a dependent variable: for example, when we want to decide whether
or not a particular external event leads to a phenomenal event. This
is an area of some controversy at the moment in psychology, where
one of the holy grails is the attempt to provide empirical evidence
for the intuitively reasonable idea that there can be a dissociation
of behaviour from consciousness. This is a phenomenon which most

of us experience from time to time, particularly when performing a highly practised task like driving a car or using a keyboard, and which the clinician often feels presents in exaggerated form in certain neurological conditions. The term 'blindsight' was coined by Larry Weiskrantz at Oxford to describe perhaps the best known example of this dissociation, in which patients with damage to the visual areas of the cortex deny being able to see a visual stimulus while behaving in some respects as if they are processing it, for instance by moving their eyes in its direction. The difficulty here is the same as the one already encountered with the attempt to relate evoked potentials to conscious events. We only have the subjects' external behavioural indicators (verbal or non-verbal) of their experiences and we have no way of validating these indicators. So we end up dissociating one piece of behaviour from another: in 'blindsight', the verbal response 'No, I did not see the light' is dissociated from the ability to move the eyes towards the light. This, I would argue, though not all would agree, may tell us something interesting about the way the brain compartmentalizes different aspects of visual processing and it may tell us that subjects are more conservative about admitting to seeing a very degraded image than about trying to move their eyes to it, but it sheds little light on the actual experiences the patients are having when we show them a light. There is an elegant circularity in trying to prove that behaviour can be dissociated from conscious awareness by using behaviour to indicate the absence of awareness.

I am not suggesting that we should be completely sceptical about the value of introspection. There are some circumstances in which accounts of conscious experiences may be very useful in suggesting hypotheses about the nature of cognitive processes. The still influential contribution of Köhler and the other *Gestalt* psychologists to elucidating the rules underlying pattern perception is a major example. But when we talk about our conscious experiences we are providing our listener with only a very crude approximation to the actual phenomenal content of experience. (Interestingly, one of the functions of art is the attempt to refine this process of communicating mental states and the accounts of the artist can sometimes be a more useful guide to the nature of cognitive processes than naïve introspection.) What I am suggesting is that introspective reports, while often providing helpful qualitative information, can never be reliable enough to use as quantitative data defining the presence or absence of conscious awareness.

Returning to the central theme of the present chapter, electrical activity can be correlated with behaviour and this helps us towards an understanding of the neural mechanisms and cognitive processes underlying behaviour. It does not enable us to say anything directly about the nature of consciousness. But then an understanding of consciousness, for all its fascination, is not necessary to the production of an adequate model of cognitive behaviour. While consciousness may be central to an understanding of one's self, it is marginal to an understanding of other people. Consciousness in other people is a hypothesis for which there is circumstantial evidence in their verbal reports which match, by-and-large, our verbal reports of our own experiences. (This implies of course that consciousness in animals is a hypothesis for which there can be no evidence at all unless we resort to anthropomorphism, which we usually do.)

Most psychologists accept that cognitive processes, and therefore 'mind' – although this is a term not widely used in the brain sciences – encompass both conscious and unconscious activities. Clearly, conscious processes are central to an individual's own experience, but most of us remain neutral as to whether they are central to cognitive processes given that many, if not most, of these are not conscious. It also follows from this that understanding consciousness would not be sufficient for understanding mental processes. So current cognitive models of language, memory, perception and so forth are also basically neutral to the question of consciousness. They discuss how information is processed to achieve a particular end (storage and retrieval in memory, for example), but they say nothing about the borderline to be drawn between the conscious and unconscious parts of these procedures.

What remains uncertain is whether consciousness is a separate phenomenon which *needs* explaining, like language or vision, or whether it is simply an attribute of certain neural processes in the same way as high reflectance is an attribute of the piece of paper you are looking at while you read this, something which is simply part of the physical characteristics of the brain or the paper. Indeed, the evidence we have from cognitive psychology of the overwhelming predominance of the unconscious over the conscious parts of mental processes suggests that consciousness may be as peripheral to the central information processing activities of the brain as the whiteness of this paper is marginal to the semantic content of the words printed on it, which are telling you what I think about the mind.

References

Campion, J., Latto, R. & Smith, Y. M. (1983) 'Is blindsight an effect of scattered light, spared cortex, and near-threshold vision?' *The Behavioral and Brain Sciences*, 6, 423–86.

Donchin, E., Karis, D., Bashore, T. R., Coles, M. G. H. & Gratton, G. (1986) 'Cognitive psychophysiology and human information processing'. In G. H. Coles, E. Donchin & S. W. Porges, *Psychophysiology: Systems, Processes and Applications*. New York: The Guilford Press, 244–67.

Gregory, R. L. (Ed.) (1987) *The Oxford Companion to the Mind*. Oxford University Press.

Hillyard, S. A. & Hansen, J. C. (1986) 'Attention: Electrophysiological approaches.' In G. H. Coles et al. (op. cit.), 227–43.

Hillyard, S. A. & Kutas, M. (1983) 'Electrophysiology of cognitive processing.' *Annual Review of Psychology*, 34, 33–61.

Libet, B. (1985) 'Unconscious cerebral initiative and the role of conscious will in voluntary action.' *The Behavioural and Brain Sciences*, 8, 529–66.

Marcel, A. J. & Bisiach, E. (Eds) (1988) *Consciousness in Contemporary Science*. Oxford University Press.

4

Cognitive Neuropsychology
and the Philosophy of Mind

J. RICHARD HANLEY

1 Introduction

Clinical neuropsychology involves the study of the effects of brain injury on human behaviour. What neuropsychologists are trying to do is to come to some understanding of the way in which damage to the brain impairs abilities such as memory, perception and the use of language.

Within the last two decades, a new approach to this subject has assumed great influence. This new approach is known as *cognitive neuropsychology*, and it attempts to explain the impairments which neuropsychological patients unfortunately experience within the vocabulary of cognitive psychology. One of my main goals in this chapter is to describe the nature of cognitive neuropsychology, and to account for its pre-eminence.

However, this is a book about the *philosophy of mind* rather than experimental psychology, and the main point that I want to make is rather more philosophical than psychological. Consequently, I am going to start off by outlining some of the philosophical beliefs about the nature of mind which underpin contemporary research in the cognitive sciences, including cognitive neuropsychology. This will involve a brief discussion of the approach known in contemporary philosophy as *functionalism*. The basic theme of this chapter will be that the success of cognitive neuropsychology provides strong grounds for believing that functionalism, or something very close to it, is actually true.

2 Functionalism as a Philosophy of Mind

The functionalist approach to the study of mind characterizes much of the work currently being done in cognitive psychology, artificial intelligence and linguistics. Unlike classical behaviourists, functionalists believe that is not possible to explain intelligent behaviour unless we make reference to processes that are taking place inside a person's head. Now, of course, nobody denies that certain processes (blood flow, neural transmission etcetera) occur in the brain and that behaviour would be impossible without them. What is controversial about functionalism is its claim that we are going to be able to make significant generalizations about behaviour only if we think about what is going on in the brain at a particular level of description. If we confine ourselves to explanations couched in the vocabulary of physics or neurochemistry, then we are going to lose, or fail to formulate, a vitally important set of generalizations about human behaviour, and science will never be able to explain or predict behaviour in a satisfactory way.

According to functionalism, it turns out that the appropriate level of description is the same as that which characterizes *folk psychology*, the psychological theory that ordinary people use when predicting and explaining the behaviour of their fellow human beings in the course of their everyday lives. Functionalists, therefore, attempt to explain behaviour in terms of mental concepts such as beliefs, thoughts, desires and memories. Behaviour comes about as a result of the interaction of these mental processes with each other and with the environmental stimuli that are constantly impinging upon our sensory systems. This is not to say that folk psychology already has adequate theories of perception, language, memory or any other cognitive process. Indeed, the data from patients with brain injury that I will be discussing in the final two sections are very puzzling indeed from the standpoint of folk psychology. The point is simply that the account of mental processes which folk psychology provides, constitutes an explanation at an *appropriate level of abstraction* for the purposes of explaining behaviour scientifically.

It should be emphasized that this level of explanation does not commit the functionalist to a belief in any non-physical substances or processes. Most, perhaps all, functionalists are thorough-going materialists who believe that mental phenomena are genuine *physical* phenomena seen at a particular level of abstraction. This commitment to materialism means that a couple of standard dualist objections must be faced.

First, there is the dualist's argument that mental processes cannot be physical processes because physical entities – such as neurons – lack certain qualities – such as intentionality or consciousness – that characterize the mental. The response to this is that intentionality and consciousness are *emergent properties* of physical systems. Neurons do not individually have the property of consciousness, consciousness emerges when a large number of neurons are interacting in the right kind of way; just as *speed* is a property not of any single component of a car, but an emergent property of the whole system when it is operating in an appropriate way. Of course, nobody as yet knows how intentionality – the property that mental phenomena have of being *about* something other than themselves – or consciousness emerge from the operations of the brain. From the perspective of functionalism (and from the perspective of other materialist theories also), however, this is a question for science rather than an imponderable problem of metaphysics.

Searle (1984, pp. 18–21) strongly supports the view that intentionality and consciousness are emergent properties, but there is at least one important difference between Searle's account of emergent properties and the one I am advocating here. I have no quarrel with Searle's claim that 'mental phenomena are caused by processes going on in the brain'. When he states subsequently that 'mental phenomena just are features of the brain', thus tying mental phenomena very rigidly to the brain itself, then I dissent. The functionalist view I advocate is that mental phenomena emerge as a result of the way that the neurons etcetera are functionally *organized* in the brain, not as a result of the physical properties of neurons *per se*. As Churchland (1988, p. 37) has put it, 'what is important for mentality is not the matter of which the creature is made, but the structure of the internal activities which that matter contains'. Consequently, mental phenomena could emerge from a physical system which does not contain neurons at all, if its physical components were arranged together in a particular way. Most important, there may be no interesting similarity whatsoever that could be formulated in the vocabulary of physics between such a system and the brain. This might even include the nature of the emergence of the mental from the physical itself. Only at the functional level would the two types of system be equivalent.

The second question which an opponent of dualism such as a functionalist must face, concerns the alleged *privacy* of the mental. It is true that we cannot observe or measure directly mental processes taking place in the brain in the way that we can measure, say, blood flow via a brain scanner. This does not mean however that mental processes are in some way divorced from the physical world, nor does it mean that they should be excluded from the subject matter of natural science. From a functionalist perspective, mental processes are inferred processes – they gain their status in our theoretical base not as a result of being directly observed or experienced, but from the way in which they enable us to understand and explain human behaviour. They exist, theorists believe, because they help us to see the world as it really is. Their ontological status is therefore every bit as secure as the status of unobserved theoretical entities in other sciences (for example quarks in sub-atomic physics).

What this means, of course, is that functionalists do not see consciousness as a defining feature of the mental. Since the time of Freud, it has been acceptable to many theorists that the way in which we behave may be powerfully influenced by mental processes to which we have no conscious access. This is not to say that functionalists would be in sympathy with Freud's belief that certain unconscious mental processes are so anxiety-provoking that they must not be allowed to enter awareness. They simply share the belief that it is not going to be possible to explain behaviour adequately if mental processes are identified with the contents of conscious awareness.

Let me emphasize here that functionalists are happy to accept that many of our mental states *are* associated with conscious awareness. They are also happy to accept that it is only because we have these mental states that we behave as we do. Behaviour is genuinely caused by the interaction of such mental states. Such views are very different from those that would be associated with behaviourism or epiphenomenalism, neither of which allows mental states any causal role in the production of behaviour. Furthermore, the work of Young and his colleagues, which I shall be discussing later in the chapter, shows that being aware of the operations of, say, one's face processing system has vitally important functional consequences. However, the functionalist view is that it would be quite misguided to attempt to explain behaviour by making direct reference to the *subjective* or *phenomenal* qualities (technically known as *qualia*) of these mental states. If it is really necessary to think of mental states as having qualitative content (and see Dennett, 1988, for some powerful arguments that it is not), then it follows from functionalism that such qualia do not have causal interactions with other mental states or behaviour and are mere epiphenomena.

3 Successful Science

The sceptic might, at this point, complain that while I may have sketched out the functionalist position, I have not provided any convincing arguments as to why one should believe it. What I now want to suggest is that there is a lot of very successful science currently being conducted which literally depends on functionalism being true. If functionalism is false, then the success of the cognitive sciences is a massive scientific fluke. My argument for functionalism is therefore critically dependent on whether or not I can convince you that progress in one of these areas – cognitive neuropsychology – is unlikely to be simply an illusion. In this section, I will set out what I believe to be the basic characteristics of a flourishing, as well as an unsuccessful, approach to science. I will then attempt to evaluate cognitive neuropsychology in terms of these criteria.

Science exists so that we can improve our understanding of naturally occurring phenomena. Understanding in this sense means being able to perceive structure amongst a set of observations that were at first sight perplexing and confusing. When we identify such a structure, then it means that we can successfully explain our observations in terms of concepts that we genuinely understand already. What are the signs that tell us whether or not we are making genuine progress in a particular area of study? First, we should be able to explain a relatively large set of observations in terms of a much smaller set of more general theoretical principles. Second, these principles should then lead us on a successful search for phenomena that we had not observed previously. Then, as we encounter fewer phenomena that genuinely puzzle us, so our faith in the explanatory adequacy of our theoretical base increases.

Why might an attempt to explain a particular set of phenomena flounder? Perhaps the most obvious cause of failure is an inability to perceive the pattern that exists in nature. There would appear to be at least two different reasons why this might be so. First, it may be that no one (as yet) has made the critical observations which would allow the pattern to become evident. In this situation, 'further research is necessary' and, when controversy arises, it is likely to occur between those who actually share a large number of fundamental theoretical assumptions. Secondly, a failure to perceive the pattern may also occur because we lack within our theoretical base the conceptual framework that would enable us to grasp the structure that is potentially available, given the observations that we have made already. For example, we apparently only came to some understanding of how the *heart* worked when we had within our conceptual framework the notion of a *pump*. In such a situation, further collection of data may be pointless in the absence of any fresh conceptual insight.

There is, however, a more fundamental reason why an attempt to perceive a structure within a given set of phenomena may fail; it may be that there actually is no structure there to be perceived in the first place. Plato said that we should attempt 'to carve nature at its joints'. The implication, contrary to relativism, is that certain things (referred to in the contemporary literature as 'natural kinds') simply belong together. If we attempt to put the wrong type of things together, or attempt separate explanations of things which are part of the same natural kind, then we are going to struggle to produce successful science. We won't produce any interesting generalizations, we won't succeed in predicting new phenomena, and the world will remain every bit as confusing as it was previously.

4 Cognitive Neuropsychology

4.1 Case Studies and Group Studies

Cognitive neuropsychology is the attempt to draw parallels between models of cognitive function and the patterns of performance observed in patients who have suffered brain injury. There are two basic questions. First, can we explain the impaired performance that these patients produce in terms of our functional models? Second, can we learn anything new about the nature of the underlying cognitive processes from studying these unfortunate individuals?

Cognitive neuropsychology is largely a European rather than a North American phenomenon. The vast bulk of the neuropsychological work performed in the United States to investigate cognitive processes uses group studies as in, for example, the investigation of human amnesia (severe loss of long-term memory function as a result of brain damage). A set of amnesics is first assembled on the basis of their low scores on a clinical memory test. Their performance on some task is then evaluated by comparing their average score with the average score of a group of matched control subjects. The purpose is to test an hypothesis about what the 'cause' of amnesia might be. This approach to amnesia has had some success. In particular there is the intriguing finding that some amnesics can learn certain new skills as quickly as normal subjects, even though they are often unable to remember the circumstances in which they learnt them. Unfortunately, though, we are not very much closer to a genuine explanation of amnesia in functional terms that we were twenty years ago.

The problem is that it is highly improbable that a group of patients with brain injury constitute a natural kind, even when they display similar symptoms on some test or other. This is because no two patients are likely to have identical injuries, and large groups of patients are even less likely to be homogenous. In fact, if you probe deeper, vitally important functional differences between patients will emerge. In amnesia, as in many other so called neuropsychological syndromes (developmental dyslexia, schizophrenia, Wernicke's aphasia etcetera) there is probably no uniform pattern in nature waiting to reveal itself. What you have are groups of people who display superficially similar symptoms for a variety of different reasons.

Where cognitive neuropsychology has had its greatest success is in areas where a detailed model of cognitive function is used to explain the pattern of performance produced by *individual* patients. Let me illustrate this via an examination of the cognitive neuropsychology of reading.

4.2 Models of Reading

According to one influential cognitive model (Coltheart, 1985; see Figure 1), there are two distinct reading routes that might come into operation when one is reading aloud. Following the terminology of Patterson (1982), these two systems are said to involve either 'assembled' or 'addressed' phonology. A pronunciation of a word is said to be assembled when it is built up piecemeal from its component letters. The letters are first 'parsed' into their appropriate graphemic units. A grapheme is here defined as the way in which a phoneme is represented in print. Graphemic parsing is necessary because a phoneme is often represented in English by more than one letter (for example, PH represents one phoneme in 'graph', OO represents one phoneme in 'boot'). Each grapheme is then translated into a corresponding phonemic representation on the basis of pre-established conversion rules (each grapheme would become associated with a particular phoneme as one's reading skills develop). Finally, the phonemes are blended together to produce the spoken response.

The alternative pronunciation route, which involves 'addressed' phonology, employs the lexical system. Initially, an entry in a reading lexicon which matches the sequence of letters that one has detected is located. The reading lexicon (or 'visual input lexicon' as it is sometimes known) contains our knowledge of written English word forms. It is built up as a result of encountering these words in print as one is learning to read, though of course new word forms will be added throughout adult life as they are encountered. This whole-word visual representation is then used to address and so locate its associated pronunciation in a lexicon of spoken word forms known as the speech output lexicon. It is known as a speech *output* system because there is evidence that a quite separate lexicon is involved in speech perception. A pronunciation is addressed either with or without the mediation of the semantic system – our store of word meanings. The fundamental difference between the two routes, then, is that a pronunciation is either built up from sub-lexical components ('assembled' phonology) or looked up as a whole ('addressed' phonology).

This model has been extremely successful in enabling us to understand acquired dyslexia. Acquired dyslexia involves a loss of reading ability as a result of brain injury. This contrasts with developmental dyslexia which is an impairment, possibly congenital, in learning to read in the first place. The model can explain a pattern of acquired dyslexia known as *surface dyslexia* which is

Figure 1

A dual route model for the pronounciation of print based on Coltheart (1985).

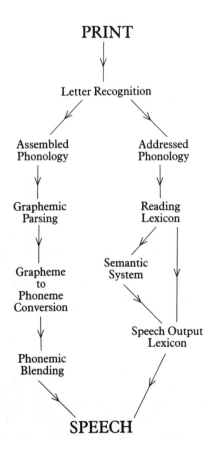

PRINT

Letter Recognition

Assembled Phonology

Addressed Phonology

Graphemic Parsing

Reading Lexicon

Grapheme to Phoneme Conversion

Semantic System

Speech Output Lexicon

Phonemic Blending

SPEECH

characterized by poor reading of irregularly spelled words such as 'yacht' or 'colonel'. These words tend to be read as if they were regular. So 'colonel' might be read COLL-OH-NELL. In one memorable instance, a patient pronounced 'LISTEN' as 'LISTON' and responded 'that's the famous boxer' (Marshall and Newcombe, 1973). Despite their problems with irregular words, however, these patients can produce a plausible pronunciation of unfamiliar non-words ('blasp', for example). What might be responsible for such an unusual pattern of performance? This impairment can be explained in a straight-forward manner if one assumes that damage has occurred to the part of the reading system that involves *addressed* phonology. This would mean that the patient is heavily reliant on *assembled phonology*. This allows them to generate a plausible pronunciation for a non-word like 'blasp', but means that they cannot pronounce many irregular words correctly. Consequently, words like 'colonel' or 'yacht' are pronounced as if they were non-words.

The success of the model does not end there. Following the discovery of surface dyslexia, it became clear that there should also exist another form of acquired dyslexia in which the ability to use assembled phonology was lost, while the ability to read a word via addressed phonology was intact. This pattern had never been noticed before, but as soon as researchers started looking for it, several case studies of what is now known as *phonological dyslexia* were reported in rapid succession in the early 1980s. In cases of phonological dyslexia, the patient finds it almost impossible to read any word with which he or she was unfamiliar prior to brain injury. However they can still read a very high percentage of pre-morbidly familiar words accurately, regardless of their spelling. This pattern of performance suggests that these patients find it difficult to assemble a pronunciation, but they can continue to read familiar words because the lexical system, utilizing addressed phonology, is still working effectively. This means that they are able to retrieve the appropriate pronunciation of a word as a whole from the speech output lexicon. The dual-route model of reading is thus able not only to explain an existing set of data within a simple theoretical model, it also successfully pinpointed the existence of an entirely new type of acquired dyslexia.

Moreover, a closer look at individual patients provides support for what was said about the heterogeneity of groups at the start of this section. So, the more that surface dyslexics are studied, the more it becomes obvious that the condition fractionates; there are important differences between individual surface dyslexics. These differences can also be accommodated by the dual route model.

For example, one surface dyslexic can accurately define the irregular words that he regularizes in pronunciation tasks (for instance, pronouncing 'colonel' as 'COL-OH-NELL'). His problem is therefore at the level of the speech output lexicon. Another, who has problems in understanding speech as well as problems in understanding print, has an impairment at the semantic level. Yet another patient's problems are at the level of the visual input lexicon itself. A different patient correctly reads irregular words aloud but fails to retrieve their meaning, responding for example to a word on a card with: 'HYENA, what the heck is that?' (Schwartz, Saffran and Marin, 1980). This patient has lost the semantic representations for many words (the brain's store of meanings), but retains the link between the visual input and speech output lexicons. In addition, Coltheart (1985) argues that other patients have impairments to the assembled phonology system. One patient pronounces every letter in a word separately, which suggests a problem of graphemic parsing. Another patient could name letters but could not sound them out, suggesting a problem at the level of grapheme to phoneme assignment.

I have gone into such detail about individual patients to try to convince you first, that it can be misleading to categorize patients too narrowly into groups, and second, that the dual-route model I described can accommodate a wide variety of data from different individual cases. There is an equally important additional point that I want to make. Since brain damage can produce these very precise differences between patients, it is difficult to avoid the conclusion that there is one part of the brain that has the precise function of carrying out each piece of information processing that is specified within the cognitive model. It seems to me to be perverse in the extreme to attempt to resist the claim that the brain is literally carrying out these functions. Cognitive neuropsychology thus provides powerful evidence that the level of analysis which functionalists use to describe brain processes is the correct one.

4.3   Models of face processing
Finally, I want to move from cognitive models of word recognition to cognitive models of face recognition. This is because I believe that one of the basic assumptions of functionalism can be successfully illustrated, and alternatives to functionalism can be successfully confronted, by a careful examination of the effects of brain injury on face processing tasks.

According to functionalism, it is useful to categorize environmental stimuli on the basis of what they mean to a subject rather than on the basis of their gross physical characteristics. In other words, when it comes to an attempt to understand how someone is likely to respond to a stimulus, a description of the stimulus in terms of its simple physical dimensions is not going to be of any value. No laws of behaviour are going to be formulated which are in any way dependent on the basic physical characteristics of a stimulus. One might think that radical behaviourists such as Skinner would advocate the classification of stimuli along purely physical dimensions. However Skinner (1957) writes of verbal behaviour as being 'under the control of extremely subtle properties' of a stimulus, but never clarifies what this might mean. This is one of the reasons why Chomsky (1959) was able to launch such a devastating attack on radical behaviourism.

The inadequacy of conceptualizing stimuli in purely physical terms is neatly illustrated in a study by Campbell, Landis and Regard (1986). They compared the performance of two patients on a lip-reading task and on a task which required analysis of facial expression. One of the patients could not categorize the expression on faces that she was shown in photographs in terms of whether the expression was one of happiness, anger, surprise and so on. However, she *was* able to judge the sounds that were being mouthed by faces in photographs, and showed other evidence of normal lip-reading abilities. By contrast, the other patient (known as 'T'), was able to judge facial expression normally but had lost the ability to lip-read. At first sight, the reader might doubt whether even people *without* brain injury usually possess significant lip-reading skills. In fact, though, McGurk and MacDonald (1976) have shown the extent to which we use information about the position of a speaker's lips to help us recognise spoken words. They showed, for instance, that if you look at someone saying 'ga' on a piece of film with the sound being removed and replaced by the sound 'ba', then subjects will actually report hearing the sound 'da'. Patient 'T' was not susceptible to the McGurk effect.

It is important to remember just how similar the physical features are that one must respond to in facial speech and facial expression judgements. In both cases it is the position of the lips that conveys much of the vital information. If it is the simple physical characteristics of a stimulus that play the key role in generalizations about behaviour, then we might expect to find patients who have lost the ability to lip-read and lost the ability to judge expression, but not patients who have lost only one of these two abilities while retaining the other. According to the functionalist, of course, facial expression and lip-reading are likely to be dealt with by distinct parts of the information-processing system because the nature of the information that they convey is so different. Therefore the dissociation which Campbell and her colleagues have demonstrated between lip-reading and expression analysis makes perfect sense from a functionalist perspective.

4.4 Phenomenology

I now turn to a consideration of some implications of the cognitive neuropsychology of face recognition for phenomenology – an approach to the mind and mental phenomena that gives prominence to introspectible 'phenomena' understood as acts of consciousness and their immediate objects. Phenomenologists such as Dreyfus (1972) argue that the level of explanation utilized in cognitive science does not truly exist. The physical brain and the world of introspectible phenomenal experience are all that there really is: 'no cognitive psychologist has succeeded in defining another sort of input between these two which would provide the ultimate bits of information to which rules are applied' (p. 199). My favourite phenomenological quote, however, comes from Jennings (1986):

> . . . social psychologists spent years conducting experiments to specify the exact parameters of a hypothetical motivational state called 'cognitive dissonance' . . . Certainly, an enormous amount of unproductive work could have been saved if phenomenological analyses were first performed to 'see' if this supposed psychological state actually existed . . . (p. 1236).

One of the most remarkable findings to have emerged from contemporary cognitive neuropsychology is the demonstration that patients can show evidence of covert recognition of faces that were known pre-morbidly, in the absence of any conscious awareness that the face is familiar. For instance, the patient PH (Young and De Haan, 1988) shows no overt recognition of faces. When he is shown a pair of faces and has to decide which of the two is a celebrity, he performs at chance level, even though he performs almost as well as normal subjects on this task when the faces are replaced by their names. In other situations, however, PH's pattern of responding makes it clear that he is recognizing familiar faces at an unconscious level. The clearest example of this is PH's performance in priming tasks (Young, Hellawell and De Haan, 1988).

Associative priming is a well known phenomenon in cognitive psychology. If one has to identify a stimulus – for instance a word – then one can accomplish this more quickly if presentation of the word is immediately preceded by an associated word or picture. For instance, when subjects have to decide whether certain names are familiar or not (say, Oliver Hardy) they respond more quickly if they are shown, a few tenths of seconds earlier, a picture of a person who is associated with the target name (Stan Laurel). Now, the remarkable finding is that PH shows exactly the same pattern. He can identify a familiar name more quickly if it is preceded by an associated face, even though he does not report finding any face familiar. What is more, he shows every bit as much priming from these unrecognized faces as he does from names (which, of course, he *can* recognize overtly).

These data are of great theoretical significance within cognitive neuropsychology. For instance the strength of the priming effect suggests that covert recognition reflects the otherwise intact operation of the normal face recognition system when it is cut off from some centre of consciousness (Young and De Haan, 1988) rather than the operation of a separate, subsidiary face recognition system. This in turn opens up some fascinating questions about the role of consciousness itself in memory and perception.

What I want to emphasize here is the impact of these findings for a phenomenologist. If all that exists in reality are low-level physical processes in the brain on the one hand, and the high-level products of phenomenological awareness on the other, then how is PH's covert recognition of faces to be conceptualized? You could ask PH to introspect into the contents of his phenomenological awareness when he is looking at faces for as long as you liked, but there would be no insight that any recognition is occurring. That PH is genuinely recognizing faces, however, cannot be seriously questioned. This pattern of findings would appear to be impossible to accommodate from the viewpoint of phenomenology. As Bauer put it in a recent BBC television discussion of covert recognition, 'Our normal experience of perception, of seeing objects or faces as an all or none process, is a trick that the brain plays on us'. It is a trick that should no longer fool anyone except phenomenologists.

Finally, as in the discussion of reading, I could point to other patients who have a wide variety of different face processing problems. For example, some have difficulties in retrieving semantic information about people (for example their occupation), some have difficulties specific to the retrieval of people's names, and some can remember old faces but cannot learn new ones. The problems which these and other patients suffer can mostly be explained in terms of detailed functional models of face processing such as that proposed by Bruce and Young (1986), in the same way that patients' different reading problems could be explained by Coltheart (1985).

Bearing all this in mind, what are we to make of Searle's (1984) claim that the brain does not identify faces via information processing of the kind described in cognitive models and that, as far as the cognitive sciences are concerned, there may simply be no story to tell? His suggestion is that 'facial recognition may be as simple and as automatic as making footprints in the sand'. If this were true, then it is hard to see how impairments in face processing could be explained so economically in terms of the cognitive modules that functional models contain. If these information-processing modules exist only in the minds of cognitive scientists, rather than in the minds of the subjects they study, then breakdowns in face recognition or word recognition should either be all-or-none, or else they should be extremely difficult to conceptualize within the vocabulary of cognitive psychology. In fact, the striking dissociations that one can observe in neuropsychological patients show us instead that skills which seem so simple and automatic in the course of everyday life are in fact comprised of a large number of functional sub-components, any of which may be impaired by brain injury. Work such as that of Young et al (1988) has even shown us how something that was traditionally assumed to be as intangible and subjective as the nature of conscious awareness itself can be disrupted by physical damage to the brain and can be successfully studied by the observational techniques of cognitive psychology. The fact is that cognitive neuropsychologists have significantly increased our understanding of the effects of brain injury on behaviour by conceptualizing mental processes in purely functional terms without regard to their subjective qualities or to physiology. This seems to me to represent good grounds for believing that functionalism itself may well be true. It is time for certain philosophers to come and take a hard look at the data which we have collected before they dismiss our models and our philosophical assumptions so glibly.

Suggested Reading

Although neither have been cited directly in the text, the philosophical ideas in this chapter have been heavily influenced by the work of Jerry Fodor and Zenon Pylyshyn. Fodor (1981) provides a very clear description of functionalism, and his book *The Modularity of Mind* discusses some of the philosophical issues surrounding cognitive neuropsychology. Pylyshyn (1984) contains an important account of the relationship between cognitive psychology and artificial intelligence, and Pylyshyn (1973) contains an interesting discussion of the differences between cognitive science and phenomenology. A very clear introduction to current work in cognitive neuropsychology is provided by Ellis and Young (1988). Churchland's *Matter and Consciousness* is an equally lucid introduction to the philosophy of mind.

References

Bruce, V., and Young, A. W. (1986). 'Understanding face recognition'. *British Journal of Psychology*, **77**, 305–27.

Campbell, R., Landis, T., and Regard, M. (1986). 'Face recognition and lip-reading: A neurological dissociation'. *Brain*, **109**, 509–21.

Chomsky, N. (1959) Review of Skinner's *Verbal Behavior*. *Language* **35**, 26–58.

Churchland, P. (1988). *Matter and Consciousness* (Revised Edition) Cambridge, Mass.: MIT Press.

Coltheart, M. (1985). 'Cognitive neuropsychology and the study of reading'. In M. Posner and O. Marin (Eds), *Attention and Performance XI*. Hillsdale, N.J.: Lawrence Erlbaum.

Dennett, D. C. (1988). 'Quining qualia'. In A. Marcel and E. Bisiach (Eds), *Consciousness in Contemporary Science*. Oxford University Press.

Dreyfuss, H. L. (1972). *What computers can't do: a critique of artificial reason*. New York: Harper and Row.

Ellis, A. W., and Young, A. W. (1988). *Human cognitive neuropsychology*. Hillsdale, N.J.: Lawrence Erlbaum.

Fodor, J. A. (1981). 'The mind-body problem'. *Scientific American*, **244**, 114–23.

Fodor, J. A. (1983). *The Modularity of Mind*. Cambridge, Mass.: MIT Press.

Jennings, J. L. (1986). 'Husserl revisited'. *American Psychologist*, **41**, 1231–40.

McGurk, H., and MacDonald, J. (1976). 'Hearing lips and seeing voices'. *Nature*, **264**, 746–8.

Marshall, J. C., and Newcombe, F. (1973). 'Patterns of paralexia: A psycholinguistic approach'. *Journal of Psycholinguistic Research*, **2**, 175–99.

Patterson, K. E. (1982). 'The relation between phonological coding and reading: Further neuropsychological observations'. In A.

W. Ellis (Ed.), *Normality and pathology in cognitive functions*. London: Academic Press.

Pylyshyn, Z. W. (1973). 'Minds, machines and phenomenology: Some reflections on Dreyfus' "What computers can't do" '. *Cognition*, **3**, 57–77.

Pylyshyn, Z. W. (1984). *Computation and Cognition*. Cambridge, Mass.: MIT Press.

Schwartz, M. F., Saffran, E. M., and Marin, O. S. M. (1980). 'Fractioning the reading process: Evidence for word-specific print-to-sound associations'. In M. Coltheart, K. Patterson, and J. Marshall (Eds), *Deep Dyslexia*. London: Routledge and Kegan Paul.

Searle, J. (1984). *Minds, brains and science. The 1984 Reith Lectures*. London: BBC Publications.

Skinner, B. F. (1957). *Verbal Behavior*. New York: Appleton-Century-Crofts.

Young, A. W., and De Haan, E. H. F. (1988). 'Boundaries of covert recognition in prosopagnosia'. *Cognitive Neuropsychology*, **5**, 317–36.

Young, A. W., Halliwell, D. A. and De Haan, E. (1988). 'Cross domain semantic priming in normal subjects and a prosopagnosic patient'. *Quarterly Journal of Experimental Psychology*, **40A**, 561–80.

5

A Critique of Neuromythology

RAYMOND TALLIS

Introduction

One of man's great intellectual adventures – the exploration and understanding of his own nervous system – is progressing at a rate undreamed of only a few decades ago. There are many reasons for this. First of all, there have been important advances in experimental methods: single cell recordings with exquisitely fine electrodes; novel methods of imaging the internal structure of neurons and the connections between them; cell culture techniques permitting the growth and development of nervous systems to be studied in great detail; and sophisticated computational and statistical analysis of data permitting better mathematical modelling of large and small scale events in the nervous system and its functional connections. Secondly, there have been important conceptual advances. Since Hubel and Wiesel began publishing their work in the late 1950s, there has been an increasing appreciation of the way in which nervous systems are so structured as to ensure that certain events of special importance to the organism have an increased likelihood of triggering activity in the relevant places. Alongside this, there has been growing awareness of the plasticity of the nervous system and of the extent to which the 'hard-wiring' of the wetware of the brain is itself modulated by the brain's own experience. At a microscopic level, the range of factors and substances believed to influence the interactions between neurones has been greatly widened. And there has been a remarkable interchange of ideas between computational theorists and neuroscientists, in which attempts to create computer models of neural function have not only generated powerful new tools for the interpreting of the brain but have also fed back into computer theory and practice. At every level – from the simple oligosynaptic circuits involved in the tropisms of primitive organisms to the complex neural activity implicit in human perception – computational models dominate scientific thought. The converging conceptual worlds of computational theory and neuroscience are expressed in the huge and powerful 'neural nets' of parallel distributed processors and in the emergent science of cognitive neurobiology in which the brain is approached as an immensely complex information processor (see Chapter 7). A third reason for the accelerating rate of advance in neuroscience is that there are simply larger numbers of better funded people engaged in research in this field today than ever before. And they come from diverse backgrounds: not only physiologists but also physicists, molecular biologists and mathematicians are attracted into neuroscience which threatens to displace physics and even molecular biology as the queen of the sciences.

It would be perverse, then, to deny that very exciting things have been happening and it is no business of this chapter to disparage these remarkable advances in understanding of the brain. My concern here is with the mythology that has accompanied these advances; the meta-physical claims implicit – and not infrequently explicit – in the way they have been described. I am concerned, that is to say, with neuro-mythology. The founding myth of neuromythology is that our more detailed knowledge of the nervous system has resulted – or very soon will result – in an increased understanding of the mind, indeed of the very nature of understanding itself. If we do not yet have the solution to the problem of consciousness, we are at least working towards it within the right framework. Any delay in arriving at a solution will be due not to our being on the wrong track but simply to the enormous complexity of the problem. (We are frequently reminded that the brain has many millions of neurones and that these have many billions of connections). When we have a complete account of the brain, we are assured, con-sciousness will be intellectually transparent and the mind will assume its rightful place as just another part of (physical) nature, obedient to the laws that hold sway elsewhere in the material universe.

This is the myth that I want to examine here. Although the majority of scientists tend to be a little coy about metaphysical matters in their professional publications, they are often less so outside when writing elsewhere, being prone to describe the framework of presuppositions about perception within which they conduct their investigations as if it were a discovery in its own right and that 'discovery' an explanation of perception. And although the majority of materialist philosophers base their belief in the neurophysiological theory of perception on arguments rather than observations, they are, nevertheless, greatly influenced by the apparent successes of neurophysiology.

The Materialist Theory of Perception

We may think of consciousness as having two components: sensation and perception on the one hand and willing or agency on the other; or input and output. For the purposes of the present discussion I am going to confine myself to sensation and perception and ignore behaviour. I do this not only because the issues are easier to grasp in the case of perception than in the case of voluntary movement, but also because neurophysiologists of movement are less prone to wild claims than neurophysiologists of perception: most of the former would admit that we do not yet have the faintest idea how voluntary activity is able to utilize or over-ride reflex pathways; how we mobilize so-called 'motor programmes' when we need them; or even where in the nervous system voluntary movement is initiated.

The metaphysical framework for the neurophysiology of perception is provided by *the Causal Theory of Perception* (henceforth referred to as the CTP). This goes back at least as far as Aristotle. According to Aristotle, perceiving an object is the result of being acted upon by it: objects of perception, acting via a medium of perception, causally affect the perceiver's sensory apparatus. As a result, the apparatus 'receives the form of the object without its matter'; the change in the apparatus *is* perception. The CTP is susceptible of a materialist interpretation and this, in its neurophysiological version, is what I am going to focus on. This explicitly materialist framework of contemporary neurophysiology originated much later than Aristotle. One of its earliest expressions is to be found in Thomas Hobbes's *Leviathan*, published in 1651:

> The cause of sense is the external body, or object, which presseth the organ proper to each sense, either immediately, as in taste or touch; or, mediately, as in seeing, hearing or smelling.

The external object

> worketh on the eyes, ears and other parts of a man's body; and by diversity of working produceth diversity of experience.

We experience the world in virtue of the fact that the contents of the world *impinge* on us. Our bodies and the world bump into one another and there is an exchange of energy between them. This exchange of energy explains how we perceive the world.

This is now so widely accepted that it seems less like a theory, or even a theoretical framework, than a piece of common sense; and in one form or another it encompasses the views of the majority of Anglo-American philosophers and neuroscientists about the basis of consciousness or, at the very least, of perception. Although some philosophers and psychologists would emphasize the role of action in controlling perception (see chapter 2) and some talk of 'top down' constraints on the interpretation of the perceived, the causal role of incident energy remains fundamental and the materialist version of the CTP essentially unchallenged.

The *neurophysiological* version of the CTP, with which we are concerned here, holds that perception is the result of the constant interaction between the material world and the nervous system. In particular, perceptual awareness, and so consciousness itself, is identified with certain events taking place in the higher reaches of the central nervous system where a chain of events, collectively described as sensory processing, and originating from the object that is perceived, reaches a terminus. For example, I perceive this flower in front of me because light which has been reflected from it impinges on my retina and causes trains of nerve impulses to travel along the visual pathways to the visual cortex. The events in the visual cortex correspond in some way (see later) to perception of the flower. It is out of such events that the visual field, indeed the visual world, is composed. And these, along with other cortical events relating to other sensory pathways, are the basis of consciousness and of our state of being 'worlded'. In other words, according to the neurophysiological CTP, sensation, perception, experience, consciousness, are intimately related to, or even boil down to, large numbers of trains or patterns of nerve impulses. We perceive what is 'out there' or what is 'around us' as a result of the transfer of energy from objects or events to specialized parts of the body known collectively as 'the sensory system'.

I shall argue that this framework is explanatorily inadequate and that the inadequacy is inherited by theories developed within it. Such theories contribute nothing to explaining the mystery of perception. At best they re-describe perception in a manner that actually generates more problems than it solves. Neuroscience, which depends upon a materialist CTP for the explanatory force of its explanations of the mind, cannot, therefore, sustain any claim to be explaining or advancing our understanding of the basis of perception, or of the mind.

The Neurophysiology of Perception: Exposition

The main task of sensory neurophysiology has been to establish in more precise detail how 'the diversity of working produceth diversity of experience' – the modern term for which is 'coding of sensory information'. The framework for the investigation of 'sensory coding' was established in the nineteenth and early twentieth centuries, when

the business of explaining perception was transformed into the more
specific project of correlating the physical properties of perceived
objects and events with patterns of activity in the nervous system
and the latter with the subjective properties of the experience:

PHYSICAL PROPERTIES   PATTERN OF NEURAL   SUBJECTIVE PROPERTIES
     OF STIMULUS   :   ACTIVITY   :   OF EXPERIENCE

It was early appreciated that, apart from, say, minor variations
in the speed of conduction, the impulses in all nerve fibres have
essentially identical characteristics. This was explicitly recognized
by the early twentieth century physiologists who saw their
fundamental task as that of discovering how the infinite variety
of the perceived world could be reflected in, or reconstructed in,
the rather monotonous nervous system. With the advent of digital
computers and the development of information theory in the 1940s
and 1950s, this job was interpreted as being that of finding out how
the nervous system 'encoded' reality in a digital form. The task of the
nervous system was seen to be a computational one.

It would not be appropriate here to attempt the impossible task
of summarizing modern sensory physiology but it is necessary to
discuss a few basic principles and laws. We can think of experience
as being differentiated both *qualitatively* and *quantitatively*. For
neurophysiologists and neuropsychologists, the way forward in
understanding perception has been to correlate these dimensions
of experience with, firstly, the material properties of the experienced
object or event (usually regarded as the 'stimulus') and, secondly, the
patterns of discharges in the sensory system.

Qualitative Aspects of Experience
The *quality* – or *modality* – of the experience depends less upon the
quality of energy reaching the nervous system than upon which
parts of the sensory system are activated: stimulation of the retinal
receptors causes an experience of light; stimulation of the receptors
in the inner ear gives rise to the experience of sound; and so on.
Muller's nineteenth-century '*doctrine of specific energies*' formalized
the ordinary observation that different sense organs are sensitive to
different physical properties of the world and that when they are
stimulated, sensations specific to those organs are experienced. It
was proposed that there are endings (or receptors) within the nervous
system which are attuned to specific types of energy. For example,
retinal receptors in the eye respond to light energy, cochlear endings
in the ear to vibrations in the air, and so on. Of course, high

energy stimulation even of the wrong kind may stimulate a sensory ending; for example, excessive pressure on the eyeball will produce a sensation of light. Contrariwise, over-intense stimulation of the appropriate kind will evoke pain. These are, however, abnormal situations; for ordinary perception, the doctrine of specific energies holds.

This early framework for sensory physiology – of a piece with the Hobbesian idea of 'the organ proper to each sense' – has undergone a good deal of refinement. Within the cochlea, for example, it has been shown that there are endings that respond preferentially to sounds of high rather than low pitch. More centrally, in the cerebral cortex the afferent fibres from groups of receptors are 'wired together' so that more complexly patterned stimuli – such as edges or lines of a certain inclination – may preferentially elicit neural activity and the corresponding subjective experience. The work of Hubel and Wiesel, in particular, put the conception of neurones as 'feature detectors', rather than simply energy detectors, on the map, supporting the idea that for each cell in the cortex there was a specific pattern of excitation that would reliably excite it. Each cell had its own stimulus requirements and when it became active this said something about the nature of the event or object in its own part of the visual field. It would not be too great a distortion of the facts to say that the main thrust of twentieth century sensory physiology has been to move the application of the doctrine of specific energies inwards from the sensory ending towards and into the cortex.

Quantitative Aspects of Experience

There are three fundamental dimensions of *quantity* in experience: (a) intensity; (b) (spatial) extensity; and (c) duration. At a neurophysiological level, the intensity of an experience is typically reflected in the number of neurones activated (the phenomenon of 'recruitment') and, more specifically, in the firing frequency of the relevant neurones. Extensity (for example the size of a patch of light) usually correlates with the number and spatial distribution of receptors activated. Finally, duration is correlated with the period of time for which the relevant neurones are active. (I am leaving aside phenomena such as accommodation, whereby a constant stimulus when sustained may activate the nervous system progressively less intensively, with a corresponding reduction in the perceived intensity of the stimulus. These, and other features of 'adaptation', do not invalidate the underlying conceptual framework.)

The earliest psychophysical observations demonstrated a correlation between the intensity of the physical stimulus and subjective reports of the intensity of the resultant experience. These were eventually formalized in the Weber-Fechner law which reported a quantitative relationship between stimulus and subjective experience, the sensation increasing in proportion to the logarithm of the magnitude of the physical stimulus. A quantitative correlation between the objective intensity of stimulus and the pattern of neural activity was subsequently demonstrated by physiologists recording from individual fibres. Since the work of S. S. Stevens in the 1930s and later, it has been recognized that, although the Weber-Fechner Law holds for many sorts of sensory experience, the exponent varies widely; nevertheless, the principle of a quantitative correlation between external stimulus, neural activity and experienced sensation remains intact and now appears to be well-established.

So much for the basic laws. The repeated confirmation of the correlation between the physical characteristics of the stimulus and the characteristics of the neural activity it triggers, and between the characteristics of the stimulus and that of the subjective sensation, has encouraged the belief that our sensations are in some sense to be understood in terms of a set of stimulation levels (spiking frequencies) in the appropriate sensory pathways. And it would seem that physiologists – working within the common-sense assumptions that we experience the world because it impinges upon our bodies and that what we experience is what, directly or indirectly, impinges on our bodies in the form of transferred energy – have made considerable progress in explaining how 'the diversity of working produceth the diversity of experience'.

Or have they? In the discussion that follows, I shall question whether:

(a) scientific, and in particular physiological, observations have provided any additional, independent evidence in support of the impingement theory of perception/experience;

(b) the impingement theory, with its physiological embellishments, goes any way towards explaining perception.

One might expect, a priori, that no *empirical* (that is perception-based) observations could provide evidence in support of a metaphysical theory of perception; that perceptions would not enable us to get to the root of perception. By unmasking the circularity of physiological explanations of perception that have been developed within the framework of the idea of the 'impingement', I shall show that the *a priori* principle is upheld.

The Neurophysiology of Perception: Critique

1) The Psychophysical Laws

According to the Muller doctrine, sensory endings are particularly sensitive to certain types of energy – light energy in the case of retinal endings, sound energy in the case of cochlear endings, and so on – and that when they, or their central connections, are stimulated a specific modality of sensation is experienced. According to the Weber-Fechner law, there is a correlation between the intensity of the energy incident on the sense ending and the magnitude of the corresponding subjective experience. These laws seem a) to provide empirical support for the neurophysiological account of perception and b) to contribute to its explanatory force. I will argue, however, that a) and b) are apparent rather than real.

a) Do the laws provide empirical support for the neurophysiological account of perception?

Both laws are derived from observations and there can be no doubt about their empirical credentials. Are those empirical credentials sufficient, however, to sustain the metaphysical implications it is thought that the laws have? Empirical observations may generate laws that correlate one type of experience with another; but can they take us 'beneath' experience to its basis? It seems unlikely that experience can take us outside of the closed circle of experience to reveal that upon which experience – experience in general, rather than particular experience – is based. Yet some writers seem to think that the laws do just that; and that the quantitative observations encompassed in the laws take us beyond (subjective) experience because they are based upon objective measures of physical energy, utilizing scientific instruments.

The objectivity of the psychophysical laws – and the escape from the closed circle of experience – is more apparent than real. For the scales on the 'objective' measuring devices used to derive the data upon which the laws are founded are not validated independently of subjective experience. In the final analysis, the scientific estimate of the intensity of light, for example, is rooted in subjective experience of brightness. Our objective measures of light intensity would be discarded if they *universally* gave answers that contradicted our subjective experiences. Scientific measurements may 'correct', 'reform' or at least question individual unaided observations but there cannot be a systematic, universal discrepancy. The cash value of scientific observations in this context must therefore be based upon subjective experience and cannot be greater than the cash value of the latter; for it is subjective experience that, ultimately, validates our objective scales of energy intensity. We may use physical methods of measuring light intensity that are apparently independent of our subjective experience – for instance photosensitive cells – but these are accepted because they correlate to a greater or lesser degree, under normal circumstances, with subjective experiences of brightness. If there were simply no correlation whatsoever between the electrical output of a photo-electric cell and some other measure of light intensity directly or indirectly related to experience, it would not have been accepted as a way of measuring light intensity. However indirectly related to sensory experience a laboratory quantification of a particular form of energy may be, in the end the rate of exchange between one form of energy and another – the way in which we compare the quantity of one with the quantity of another – reposes upon the gold standard of subjectivity. The observation that a sensory system has a relatively low threshold for the form of energy which it transforms into experience is not only a pre-scientific empirical observation but also one that science could not reform – if reform were necessary – nor independently validate.

It would seem therefore that the contingent or empirical links uncovered by experimental science between the nature of the stimulus and the intensity and distribution of neural activity on the one hand and between the properties of the stimulus and those of the evoked sensation on the other are not based on discoveries that go beyond, or arise outside of, ordinary experience. Ultimately, the two variables of impinging stimulus and evoked sensation are internally rather than externally related; for our estimate of the properties of the impinging stimulus – and the decision as to whether or not those properties 'justify' the sensation they give rise to – is based upon the norms of, necessarily subjective, experience. The psychophysical laws relate sets of experiences, rather than relating experiences to something external to experience.

Interestingly, the psychophysical laws may be even more entrained in subjectivity than I have suggested. Recent work has confirmed that it is not possible to measure intensity of subjective sensation in a way that is distinct from and independent of measurement of the physical stimulus from which it is derived; that Fechner's logarithmic transform exists only as a mathematical construction to link reports of sensations with measurements of stimuli; and an experimental subject's conformity to Stevens' power law depends on his getting the experiment 'right'.

Even if the laws of psychophysics are empirical laws in the sense of correlating one type of observation or experience with another, they are *not* laws about the relationship between experience and that which lies outside of experience and is its trigger or basis – 'pure', objective, material energy. Psychophysical laws, in other words, provide no independent evidence for a physical basis of perception. To assert this is merely to reiterate a point that should be obvious: that science, however sophisticated its instrumentation, cannot generate observations that somehow enable us to look at the relationship between experience and the world as it were from outside of experience.

(b) The lack of explanatory force of the laws

The lack of explanatory force of neurophysiological and psychophysical observations is explicitly admitted by some scientists. It has been well expressed by the biologist Richard Dawkins:

> The sensation of seeing is for us very different from the sensation of hearing, but this cannot be directly due to the physical differences between light and sound. Both light and sound are, after all, translated . . . by the respective sense organs into the same kind of nerve impulse. It is impossible to tell, from the physical attributes of a nerve impulse, whether it is conveying information about light, about sound or about smell.

A similar point was made by the seventeenth-century philosopher John Locke, who saw it as an insoluble mystery. Dawkins, however, feels he has an answer. He asserts, rather cryptically, that

> It is because we *internally use* our visual information and our sound information in different ways and for different purposes that the sensations of seeing and hearing are so different. It is not directly because of the physical differences between light and sound

This is not a very convincing escape from the circularity of the psychophysical laws. On the contrary, it exposes the explanatory weakness of the Muller Doctrine, if it is offered as an advance in our understanding of the origin of different modalities of sensation, of why the world feels as it does; and, even more, if it is offered as an account of our being able to feel the world at all. The Doctrine is at best a circular re-statement of the obvious: Why did I experience those vibrations in the air as sounds? Because they stimulated my auditory, rather than my visual, system. But why do those particular nerve endings count as part of the *auditory* system? Because they are connected with the area of the cortex that is designated the auditory cortex. But why is that particular area of the cortex designated the *auditory* cortex? Because it is concerned with the reception of sound. But what evidence is there that this bit of the cortex *is* concerned with the reception of sound? Well, there is the fact that it is connected to sensory endings that are designed specifically to respond to vibrations in the air. And so we are back to the beginning . . . The circularity is obvious: the destination of the particular sensory pathway defines/explains the starting point, the starting point defines/explains the destination.

(2) Metaphysical Problems
We are now close to the fundamental inadequacies of the neurophysiological explanation of perception. Consider the physiologist's intuition that an increased neuronal firing frequency *explains* increased intensity of experience. This depends for its *prima facie* plausibility upon the assumption that there can, should or must be a correlation between the quantity of energy incident on nervous tissue and the intensity of experience. But to *begin* with this assumption is to by-pass, rather than explain, the mystery of perception as it presents itself to us if we assume that perception occurs because the perceived object impinges directly or indirectly upon the nervous system. The mystery that it by-passes is that of *how energy is transformed into sensation, experience, information* or whatever. Only when *that* has been explained might the Weber-Fechner Law and the Muller doctrine – connecting the quantity and modality of energy with the quantity and modality of sensation – have any explanatory value. The specific observations of neurophysiologists, correlating stimulus properties, neural activities and the characteristics of subjective reports of sensation, contribute to explaining how 'the diversity of working produceth a diversity of experience' *only if we have already explained how 'working' produceth 'experience' at all*. Or how energy impinging on the nervous system is transformed into information in, or addressed to, the nervous system. I would argue that physiologists of perception, working within the framework created by the Muller Doctrine and the Weber-Fechner Law are in a position of dotting the i's and crossing the t's in a text that has not yet been written.

This is only the beginning of the neurophysiologist's metaphysical problems. For the materialist version of the CTP is beset with many difficulties that ultimately make its claim to have explanatory force somewhat vacuous. I should like to deal briefly with the most important of these.

a) How do the neural events in the brain actually relate to
perceptions?

There are several rival accounts of this, some of them not compatible
with materialism. For example, *substance* and *bundle* (or *event*)
dualism assert that the neural events *cause* the perceptual events.
In other words, the perception is a mental *effect* that is at one
step in the causal chain beyond the physical events. Since the
causal chain passes through perception and on to the rest of the
nervous system, perhaps triggering action, it must become physical
again. So one is left with the impossible task of explaining why a
perfectly respectable causal chain should 'go mental' for a while
and then, recovering its non-senses, should return to being purely
physical. Substance and bundle dualism for this and other reasons
are rather unpopular. *Property* dualism holds that the perception and
the neural events which are its physical basis are simply different
aspects, properties or attributes of the same (physical) events: what
the physiologist observes on examining the brain and what the
owner of the examined brain feels are two aspects of the same
event. This interpretation in no way diminishes the enigma of the
relationship between electrochemical events in the nervous system
and conscious experiences. For the idea of an object or an event
with two metaphysically different aspects – with, as it were, an
unextended mental front end and an extended physical rear end
– is deeply puzzling. Moreover, rather as substance dualism tends
to do, it seems to undermine the causal role of consciousness in,
for example, bringing about or influencing actions. For the causal
relations of events would be just the same irrespective of whether
or not the causal chain temporarily took on a mental aspect (as in
property dualism) or (as in substance dualism) 'went mental' for
a while. A further telling argument against the dual aspect theory –
and one that has been rarely noticed – is that 'aspects' are relative
to viewpoints; in other words, they emerge posterior to perceptions.
They cannot, therefore, be invoked to explain perceptions, even less
the manner in which perception is related to matter.

Most scientists implicitly, and the many philosophers explicitly,
prefer *identity* theories. These assert that perceptions are *strictly*
identical with certain events in the nervous system. Such theories
have to face the obvious objection that brain processes and mental
phenomena seem utterly unalike. For example, one can say of a brain
process that it occupies a particular point in space or that it can be
displayed on an oscilloscope screen; whereas neither of these things
could be said of, for example, the subjective sensation of the colour
blue or of the thought that I hate Monday mornings. It is difficult

to comprehend an object that is utterly unlike itself. This, in fact insuperable, difficulty is said to be overcome by proposing that mental phenomena and brain processes are the same stuff viewed within different theoretical frameworks. But this apparent escape is only another version of the dual aspect theory and inherits the latter's problems.

b) How/why does the causal chain linking object and perception have a beginning and an end?

The materialist versions of the CTP assume that there is a causal chain that begins with the perceived object and ends with the perception. The perception then 'reaches back' to the perceived object. Since this causal chain is but part of a boundless nexus of causal chains that originate before and outside the perceived object and end beyond the perceiving body, it is not very clear why the former should count as an 'origin'. Why, in other words, should perception be of the perceived object rather than any other object in the causal chain further back in the causal chain; why every perception should not be of the Big Bang that started off the Universe. Nor is it clear why the events in the cerebral cortex should count as a terminus; why they – rather than other events up- or down-stream – should constitute the perception. The CTP proclaims that the link between the perceived object and the perception is just an ordinary bit of the great causal nexus of nature (it needs to believe this, as we shall see presently) and yet it is prepared to accept that this segment of the chain has a rather privileged status; at the very least, that it has a beginning and an end.

c) How does the nervous system construct stable objects out of transient events?

The neurophysiological CTP asserts that perception consists of neural events triggered by events in the perceived object. The perceived world, however, seems to consist of stable objects as well as events occurring in them. The CTP requires, therefore, that transient events triggering transient events should give rise the idea of (permanent) objects as well as that of transient events within them. There is as yet no way of explaining how objects are constructed out of events; even less how the contrast between objects and events – one of the most pervasive features of everyday experience – is perceived.

d) The monotonous nervous system and the infinitely varied perceived world

As Dawkins pointed out in the passage quoted earlier, nerve impulses look pretty much the same whatever 'information' they are carrying. There is a sharp contrast between the monotony and similarity of the event in the nervous system and the variety of the perceived world. The perceived world is infinitely various, within and across modalities of sensation. Moreover, there is a clear distinction between present and past perception (memory); between memory and thought; between passive and active states of mind (daydreaming versus active recall, association of ideas versus directed meditation); and between the content and the level of consciousness. For causal theorists there are only nerve impulses, all of which are essentially the same. Perception, that is to say, boils down to the passage of sodium, potassium and other ions across semi-permeable membranes. It is legitimate, therefore, to ask what it is that is special about flea-bitten membranes that they should open up one object (the body) to all others, to a world. That they should make of one body a site where the variousness of all other bodies is in some way received.

There are several responses to this puzzle. They all involve the use of terms, or an appeal to concepts, that are illegitimate within the physicalist terms of reference of the neurophysiological CTP. Yes, it will be conceded, there *is* an apparent discrepancy between the rather simple nerve impulses nervous system and the complex representations of the world they afford us. This discrepancy, however, disappears when we recognize that it is not in individual nerve impulses that we must seek our representations of the world, but in their *patterns*. We must think of the nervous system encoding the perceived world; and in trying to understand this process we should consider not individual spikes but their potentially infinite combinations. The monotony of the individual neurones is irrelevant; what matters is the infinite variety of their combinations, of their patterns, which will become evident when we look at the nervous system at the right level.

I shall deal with the language of neurophysiological description shortly. However, it is necessary to say a word or two here to refute this seemingly compelling argument. We are so used to hearing talk about the nervous system 'encoding' the outside world that it is easy to forget that this is a metaphor and it is one that has no place in serious philosophical discussion of the mind-body problem or the philosophy of perception. The reason the coding metaphor has such currency in contemporary talk about perception is that it seems to suggest a way in which very simple and apparently homogenous elements such as nerve impulses can generate the richness and variety of consciousness.

Consider morse code. Using this very simple code, constructed out of dots and dashes, it is possible to encode a text of any degree of richness – even, for example, the works of Shakespeare. We may imagine therefore that neural dots and dashes – trains of impulses – can encode the variousness of experience. The analogy is attractive, but illegitimate. For the richness of morse code is a borrowed richness. First, it is parasitic, as all codes are, upon a primary, natural language. The meanings of morse are borrowed from the meanings of, say, English and messages encoded in it are meaningful only when they are interpreted, that is, decoded. Where is the decoder in the nervous system? In so far as it 'translates' at all, the nervous system 'translates' only from nerve impulses into nerve impulses, from sodium fluxes into sodium fluxes. This would not count as decoding unless muscular activity and other outputs were regarded as translations out of 'impulsese' into an interpreted language. But to interpret decoding in this way would be to espouse behaviourism and to by-pass consciousness altogether.

There is a second, yet more damaging, objection to the coding metaphor. Even translation from morse into natural language does not take us all the way to consciousness; for, in the absence of consciousness, language is merely variegated sound, rather than the rich varieties of meaning that are embodied in, for example, Shakespeare's texts. No one outside of the wilder sects of the artificial intelligence fraternity would suggest that a device that translated morse into natural language characters on the screen of a computer was releasing the consciousness implicit in morse. Natural languages such as English in turn owe their meanings to the conscious experiences of language users. Codes, in short, owe their meanings – and the variety that is constructed out of their monotonous elements – to consciousness. If the nervous system, therefore, owes the richness of the experiences which its activity embodies to the complexity of its codes, it must, ultimately owe its consciousness – to consciousness; for this will be required ultimately to turn its codes into complex experienced meanings, into experiences.

e) The unities of consciousness

Neurophysiological accounts of consciousness fail to address the problem of the unities of human consciousness. These unities are evident at different levels. There is the unity of the moment: different tactile and proprioceptive sensations amount to a coherent body image; different visual sensations cohere to a visual field; and sensations from different modalities converge to a general sensory field, an organized moment-by-moment presence of a world, so that the feeling in my hand as I hold a stone, the sight of the sea and the sound of the seagull behind me are all not merely present but co-present. Beyond this, current sensations converge with knowledge and memory and desire to make sense of the experience of the present: I not only experience this object but I recognize it – as something of a certain kind; as yours, as mine, as something I have seen before; and it means something to me in terms of my appetites and needs and ambitions. Beyond the unities of the present moment, there are unities over time. There is a self that coheres over time, so that a person p_2 at time t_2 is in some sense identical to the person p_1 at time t_1. This identity operates at a much higher level than mere identity of the body or continuity of habits. It is an explicit sense of continuing self which includes a sense of responsibility over time ('*I* did that') and, beneath this, a deep sense of psychological continuity ('I remember having that experience', 'I was there then'). Sensations and memories converge to create a continuing, if interrupted, sense of a coherent self. This sense of self is quite robust: when we wake up, we not only remember what we know, but also who we are. We are able to resume ourselves after sleep, after an alcoholic stupor, after an epileptic fit, after prolonged coma. In the light of these unities, it seems necessary to postulate a systematic set of relationships between the patterns of memory and the sense of 'I', the qualitative interior of mental experience.

The basis of these unities does not seem to lie within the nervous system as it is currently conceived. Since Sherrington's classic *The Integrative Action of the Nervous System*, there has been much talk of 'the integrative activity of the nervous system', based upon the convergence of nervous pathways. But the scattered activity of different parts of the nervous system seems to converge only at the cost of merging, and so losing, the components that come together in the process of convergence, rather in the manner of snowflakes joining a drift. There is no neurophysiological model of the kind of convergence that would seem to be necessary for the many different sensations of the moment to be brought into synthetic unity, without loss of their individual distinctiveness and specificity, into the instantaneous sense of 'being here'; or of the manner in which experience of many different moments can be synthesized into a sense of continuing self without those moments losing their separateness in memory. As for the recovery of consciousness, or wakefulness, there is no imaginable physiology of this 'light dawning over the whole'. Neural activity, triggered by a thousand scattered occasions, temporally and spatially dispersed, has nothing within itself to create the basis of these fundamental unities of consciousness.

f) Intentionality

The final and the greatest problem of the neurophysiological version of the CTP (or, indeed, any version of the CTP), is that it cannot explain the *intentionality* or *'aboutness'* that connects the neural events with the object they are supposed to be perceptions of. The causal theory of perception relates the object and contents of perception in two directions: there is an afferent limb connecting the object with the nervous system in which perception is generated; and an efferent limb in virtue of which the neural events 'reach out to' or 'are about or of' the object. The efferent limb carries the intentionality or aboutness that is fundamental to perception:

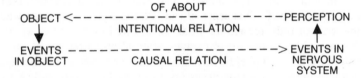

EFFERENT LIMB

OBJECT <-- OF, ABOUT INTENTIONAL RELATION --> PERCEPTION

EVENTS IN OBJECT -- CAUSAL RELATION --> EVENTS IN NERVOUS SYSTEM

AFFERENT LIMB

It is clear that the inwardly-directed causal, connection does not explain the outwardly-directed intentional relation.

Intentionality is usually overlooked by causal theorists who tend to see their job as being to sort out the afferent limb. It is therefore especially ironical that the neurophysiological CTP, which locates the basis of perception literally in the head, at a particular place away from the perceived object, actually sharpens the mystery of intentionality. For nature, after all, offers no other examples of causal chains in which events causally downstream refer back to the objects that are involved in producing their causal ancestors. The intentionality of perceptions – and indeed of other mental phenomena – makes them non-analogous to material phenomena outside of the nervous system. And nothing that takes place within the nervous system can explain why this property of intentionality should emerge there.

The Attractions of the Materialist Causal Theory of Perception

If, as I have argued, neurophysiological explanations of mind explain nothing and if physiological observations give us no purchase on the essentially metaphysical question of the nature of mind, how has the myth become so powerful that many people within and outside the scientific community do believe that neurophysiology has advanced (or will advance) our understanding of mind and the mind-body relationship? The CTP itself is attractive for many reasons.

For a start, it promises to biologize consciousness; to make it part of the natural world. This, in turn, opens up the possibility of a unified account of the world that encompasses not only physical but also mental events. The causal thread that reaches from the perceived object to the perception and on from that to the overt activity of the perceiver symbolizes the ontological homogeneity of the world. The CTP, or something like it, is thus crucial to the over-riding scientific project of describing the whole of reality in terms of a single set of (physical) mechanisms.

Secondly, the neurophysiological CTP is consistent with scientific and everyday observations about the interdependence of mind and brain. Ordinary experience seems to indicate that brain position determines experience content: where my head is (in space and in time) is the most important determinant of the content of my consciousness. Moreover, the state of my sense endings – whether they are covered or uncovered, damaged or undamaged, pointed in one direction or another – also influences experience content. Changes in electrical activity of the brain are associated with changes in the level and content of consciousness: you can tell whether someone is asleep or awake by looking at his electro-encephalogram. And we have already discussed the correlations described by the Weber-Fechner law between impinging energy and sensation.

The most striking demonstration of the interdependency of brain and mind are observations, ranging from the most crude to the most refined, that brain dysfunction leads to abnormalities of or absence of perception. Decapitation, with associated brain removal, leads to a perceptible decline in I.Q. in most instances. Indeed, brain removal leads to mind removal. Brain injury, due for example to trauma or to stroke, or to experimental lesions, seriously interferes with perception and may remove perception completely, either temporarily or permanently. There are rough correlations between the kinds of brain injury and the kinds of deficits observed in consciousness, as are described in a vast neuropsychological literature. Brain dysfunction – due to uncontrolled electrical discharges as in epilepsy or due to the effects of drugs or toxins damping down electrical activity – will lead to disturbance or loss of consciousness. Contrariwise, pseudo-perceptions, ranging from crude, unformed noises and flashes of light through to complex scenes with accompanying meanings and emotions, can be generated by spontaneous discharges of the brain or in the laboratory by stimulating electrodes.

All of these observations seem to fit with, and to give support to, the idea that perception is the result of the impact of the perceived objects on an appropriately tuned nervous system. It would be perverse to deny this. But it has to be reiterated that the CTP does not *explain* these observations: it does not explain how the impinging events give rise to awareness of those events. At best, the CTP is a vacuous summary of these observations, a framework within which they can be gathered together. Conformity with observations about the interdependence between mind function and brain function does not support the claim of the neurophysiological CTP to explain mind or point the way to such an explanation.

A parallel attraction of the theory is that it seems to *constrain perception to be true* – to be only about things that impinge on the nervous system; that are, in other words, 'really there'. This is important for the biologizing of consciousness: consciousness will evolve only if it improves the survival chances of creatures endowed with it; and it will have survival value only if it accurately reports what is actually 'there'. If perception has to be triggered off by what is actually there, then it is constrained to be true. False perception can arise only if the nervous system has spontaneous activity independently of any causative external object.

Unfortunately this evolutionary attraction of the causal theory is also illusory, for reasons that similar to those that established the circular nature of the Weber-Fechner and other psychophysical laws. The constraint that we shall perceive only that which is 'really there' is a true constraint only if 'really there' can be defined independently of the usual constraints of perception. Unfortunately, as I have demonstrated elsewhere (see Chapter 3 of my *Explicit Animal*), it cannot. So the constraint boils down to: we can perceive only that which we usually perceive. This, of course, is no real constraint at all. Moreover, what we perceive far exceeds what actually interacts with our nervous system; for what interacts with our nervous systems is occurrent energy and what we perceive are continuant objects (see earlier, p. 98).

Since the CTP is so flawed as an explanation of the mind and since its apparent attractions are apparent rather than real, how does the claim of that science to advance our understanding of the mind command such a following? To answer this question, we need to understand the language of neuromythology.

The Language of Neuromythology

The fundamental reason why the neurophysiological version of the CTP does not count as any kind of explanation of perception, or provide a framework within which such an explanation might be sought, is that the transformation of, say, light into electrochemical energy and the subsequent redistribution of electrochemical activity in the nervous system is in no way analogous to the transformation of energy into information, to the process by which unconscious events become conscious experiences, such that one type of body (the living human body) is 'worlded' in the way that other bodies (rocks, for instance) are not. There are many transducers that are not sense organs – for example photo-electric cells – so transduction is not itself sufficient to create sensations out of the impingement of energy arising from one body upon another. Since this *is* so obvious, we have to ask ourselves how the illusion that the events in sensory endings and their proximal connections explain perception could have been sustained for so long.

The power of neuromythology resides in the subtlety with which it juggles descriptive terms. Neurophysiological observations seem to provide an explanation of perception only because those observations are described in increasingly mentalistic terms as one proceeds from the periphery to the centre of the nervous system. The gap between the physical and the mental is bridged by describing end organ events in rigidly physical terms and events occurring more centrally in psychological terms. As a nerve impulse travels along an afferent fibre, it also propagates from one part of Roget's Thesaurus to the another. As the impulse propagates centrally, it leaves the world of 'energy transformations' and enters the world of 'signals' until, two or three feet and two or three synapses later, it has become 'information', or part of a pattern of impulses that count as information. In short, electrochemical activity leaves the sense ending as physical events and arrives somewhere in the cortex as information. No explanation whatsoever is offered as to how this happens – and yet it cries out for explanation as all parties are agreed that the electrochemical activity remains electrochemical activity throughout.

The problem is to some extent concealed because of a certain flexibility in the terminology used to describe an impulse at any particular point in the sensory path. Prolepsis and regression are the important rhetorical devices here. An event in a sensory receptor may sometimes be described quite mentalistically – as a 'signal', for example – in anticipation of its causal successor's ultimate spiritual elevation (prolepsis). Alternatively, the most central events, which are supposed to be identical with, or the basis of, perceptions are described in unreconstructed physicalistic terms (regression). Mentalistic descriptions are sometimes taken even further back than the most peripheral neural events, into the energy in the outside world even before it impinges on the nervous system. The metaphysical duties of the nervous system are thereby greatly lightened; for the energy/information barrier – or the body/mind gap – may be crossed simply by referring to light, for example, not only as 'energy' but also as 'information', so that at the very least, it possesses *intrinsically* the subjective qualities of the experience of it, such as brightness. This may sometimes reach the point of absurdity; for example, the psychologist J. J. Gibson asserted that 'light reflected from surfaces and focused on the retinae contains a large amount of information'. On the other hand, events in the cerebral cortex – even in the 'highest levels' of the cortex – sensory association areas or whatever – may be described both in brutally physicalistic terms – as 'electrochemical events' or as 'complex information processing'.

Since it is rarely made clear at what place in the nervous system a train of nerve impulses is supposed to pass over spiritually to the other side, it becomes more difficult to pinpoint the absurdity or explanatory weakness of neuromythological discourse. It used to be said that nerve impulses 'entered consciousness' in the thalamus, but this suggestion has been quietly shelved. Even neurophysiologists find the idea of the thalamus as the back door or ground floor of consciousness embarrassingly naïve. But superficially more cunning neurophysiological theories of consciousness suffer from the same fundamental naïvety. They are rooted in the belief that the transduction of unconscious energy understood in physicalistic terms from one form to another and its redistribution within the nervous system somehow accounts for the emergence of consciousness of that energy, for its transformation into information; that energy transduction will explain how, in the human body, matter becomes conscious of itself.

Both biological and computational models of consciousness depend for their apparent plausibility upon the liberal use of terms such as 'information' that have a multiplicity of meanings. The most important characteristic of these terms is that they have a foot in both camps: they can be applied to material processes, in particular those taking place in the brain, which is thought of as an unconscious machine, as well as to human beings. Their deployment in this fashion erodes, or elides, or conjures away, the barriers between man and machine, between consciousness and mechanism, between mind and matter. The typical sequence of events is that a term most usually applied to human beings is transferred to physical machines such as telephones or computers. This begins as a consciously metaphorical or specialist use but the special, restricted, basis for the anthropomorphic language is soon forgotten: the metaphorical clothes in which thinking is wrapped become its skin. Machines described in human terms are then offered as models for mind (described in slightly machine-like terms).

To see what is wrong with the vast majority of philosophical discourse in the field of cognitive science, and what is amiss with physicalist accounts of the mind generally, we need to look particularly carefully at the first step: the application of human terms to machines, in particular to brains understood as machines. In most cases, as we shall see, the process of epithet transfer is no more valid (or no less metaphorical) than referring to the place used to house candidates for execution as 'a condemned cell'. When we hear of a man who has spent the last year in a condemned cell, we know that it is the man, not the cell, who faces execution. It is the man, not the cell, who should have right of appeal. It is the man, not the cell, on whose behalf we grow indignant. When we are told that a telephone – or a peripheral nerve – receives information, however, we fail to notice – or at least fail to be alerted by – the fact that it is we, not the telephone, who require, are able to receive, and are glad of, information. This is not because there is more justification in taking the transferred epithet literally in the case of the telephone than in the case of the prison cell but because 'information' has a multiplicity of meanings that 'condemn' does not. In the case of the telephone, the transferred epithet adopts a protective colouring to suit its new surroundings.

It is not too much of an exaggeration to claim that the greatest advances in breaking down the mind/body, consciousness/mechanism, man/machine barriers have come not from neurobiology or computer science but from the use of such transferred epithets. The engineer's customary courtesy in his dealings with his machines has permitted many assertions to pass 'on the nod' that would otherwise be challenged. Indeed, such courtesies have come so to dominate our language that it is almost impossible to look critically at the idea that machines have memories, that they 'store information' and do calculations, or that different parts of the nervous system 'signal' to one another. We are accustomed to hearing that radar 'sees' an enemy plane or that it 'hunts' a target. We cease to notice that we are conferring intentionality upon systems that are themselves only prosthetic extensions of the conscious human body.

This journeying of terms between the mental and the physical realms lies at the root of the myth that modern neurological science has somehow explained, or will explain, or has advanced our understanding of, what consciousness truly is. 'A *picture* held us captive', Wittgenstein said, 'And we could not get outside of it for it lay in our language and language seemed to repeat it to us inexorably'. The application of this observation to the neurophysiological versions of the CTP seems self-evident.

Conclusion

The belief that scientific investigation of the brain is leading – or will lead – to a full understanding of the mind is, therefore, without foundation. Does this false belief matter? I am sure that it does; for the version of consciousness served up by scientific theory is one that is drained of virtually everything that makes us, as conscious beings, distinct. The scientific account of consciousness cannot accommodate subjective experience, qualia, and all that makes being a conscious entity different from being a stone. If, as many modern thinkers seem to believe, mental contents such as qualia can be defined in terms of, and their essence reduced to, their causal relations to inputs mediated by sensory endings and to behavioural outputs, then consciousness is utterly emptied. Next to such interpretations of the mind, even Freudian, Marxist, Durkheimian, Derridan and Helmholtzian marginalizations of consciousness seem positively humanistic. The delusion that neuroscience is explaining consciousness – and that mind can be assimilated to the workings of largely mindless nature – is rooted in a signal failure to appreciate its true nature and an overlooking of its essential mystery. And that, in turn, means misconstruing our nature and our mystery, who are of all of nature's creatures the most conscious and the most mysterious. The larger cultural implications of this do not need spelling out.

Bibliography

The best short account of contemporary materialist philosophy of mind is Paul Churchland's up-to-date, clear and rigorous *Matter and Consciousness* (Bradford Books: MIT Press. Revised edition, 1988). Patricia Churchland's *Neurophilosophy* (Bradford Books: MIT Press, 1986) incorporates a good deal of interestingly presented contemporary neurophysiology but does not, in this reader's opinion, show how it relates to the philosophical arguments. *The Mind/Brain Identity Theory*, a collection of papers edited by C. V. Borst (Macmillan, 1970), remains one of the best anthologies on the central question of whether mental states could be brain processes. The two classic physiological texts are Lord Adrian's *The Basis of Sensation* (Oxford University Press, 1928) and C. S. Sherrington's *Integrative Activity of the Nervous System* (Oxford University Press, 2nd edition, 1948). Two other sources are strongly recommended. *Mindwaves* edited by Colin Blakemore and Susan Greenfield (Blackwell, 1987) is large collection of attractively written essays by a wide variety of experts approaching the mind-body problem from both the physiological and the philosophical standpoints. *The Oxford Companion to the Mind*, edited by Richard Gregory (Oxford University Press, 1987) contains many user-friendly entries relevant to the theme of this chapter. Finally, my own defence of human consciousness against materialist interpretations, *The Explicit Animal* (Macmillan, 1991), deals with the themes of this chapter in greater detail.

6

The Consciousness of Animals

STEPHEN R. L. CLARK

1 *Introduction*

Common sense assures us that many non-human animals have desires, thoughts and plans much like our own. But common sense can be challenged. The chief principle of a properly scientific Enlightenment is that nothing is to be believed merely because 'common sense' would have it so, or because we *feel* its truth. Only what can be proved to the satisfaction of someone determined not to practise a potentially misleading empathy can be trusted: animals must be treated 'objectively', for the real world is one of mere, indifferent objects unaffected by our casual or conventional likes, sympathies and identifications. This 'modernism' is itself under challenge from 'post-moderns', inclined to doubt that there are any truths at all outside the sphere of what 'we' happily endorse: 'the objective world', by that account, is only another fanciful creation, and those who insist that we must only think 'objectively' are pretending to a mystical insight into 'reality itself' that post-moderns 'know' (or choose to say) is quite impossible.

It follows that any sensible examination of the problems posed by an enquiry into the consciousness, or otherwise, of animals (which is to say, non-human animals) must begin by considering the Enlightenment project that has given us modernity and, more recently, post-modernism. That project is founded on the twin postulates that knowledge is only possible if we divest ourselves of our human emotional nature, and that what is really knowable has no prescriptive force. It is founded, in fact, on the rejection of moral objectivism. My argument will be that a satisfactory solution to the question whether, and how, animals are conscious can only come by a return to moral objectivism, to the doctrine that knowledge arises from a loving attention to what is knowable, and that what is known makes its own demands on those who know. My enquiry must begin from moral philosophy rather than philosophy of mind.

2   Moral Objectivism and the Opposition

Moral naturalism – so to call a tradition of ethical thought that has been central to the last two thousand years of civilized endeavour – has two main themes. First, that moral judgements can be really true or false, and not merely acceptable or unacceptable to this group or that. Second, that merely conventional or historically grounded distinctions are of less significance than natural ones. Thus:

1. *Some acts would be wrong, some states of affairs evil, even if no one judged as much.* It might be true, of course, that there could be no acts at all unless there were agents (and therefore moral judges), just as it might be true that no state of affairs would be evil unless someone or other found it disagreeable. It is a substantive (and therefore questionable) moral claim that all and only what someone or other finds disagreeable is therefore an evil; but that there are real evils, whether or not anyone does judge them evil, should not be in doubt. In the most extreme forms of moral naturalism, God himself can only observe the wrongness or the rightness of this act or that. He may create the conditions under which it has the properties that fix its moral value, but it is no more open to him to make what otherwise would be wrong right than to make $7 + 5$ equal 13.[1]

2. *What matters at least at the beginning of moral decision-making are those properties that are independent of human discourse.* One man may be, conventionally, 'of gentle birth', and another 'of base stock', but this difference cannot be a good reason to treat them differently. Instead we should have regard to their God-given natures, what they are in origin. Merely conventional moralists of course may insist on these conventional distinctions, but what matters so far as the objective moralist is concerned must be what is true apart from such convention. Obviously enough: if it could be right to enslave one and wrong to enslave another merely because the one was *described* differently from the other, then that moral judgement at least would be true only in virtue of what 'we' said, and therefore not be objective. Objectively valid judgements can be grounded only on what is objectively true (though even objectivists will usually agree that there is a place for derivatively binding by-laws).

Many of our actual judgements are still rooted in conventional beginnings, but would-be objectivists usually then pretend that the conventions in turn reflect 'real' divisions, that, for example, gentle or Caucasian birth actually determines character or ability. Once it is clear that there are no real or natural divisions between people of a different caste, creed or colour (or none that rationally warrants different treatment when it comes to matters germane to us all), we should abandon those merely conventional discriminations. Justice is the moral entitlement of anyone, no matter where she lives or what her accidental caste may be. Natural equals should be treated equally.

This sort of moral naturalism has had a poor press in recent years; and those who would relativize or historicize our moral beliefs seem to have made all the running; but those who oppose moral objectivism do not always realize all the implications of their preferred position. If there are no 'real', no natural, moral obligations, but all such obligations rest upon 'our' serious preference, then it is no longer easy to insist that only 'natural' divisions count. Where all is convention, merely conventional divisions are as good (or bad) as any. Why should it matter any longer that merely naked humans, stripped of their historical and cultural baggage, are only and entirely human? It takes a moral effort to remember this, and why should we make that effort if the only rules that bind us are our own?

There is a further problem. It may at first seem easy to distinguish the moral (which is conventional) from the merely natural (which carries no prescriptive force). We may conventionally decide that the cassowary is not a bird[2] – that is, is not to be treated like more usual birds – or that pets and pigs are treated differently. Whatever we decide will not be *false*. The facts of the matter, though, are otherwise: whatever it is we say or do, the cassowary *is* a bird (that is, cassowaries are winged things descended from the same common stock as blackbirds and penguins) and pigs need not be naturally different from the creatures we make 'pets'. We may not choose to attend to what pigs feel or fancy, but it will still be true that they feel pain when burnt, as much as pets do. But recent writers have begun to deny that facts are natural, any more than values: 'to attribute feelings to X is only to remind ourselves that it is wrong to hurt X [which is to say, respectable people don't usually approve of doing it]'.[3] Can we still insist that *our* conventional divisions are more rational than those of others?

In the remote past, maybe, people believed that 'weeds' or 'creepy-crawlies' named true natural kinds that were intrinsically evil. Then we began to think that these were very partial judgements, that the things we named as 'weeds' were not intrinsically weeds, nor evil. A true morality sought to discover natural kinds of a less subjective sort, the real divisions between this and that. The dogs we pet and the pigs we keep in pens are not so different (except in conventional value) that we should treat them very differently. Then we abandoned moral objectivity, including – though we did not always notice it – the obligation to treat natural equals equally and think less of all merely conventional discriminations. And finally, some few of us begin to deny even the old truth that there are natural kinds at all, that there are 'real equals' that should – on liberal views – be treated equally. We can no longer maintain the distinction between 'merely conventional' divisions and real ones. On this basis it becomes a sufficient defence of discriminatory practices that 'we' identify the victims thus and so. There are no objective rules of justice stipulating that this is wrong, nor any objective distinction between real and merely conventional distinctions. 'Rationality [in matters moral] is a myth'.[4]

The new anti-realism is in one respect more realistic than the old anti-moralism. Anti-moralists could agree that burning a pig alive would cause it pain, but deny that such an event was intrinsically wrong. Wrongness, they said, was neither a logically necessary corollary of causing-to-die-in-pain (for we could all *understand*, even if not admire, someone who said that acts like that were good), nor yet an identifiable property naturally occasioned by non-moral properties and having its own effects on future history. The 'wrongness', they said, was only 'our' projection. But what can it mean to say that something is in pain, if not that it is in a state worth fleeing from? And how could we decide that something was in pain except by acknowledging its screams, squirms and bloody sweats as pleas to desist? Malebranche heard a yelping dog impassively, as uttering no more than squeaking gears: to hear the yelps as evidence of pain would have been to be moved by sympathy. Ordinary descriptions are both factual and moral in their implications: to hold the moral implication off (with a view, maybe, to contradicting it) is to diminish our understanding even of the fact. What sort of pain is it that is not to be avoided? Can we distinguish between philosophers who deny that dogs feel pain, and ones who deny that we should ever mind? More generally: if what there is can never show us what to do, why trouble about what is? If there are no objective values, what value has the truth?

3 Animals within the Text

The new anti-realism is realistic also in this: our actual, lived worlds are structured by convention. 'Weeds', 'creepy-crawly things', 'pests', 'pets' and 'sacred cows' and 'people' are all terms at once strongly relativistic ('Everything green that grew out of the mould/Was an excellent herb to our fathers of old'[5] – but not to the average surburban gardener) and strongly prescriptive (they carry their recommendations on their faces). It is always a slight shock to realize that other peoples think us odd or filthy for those practises that seem entirely 'natural' to us – but that is merely evidence, for most of us, that *they* are odd or filthy. Older moral realists would often say that other people's discriminations are all superstitions – a position that is sublimely unaware that the speaker has her own absurdities. Hindus are superstitious for defending sacred cows; Koreans are bestial for killing and eating dogs.[6]

The world we live is full of accidental and historically grounded associations and taxonomies. Churches and council chambers are more than piles of bricks, and more than buildings for crudely commercial purposes. People – even in these liberal days – are also family members and name-bearers, who learn their tasks in life from ceremonials as much as from a would-be systematic course of study. Ancient trees and hedgerows are not replaceable by plastic replicas. Horses and dogs and cows and sheep carry along with them a story dating back to neolithic times, and subtly modified in every generation by the tales we tell. Horses are imagined into being, as much as ridden: cousins to the centaur and the pegasus. Animals inhabit the same story as ourselves.[7]

Individual animals of that kind also have their own biographies. O'Donovan, commenting on Abram's sacrifice to feed three visiting angels, remarks that no one ever needed to ask 'which calf?'.[8] But this is in error: many individual animals are and have been known as such, from the First Cow Audhumla (from Norse stories of the Very Beginning) to the latest champion. When the prophet Nathan confronted David with his sin, it would have been no answer for the king to have said that the poor man's ewe should be replaced: individuals are irreplaceable, even if someone, something else could play their part as well. Animals, like human beings, are identified as individuals in being attended to, in being irreplaceable for good or ill. In that sense even Alexander Beetle is an individual: not that there is or would have been a beetle of that name without a human act of naming, but that – once named and attended to – he is more than 'just an animal', more than a replaceable part. Does that naming make a difference to *him*? Who knows? It makes a difference to dogs and horses.

The realm of human story gives being and significance to landscape, seascape and townscape, to trees and animals and peoples. In the days when there were *real* distinctions to be made, of more importance than the merely fictional, it mattered that – we thought – all humans were alike in being human, all animals in being unthinking brutes. But if that vast distinction is a literary trope, we are released to notice that the world of our 'significant individuals' is populated not only by individual human beings but also by dogs, cats and horses with particular names and values; that the world contains innumerable avatars and images of the Red Bull and the Horse of Heaven. Not all insects are creepy-crawlies; some are 'singing masons building roofs of gold', the image of ideal community.

Human beings and human speech are historical inventions as well: our actual experience for long enough was of 'ourselves', the local tribes of people, dogs and horses, and of the 'others', *theria* (wild beasts) and *barbaroi* (who make noises that only vaguely sound like speech, as 'rhubarb, rhubarb'). Slowly we have invented the idea of 'humankind', a universal human essence discoverable over centuries and thousand-miles, distinct from all the other nations of the world, the only 'speaking peoples'. Other ages had no doubt that the other, non-human inhabitants of earth had voices, that their lack of human speech was only a sad disability, on a par with our own ignorance of other human and non-human tongues. The common speech was lost at Babel, but could be recovered.

An appreciation of the historical roots of our present attitudes enriches our present experience of human and non-human neighbour. Attempts to eliminate them on the plea that dogs are only canine, ancestral lands just earth, or spring flowers only 'genital and alimentary organs of plants' were always barbarous.

> Don't you see that that dreadful dry light shed on things must at last wither up the moral mysteries as illusions, respect for age, respect for property, and that the sanctity of life will be a superstition? The men in the street are only organisms, with their organs more or less displayed. For such a one there is no longer any terror in the touch of human flesh, nor does he see God watching him out of the eyes of a man.[9]

Even of a fish it is blasphemous to say that it is *only* a fish.[10]

A foolish work of elementary English criticism sought to 'debunk . . . a silly piece of writing on horses, where these animals are praised as the "willing servants" of the early colonists in Australia' (on the plea that horses are not much interested in colonial expansion). C.S. Lewis comments that its actual effect on pupils will have little to do with writing decent prose:

> some pleasure in their own ponies and dogs they will have lost: some incentive to cruelty or neglect they will have received: some pleasure in their own knowingness will have entered their minds'

– but 'of Ruksh and Sleipnir and the weeping horses of Achilles and the war-horse in the Book of Job – nay, even of Brer Rabbit and of Peter Rabbit – of man's prehistoric piety to "our brother the ox" they will have learnt nothing'.[11]

If there is no truth-by-nature, or none that we need acknowledge, such reductivism is ridiculous as well as vulgar. Koreans may not be factually wrong to think of dogs as dinner: neither are we wrong to think of them as friends. Which story would we rather tell, which story choose to live in? Better: which story is already telling us? Maybe we ourselves, no less than Black Beauty or White Fang, are characters in a novel?[12] 'We enter human society, that is, with one or more imputed characters – roles into which we have been drafted – and we have to learn what they are in order to understand how others respond to us and how our responses to them are apt to be construed . . . Mythology is the heart of things'.[13] The really important supplementary is: whose is the story? Ours? No one's? Nobodaddy's? God's? Saga, tragedy or farce?

4   *The Reach of Empathy*[14]

But can this anti-realist narration be the whole? There are some animals that feature, quite as much as humans, in the never-ending story, whether as faithful friends, or dreadful enemies. Dog and Wolf are one and the same species; so are pariah and guide-dog. White Rat and Black Rat are the same beneath the skin. Other animals are more distantly endorsed: koala bears are cuddly toys, but not so that they'd notice. It is a feature of those creatures whose ancestors our neolithic ancestors once tamed (or was the taming all one way?) that they are judged to participate in the story as something more than dummies. They act a part, no doubt, but one they understand and can exploit.

Other scholars, as well as anti-realists of the fashionable, literary kind, have denied the possibility of thought before speech. No one could think wordlessly, without a grasp of rules to identify those thoughts as sometimes incorrect or false. But this is to make the acquisition of speech a standing miracle in every growing child, and in the first beginnings of the human kind. If there never was a world outside of human language, and never a First Human (save the Very First, or God), we need not bother to explain how the human, thinking, kind first came to be. But how do individuals begin to speak without ever having thought before they spoke? Must we suppose some doctrine of eternal souls who never *need* to learn to speak, but only to speak a given language? It seems easier to believe that, after all, unspeaking creatures, creatures that don't speak *our* tongues, can think and plan, that they could be characters in their own unfolding story even if they weren't in ours. Human infants could not learn to speak unless they already experienced and thought about their worlds.

Those who know them best (because they love them best) are in no normal doubt that babies, dogs and horses do respond and think. According to Searle, 'only someone in the grip of a philosophical theory would deny that small babies can literally be said to want milk and that dogs want to be let out or believe that their master is at the door',[15] even though the baby has no conception of milk as such, and dogs no grasp of the indefinitely many logical implications of the proposition that so and so is at the door. The standard response that this is sentimental fancy might deserve respect if those who made it showed themselves well able to rear children or train animals. But consider the effort to exclude 'anthropomorphic' language in describing chimpanzees outlined by Hebb. 'All that resulted', he says, 'was an endless series of specific acts in which no order or meaning could be found'.[16] Even such evidence as does exist against too 'anthropomorphic' an understanding of the wordless actually counts against the notion that they do not think. The really significant thing about Clever Hans was not that he failed at elementary maths, but that he showed a superb understanding of his human's concealed wishes.[17] Animals cannot be trained unless they understand what we are after. Understanding that, they move to manipulate us in their turn.[18]

Such mutual understanding and would-be control, born in any close communication of the wordless and the wordy, may well be founded on 'shared forms of life'. Wittgenstein's too-often quoted aphorism, that 'if the lion could talk we could not understand him',[19] is implausible because lions, after all, are social animals, predators, cousins of the familiar cat who has no difficulty speaking to us and being understood. Another remark of Wittgenstein's is more apposite: 'What is the natural expression of an intention? – Look at a cat when it stalks a bird; or a beast when it wants to escape'.[20] If Wittgenstein could not understand that cat, how could he interpret it as 'stalking'?

One way of resolving an apparent contradiction between doctrin-aire rejection of mentalistic description of the wordless and the ordinariness of just such description is to suggest that words may be used 'metaphorically'. 'The attribution of anger to infra-human animals is largely metaphorical',[21] apparently because the attribution of anger to adult humans is part of a complex social, and even legal, activity. Anti-realists of the kind I have described before can have no recourse to this move, as it involves just the distinction between literal and metaphorical meaning that is now, fashionably, rejected. There are no 'central' meanings. But other commentators, of a more realistic kind, see no reason to deny that, for example, chimpanzees show the 'full picture of human anger in its three main forms: anger [i.e. aggressive action], sulking, and the temper tantrum'.[22] Similarly: 'anyone would surely judge [Harlow's monkeys] as looking severely depressed and regressed (in a clinical sense). The parallel behaviours observed in children and in monkeys exposed to somewhat similar deprivations strongly suggests that the same emotional system, grief or depression, has been activated'.[23] Even if a somewhat different physical structure or process is involved (and there seems no reason, *a priori*, to suppose this here), we need not shrink from labelling it 'depression' any more than we refuse to call a cephalopod's light-receptors 'eyes' merely because they have a different evolutionary ancestry from vertebrate 'eyes'.[24] Similarly: the *wings* of bird, bat and butterfly. In all these cases we recognize what the organ or the behaviour is about, and could understand a talking beast as well as any talking person. Ethologists schooled to avoid 'anthropomorphism' resort to scare-quotation marks when writing for their peers, but rarely explain, for example, how 'rape' by an orang-utan or by a drake is different from rape.[25] Nor do they usually (as in principle they should) place words like 'see' or 'seek' within such markers. Rhetorical tropes like this are ways of saving face, while the researchers still rely on their empathetic identification of what the animals are doing.[26]

But maybe there are limits to our understanding, and our incorporation of the 'alien' into the humanly intelligible universe. Washburn's level-headed and unjustly neglected study of 'the animal mind' raises the serious question, 'what is it like to be a wasp?'.

Anger, in our own experience, is largely composed of quickened heart beat, of altered breathing, of muscular tension, of increased blood pressure in the head and face. The circulation of a wasp is fundamentally different from that of any vertebrate. The wasp does not breathe through lungs, it wears its skeleton on the outside, and it has the muscles attached to the inside of the skeleton. What is anger like in the wasp's consciousness? We can form no adequate idea of it.[27]

So is there something it is like to be a wasp, if it is so far beyond our grasp? Why should there not be? That wasps are sometimes angry is an observation well worth remembering: that they feel emotions appropriate to their enraged behaviour (different as they must be from ours) is something I have no difficulty in imagining. Serious inquirers are regularly warned not to multiply entities beyond necessity, nor to attribute more complex or anthropomorphic modalities to what we see than are strictly needed.[28] Useful rules, but not so obvious as to justify the blank insistence that we know such creatures are unfeeling, merely because – with a sufficient hardening of the heart – we can imagine them to be unfeeling. The withdrawal of our failed projections, and the concomitant 'objectification' of the things that are left behind, should often lead to an acceptance of ignorance. The impulse to avoid that pain by saying that what we don't know is not knowledge, that our inability to prove one thing is a proof of its opposite, that what 'we' no longer 'identify' with may properly be treated as 'mere things', may often be very powerful. If anger is a socially defined role, so also is a pitiless 'objectivity'.

But the attribution of emotion to another does indeed involve that other in a definite moral universe: in identifying another's emotional state as mere crossness or anger, rather than indignation, we may be endorsing or excusing what that other does. Thus Plutchik's supposition that a whale is 'paralyzed with fright' at the approach of 'killer whales'[29] is a judgement that a more Buddhistic sensibility might not endorse; maybe the whale gives herself for food? To that extent, moralistic or emotional description of 'bad animals' or 'good animals', ones that don't or ones that do do what we demand of them, is often 'sentimental' in an opprobrious sense. We would do well not to leap to too many conclusions: I doubt if a dog that savages a child is really or importantly vicious or filled with hatred, nor yet complacently filled with the loving desire to defend her master. The dog may be so far 'emotional', so little able to discriminate objects independent of her own behavioural cues, as not to be emotional at all. What she is doing, often enough, is something that would – for us – be playing: the thing she plays with may, disastrously, be a human child, but for her it is only 'a thing (a toy) to be played with here-and-now', not 'the very same thing (or person)' as the friendly playmate of another moment. Of which more below.

The Wittgensteinian claim that 'dogs cannot simulate pain'[30] is some evidence that Wittgenstein knew as little about dogs as about lions, but the connection between the possibility of truth-speaking and sincerity and the possibility of play-acting is a real one. Only those who can 'pretend' to be in pain can know what they are doing (though it by no means follows that those who can't are never in pain). Only those can pretend who can play a part. It follows that Derrida is right (though deeply and perhaps culpably obscure) in his claim that false and fictional discourse is not strictly *parasitic* upon sincere or truthful discourse: truth and lie are twins.[31] But the birth of truthfulness (and fiction) precedes the birth of humankind. Bateson points out that game-playing (and pretence) is a skill more widely spread than our own species: many social mammals signal that what comes next, pretend attack or fury, is play. Some can use those very signals to distract their companions from a real attack or fraud.[32]

There is good reason to think that we can understand our fellow humans largely because we are all engaged upon a similar life, that there are innate patterns of behaviour and expression that ground our more sophisticated speeches. I can often see what someone is on about, what she is doing, before I think I understand her speech. Without that prior understanding nothing that she said (no noise she uttered) would be meaningful. But the same is true of other creatures than our conspecifics: there are ancestral traits we share with them, and also traits that have emerged by convergent evolution. Who doubts that cephalopods do, 'literally', have eyes, and appetites? Rorty may well be right to say that 'writhing is more important to our ability to imagine that the koala is asking us for help than what is going on in the koala . . . So we send pigs to slaughter with equanimity, but form societies for the protection of koalas'.[33] But his imagination here is limited: others can understand our cousins' signals more astutely. Even Rorty thinks it 'paradoxical' to suppose, as Descartes did, that 'the feeling of terror which accompanies our flight has no parallel within the sheep'.[34] Where neither analogy nor homology can help us we shall be astray: true aliens would not even be as easy to describe, let alone to understand, as some (not all) science fiction writers have assumed.

5   *Sensation, Perception, Umwelt*

We get our grip on the intelligence of others by seeing what they are on about, and without a capacity to see the world in something like the way they do our chance of doing so is small. Often enough we get things subtly wrong. The hunting wasp that seems to be providing caterpillars for her growing young turns out to have more of an aesthetic interest: at any rate she does not care to restore a missing caterpillar to the nest before she seals it up. To state what should be obvious: this does not confirm that wasps are stupid creatures, any more than a Betelgeusean explorer's observation that humans often copulate when they can't procreate proves that we don't know or care what we are doing. The usual or expectable effect of actions is one thing, the intention of the agent is another. Though these will usually be connected, an act may be performed independently of its expectable effect, for its own sake.

Too much attention of a romantically pessimistic kind has been paid to questions about animal *sensations*. What is it that animals immediately sense and feel? What role do such sensations play in explaining what then happens? What difference could it make if there were systematic differences in sensational qualia, or if some animal sensed none at all? If an environmental quality can have a direct, physically measurable effect on an organism's motions, what additional purpose would be served by its being *represented* in that organism's sensorium at all? Do woodlice feel attracted by the dark and damp, or have dark, damp sensations? Or are they simply caused to change direction more often when they venture into dry, bright places (which they do not sense as such)? After all, we can be affected by things we do not sense, and perhaps more effectively because we do not sense them: witness bad-tempered conduct consequent on damp, hot days and their attendant salt-loss unmitigated by the cooling effect of evaporating sweat.

That there are sensations is a truism, and that some of these 'give pain'. But the painfulness is not – most fortunately – a sensation we can recall at will: we can remember being in pain, but we do not call a new sensation 'pain' because it resembles a remembered sensum. The 'private language argument' has thrown doubt on the possibility of speaking intelligibly of any sensa,[35] but even without it it is clear enough that calling something painful can't be a matter of comparing sensa. As I remarked before: what is it to say that someone is in pain if not to recognize her screams, squirms and bloody sweats as pleas to desist? Which is *not* to say that this behaviour is all that 'being in pain' amounts to.

Nothing, that is, is likely to 'feel pain', and nothing is even likely to have sensa, that is not engaged in some project or other. Perception is unlike sensation, commonly so called, because our percepts are formed and directed by the ground plans of our lives. To perceive something is always to incorporate it within a view of things. Without such plans and projects creatures would indeed be limited to unanalysable sensa, momentary stimuli that had magical effects. There might indeed be little reason to expect that there 'really were' such sensa at all, since any effect they had could as easily be produced by merely physical changes. The difference between a stone that is warmed up, and an animal, is that the animal may take note of the warming (as it is represented in its sensorium) as a significant event. The animal perceives what the stone only receives.

Fortunately it is easier to discover what an animal perceives than what it merely senses. We find out about the world it lives in by identifying what it does, what routes it prefers and what priorities it has. Obviously our knowledge of what it perceives, and of what it is doing, will be incomplete if it has access to a wider (or at any rate a different) range of qualities: what strikes us as random or inane behaviour may well be a response to hidden variations, or differing goals. Clearly, we shall not know what it is doing unless we have some grasp of what its organs are. But loving attention to the creature's particularity (which is as necessary in understanding our conspecifics as in understanding baboons or bees, and sometimes more difficult) gives us hope of discovering the creature's *Merkwelt* and *Umwelt*.

The terms are Uexkuell's,[36] and signify the world of cues that are significant for a given animal, and that it notices.[37] Different creatures do genuinely inhabit different worlds, and it takes an effort to identify what things are like *for others*. What is worth emphasizing, and should be noticed by epistemologists, is that not all marks are merely natural. The sheep tick who waits 'patiently' for up to eighteen years until butyric acid triggers its leap from a grass stem to a sheep responds – perhaps – only to fixed stimuli. Perhaps there is no need to imagine that it *senses* anything at all, any more than a photoelectric cell. The chemical causes the muscles to twitch in a way moulded by millions of years of selective pressures. Any awareness of the event might really be epiphenomenal. But some marks – and we know far too little about ticks to know whether this applies to them – are actually created by the animal. Scent markers create a map embedded in the physical, a set of directions laid down by the animal and by its peers. Derrida, though not for reasons that he would or could endorse, was right to suspect that 'writing' (largely so-called) is older than mere speech. It is by the use of scent-marks and scratches that we create enduring objects. What is it to be the *same* lamb as the ewe has known before? For the ewe, it is to smell the same, to blend with her own smell. So when we, being vocal animals, at last begin to speak of things, we are speaking of our own markers (as well, no doubt, as markers placed 'by nature').

There does seem to be evidence that many animals have a very 'practical' perception of the world, that they are confronted not by continuing objects but by occasions for specific actions, marking out routes through immensity. We suppose that there is a physical universe surrounding us and them, a world where continuously existent objects are available for any purpose of ours but are not defined by those purposes. Male robins can be deceived into attacking any piece of red rag, but fail to respond to models that are – to our eyes – much more like male robins. Robins are no more stupid than the wasps I described before: what is 'enough like' a rival to deserve attacking is not the same for us and them. But perhaps they do not imagine robins, or male robins, at all: there are only occasions in their universe.

But of course the same is true of us. We too inhabit a world marked out for use, composed of things that are judged 'the same' by virtue of their natural and man-made significance. Would an intellectualizing robin be amused to find us responding in 'the same way' to a line of lights, a scrawl of chalk, a string of vocables that all say (so we say) what 'male robins are red-breasted' says? The sameness is so obvious to us that we forget its conventionality. Again: the standard examples, in much modern philosophical discourse, of real, material objects turn out to be artefacts: as tables, chairs and houses. The point is not only that these things are *made*, but that they are perceived as tables, chairs and houses because 'we' choose to use them so. We live in world of *Zeug*, of implements, fenced off from our occasional imagining of a world-in-itself by our wish to complete our projects. Weeds, trees and creepy-crawlies are as conventional. Understanding other creatures' worlds (whether those creatures are of our species or not) is to share, imaginatively, in what they are doing.

6   Outside the Text

So what is it that lies outside our text? One answer is that the 'real world' is the one and only universe revealed to an objective, scientific eye. We must exclude all morally loaded (and so all mentalistic) description if we are to approach the Truth. Such a truth, of course, will have little to do with our ordinary living.

> We may if we like, by our reasonings, unwind things back to that black and jointless continuity of space and moving clouds of swarming atoms which science calls the only real world. But all the while the world *we* feel and live in will be that which our

ancestors, and we, by slowly cumulating strokes of choice, have extricated out of this, like sculptors[38].

Even as an ideal limit the jointless universe is lacking: in what sense, after all, is it ideal? Why should such a truth concern us, and what grounds the devotee's conviction that it is the truth at all? The attempt to think it through consistently must in the end require us to abandon the strange superstition that we *think* at all. Eliminative materialists profess to believe that neither they nor anyone else *believe* anything at all, but they thereby render their own motions unintelligible.[39]

It seems more likely that the 'real world' be taken as the ultimate sum of life-worlds than that it be an unmeaning and strictly indescribable abyss. Uexkuell indeed concluded that astronomy itself was a biological science, concerned with points of light displayed within a human *Umwelt*. That doctrine, even though it was endorsed by Frank Ramsey, does not appeal to me.[40] If Rorty is right to identify his own position as a response to the supposed collapse of Platonism, perhaps it is time that we reconsidered that collapse. Those who would clamber from the cavern of their idiosyncratic dreams, and recognize the power of puppeteers to organize those dreams, may still hope to discover what is really real, not by rejecting what at first appears, but by surpassing it.

Both eliminative materialists and anti-realists deny that possibility, of reaching out to what is other than our dreams and finding it familiar. Both say that the folk-world and its members are only stories told by us, even if anti-realists then go on telling stories, and eliminative materialists pretend to stop. They both seek to spare themselves the possibility of error: anti-realists deny that 'we' could ever be wrong in what 'we' seriously say (for 'being wrong' is only being in the wrong, by our own standards); materialists end by denying that there is any 'we' to be right or wrong. Either way there is no division between what we think and what most truly is. But that risk, of being wrong, is the price we pay for sometimes being right. If it 'makes no sense' to wonder whether people are sentient and pigs are not (because such sentience is either a mirage or – equivalently – a projection of our arbitrary concern), we have evaded a danger, doubtless: but only at the price of surrender. We have lost that sense of Otherness that is the root of love and knowledge. Murdoch's judgement is the better path: 'we take a self-forgetful pleasure in the sheer alien, pointless [?], independent existence of animals, birds, stones and trees . . . Good art, not fantasy art, affords us a pure delight in the independent existence of what is excellent.'[41] Art is not all that suffers when we forget that excellence. We have not learnt the right lesson from the private language argument: where there is no chance of error, nothing has been said. So we must hope to mould our thought to what is genuinely Other than our thought. 'To be fully human is to recognize everyone and everything in the universe as both Other and Beloved, and . . . this entails granting that the world is authentic and meaningful without demanding proof . . . Animals are the only non-human Others who answer us'.[42]

What is outside the text, and much to be desired? Each transformation or escape from our own private story may be welcomed, every realization that the world is wider than our hearts. Why else have we so often imagined fairies, angels, aliens to give a new perspective on a world, our world, grown old? The great discovery we have now almost made is that there are indeed other perspectives on all our human world, that we are the objects of a patient or impatient gaze from animals that share our world and story. It is indeed a difficult task to see through the merely conventional animals with simple moral properties (inquisitive and imitative apes, greedy pigs, proud peacocks, cruel wolves). To evade those traps it is even worth adopting – temporarily – as physicalist a description of the actual behaviour of the animals as we can manage. But it would be as absurd (and perhaps as damaging) to settle for those descriptions as it would be for ardent bachelors to describe the actions of young females 'physicalistically', so as to avoid imputing motives and desires to them that are really only the males' own. To turn aside from the discovery that there are really Others in the world that we can come to know, and to pretend that pigs, dogs, pigeons, people are only pretence, only cuddly toys animated solely by the stories that we (who?) tell with them, is a radical defeat, as dreadful as the other error, which is to pretend to a romantically pessimistic doctrine that we could never ever find out real truths (except that one?). Fortunately for us (and maybe for our immortal souls) neither cats nor infants nor our adult neighbours are so tractable as to support either fancy. Yes, there really is a real world 'out there', and the fact that it is so often not what I would wish is exactly what reveals, and endears, it to me!

References

1. See my 'God's Law and Morality', *Philosophical Quarterly* 32 (1982), 339–47; and 'God's Law and Chandler', *Philosophical Quarterly* 37 (1987), 200–6.

2. R. Bulmer, 'Why the cassowary is not a bird', *Man* 2. (1967), 5–25 (discussing the taxonomy preferred by the Karam people of New Guinea). Other Karam folk-taxa include flying birds and bats (*yakt*), dogs, pigs, rats from homesteads and gardens (*kopyak*), frogs and small marsupials and rodents other than *kopyak* (*as*), tadpoles, weevils and snails. I doubt if our own folk-taxonomy is much more rational.

3. D. A. Dombrowski, *The Philosophy of Vegetarianism* (Amherst: University of Massachusetts Press, 1984), 129, summarizing R. Rorty *Philosophy and the Mirror of Nature* (Princeton University Press, 1979), 182–92. Words within square brackets are my own summary of what conventionalism must mean.

4. Rorty op. cit., 190.

5. R. Kipling, *Collected Verse 1885–1926* (London: Hodder & Stoughton, 1927), 547.

6. The two condemnations, to be fair, are not entirely incompatible. Some would say that what was relevant was simply pain. Sacred cows, because nobody kills them, suffer protracted deaths; Korean dogs perish by slow strangulation.

7. See V. Hearne, *Adam's Task: Calling Animals by Name* (New York: Alfred A. Knopf, 1986).

8. O. O' Donovan, *Begotten or Made* (Oxford: Clarendon Press, 1987).

9. G. K. Chesterton, *The Poet and the Lunatics* (London: Darwen Finlayson Ltd, 1962; 1st published 1929), 70.

10. Chesterton op. cit., 58.

11. C. S. Lewis, *The Abolition of Man* (London: Bles, 1946, 2nd edn), 12f.

12. See my 'On Wishing there were Unicorns', *Proceedings of the Aristotelian Society* (1989–90).

13. A. MacIntyre, *Against Virtue* (London: Duckworth, 1981), 201.

14. I have also discussed some of the following material in 'The Reality of Shared Emotion', in M. Bekoff & D. Jamieson (eds), *Interpretation and Explanation in the Study of Behavior: Comparative Perspectives* (Boulder: Westview Press, 1990).

15. J. R. Searle, *Intentionality* (Cambridge University Press, 1983) 5.

16. D. O. Hebb, 'Emotion in Man and Animal', *Psychological Review* 53 (1946), 88–106: p. 88. See R. M. Gordon, *The Structure of Emotions* (Cambridge University Press, 1989), 1f.

17. Hearne op. cit., 5, 115.

18. See R. A. Mugford, 'The social skills of dogs as an indication of self-awareness', in D. G. M. Woodgush, M. Dawkins, R. Ewbank,

(eds), *Self-Awareness in Domesticated Animals* (Potters Bar: UFAW, 1981), 40ff.
19. L. Wittgenstein, *Philosophical Investigations*, tr. G. E. M. Anscombe (Oxford: Blackwell, 1958) 223e.
20. Wittgenstein op. cit., 165e: 647.
21. J. R. Averill, *Anger and Aggression* (New York: Springer-Verlag, 1982), 282.
22. D. O. Hebb, *Textbook of Psychology* (Philadelphia: W. B. Saunders, 3rd edn, 1972, 202.
23. R. Plutchik, *Emotion: a psychoevolutionary synthesis* (New York: Harper & Row, 1980) 107.
24. K. Z. Lorenz, *The Foundations of Ethology*, tr. K. Z. Lorenz & R. W. Kickert (New York: Springer-Verlag, 1981), 90.
25. There might well be a difference, namely that human rapists, but probably not drakes or orang-utans, may be moved by hate as much as lust. But the act is still rape even if this is not so.
26. See D. R. Crocker, 'Anthropomorphism: bad practice, honest prejudice?' in Georgina Ferry (ed.), *The Understanding of Animals* (Blackwell: Oxford, 1984), 304–13.
27. A. L. Washburn, *The Animal Mind* (New York: Macmillan 1917, 2nd edn), 3f.
28. See B. E. Rollin, *The Unheeded Cry* (Oxford University Press, 1989) for an historical account of these maxims and their bad effects on the study of animal psychology.
29. Plutchik op. cit., 105.
30. Wittgenstein op. cit., 250.
31. J. Derrida, *Margins of Philosophy*, tr. A. Bass (Brighton: Harvester, 1982), 321ff.
32. G. Bateson, *Steps towards an Ecology of Mind* (London: Paladin, 1973), 150ff.
33. Rorty op. cit., 190. I do not quite understand who 'we' may be: I have a lot more sympathy for pigs than for koalas, and it is not true that only 'cuddly animals' are protected or preserved by people wide-awake enough to realize their duties.
34. Rorty op. cit., 53.
35. Unless there is an omnipresent and omniscient God who shares our sensa: true Cartesians never did believe in the 'privacy' of our own subjectivity. But that is another story.
36. J. von Uexkuell, *Theoretical Biology*, tr. D. L. Mackinnon (London: Kegan Paul, 1926). See also his 'A stroll through the worlds of animals and men' in C. H. Schiller (ed.), *Instinctive Behaviour* (New York: International University Press, 1957), 5–80.
37. D. Bloor, *Wittgenstein: a social theory of knowledge* (London:

Macmillan, 1983), 174–6, points out that Wittgenstein's observation is founded in a 'quite proper sense of the biological basis of social life'.

38. W. James, *The Principles of Psychology* (London: Macmillan, 1890), 288.

39. See the article previously cited, in Bekoff & Jamieson.

40. Uexkuell, *Theoretical Biology* op. cit., 35ff; F. P. Ramsey, *Foundations of Mathematics* (London: Kegan Paul, 1931), 291: 'I don't really believe in astronomy, except as a complicated description of part of the course of human and possibly animal sensation.'

41. I. Murdoch, *The Sovereignty of Good* (London: Routledge & Kegan Paul, 1970), 85.

42. Hearne, op. cit., 264.

7

Connectionism:
the structure beneath the symbols

ANDREW CLARK

1 A Fluid Landscape*

The musician's talent, it is sometimes said, lies not in playing the notes but in spacing them. It is the silences that makes the great musician great. As it is with music, so it is with connectionism. The power of a connectionist system lies not in the individual units (which are very simple processors) but in the subtly crafted connections between them. In this sense such models may be said to be examples of a brain's eye view. For it has long been known that the brain is composed of many units (neurons) linked in parallel by a vast and intricate mass of junctions (synapses). Somehow this mixture of relatively simple units and complex interconnections results in the most powerful computing machines now known, biological organisms. Work in parallel distributed processing (PDP) may be said to be neurally inspired in the limited sense that it, too, deploys simple processors linked in parallel in intricate ways. Beyond that the differences are significant. Neurons and synapses are of many different types, with properties and complexities of interconnection so far untouched in connectionist work. The PDP 'neuron' is a vast simplification. Indeed, it is often unclear whether a single PDP unit corresponds in any useful way to a single neuron. It may often correspond to the summed activity of a group of neurons. Despite all the differences, however, it remains true that connectionist work is closer to neurophysiological structure than are other styles of computational modelling.[1]

Neurally inspired theorizing has an interesting past. In one sense it is a descendant of *Gestalt* theory in psychology.[2] In another, more obvious, sense it follows the path of cybernetics, the study of self-regulating systems. Within cybernetics the most obvious antecedents of connectionist work are McCulloch and Pitts, Hebb and Rosenblatt.[3] McCulloch and Pitts demonstrated that an idealized net of neuron-like elements with excitory and inhibitory linkages could compute the logical functions 'and', 'or', and 'not'. Standard results in logic show that this is sufficient to model any logical expression. Hebb went on to suggest that simple connectionist networks can act as a pattern-associating memory and that such networks can teach themselves how to weight the linkages between units so as to take an input pattern and give a desired output pattern. Roughly, Hebb's learning rule was just 'if two units are simultaneously excited, increase the strength of the connection between them'.[4] This simple rule (combined with an obvious inhibitory variant) is not, however, as powerful as those used by modern day connectionists. Moreover, Hebb's rules were not sufficiently rigorously expressed to use in working models.

This deficiency was remedied by Rosenblatt's work on the so-called perceptron. A perceptron is a small network of input units connected via some mediating units to an output unit. Rosenblatt's work was especially important in three ways, two of them good, one disastrous. The two good things were the use of precise, formal mathematical analysis of the power of the networks and the use of digital-computer simulations of such networks.[5] The disastrous thing was that some over-ambitious and politically ill-advised rhetoric polarized the artificial intelligence community. The rhetoric elevated the humble perceptron to the sole and sufficient means of creating real thought in a computer. Only by simulating perceptrons, Rosenblatt thought, could a machine model the depth and originality of human thought.

This claim and the general evangelism of Rosenblatt's approach prompted a backlash from Minsky and Papert. Their work *Perceptrons* (MIT Press, 1969) was received by the alienated AI community as a decisive debunking of the usurping perceptrons. With the rigorous mathematical analysis of linear threshold functions, Minsky and Papert showed that the combinatorial explosion of the amount of time needed to learn to solve certain problems undermined the practical capacity of perceptron-like networks to undergo such learning. And they further showed that for some problems no simple perceptron approach could generate a solution. Rather than taking these results as simply showing the limits of one type of connectionist approach, Minsky and Papert's work (which was as rhetorically excessive as Rosenblatt's own) was seen as effectively burying connectionism. It would be some years before its public resurrection.

But the miracle happened. A recent three-page advertisement in a leading science journal extols the slug as savant, claiming that the parallel neural networks of the slug suggest powerful new kinds of computer design. The designs the advertisers have in mind are quite clearly based on the work of a recent wave of connectionists who found ways to overcome many of the problems and limitations of the linear-thresholded architectures of perceptrons.[6]

These contemporary connectionist systems, like marshmallows, are chiefly admired for their softness. Their distinctive modes of knowledge, representation and search enable them to tolerate more inhospitable epistemic climates than their symbol-processing cousins. They are able to function well when given inconsistent or incomplete information, to break the 'rules' when necessary, and to maintain a useful degree of functionality after physical damage ('graceful degradation'). They are also able to solve an interesting class of problems (the kind involved in low-level vision and motor control) in ways which make for the kind of fast, fluent responses characteristic of evolved living systems engaged in the battle of natural selection. In addition these systems are powerful learners, able to adapt their own internal representations to meet the requirements of the task. As one of their chief exponents puts it, they are soft, fluid, adaptable, generally 'easy-going' systems which are none-the-less able to mimic, at times, the behaviour of systems which follow rigid rules operating on symbols. They may thus help solve what that same exponent calls the 'paradox of cognition', viz. that

> On the one hand cognition is 'hard': characterized by the rules of logic, by the rules of language. On the other hand cognition is 'soft': if you write down the rules, it seems that realising those rules in automatic formal systems (which AI programs are) gives systems that are just not sufficiently fluid, not robust enough in performance, to constitute what we want to call true intelligence.[7]

For all that, connectionism is not the wonder drug of artificial intelligence. The power and scope of connectionist learning is uncertain; it is by no means obvious that high level cognitive tasks can be performed without the aid of more recognizably symbolic structures; and the kind of softness and flexibility which such systems exhibit may be more limited than at first appears. Moreover, it may be impossible to *understand* cognition except in terms of a more traditional information processing analysis, even if such analysis is regarded as some kind of approximation to the truth.

In the pages which follow I try to do three things. First, to convey something of the flavour and excitement of connectionist work – an excitement not limited to AI technologists but shared, for varying (good and bad) reasons by psychologists, philosophers and social scientists. Second, to keep the enthusiasm in check by noticing some quite thorny problems. And third, to speculate (just a little) about the future of connectionism and artificial intelligence in general.

2 *Emergence and learning*

To see what's distinctive about connectionist approaches we need to get a grip on non-connectionist ones. This is harder than it looks, because 'traditional' Artificial Intelligence is a broad school encompassing many radically different approaches. As a result there are many cases where the distinction I focus on will still fail to pick out all and only the class of connectionist models. None the less, it is the right distinction to highlight the main difference in spirit or emphasis between the two approaches. It is the distinction between two conceptions of the essence of intelligence and thought. According to the first ('traditional') conception, intelligence depends on the manipulation, by computational means, of structural strings of quasi-linguistic symbols. (This is a version of Haugeland's definition of Good Old Fashioned Artificial Intelligence, which is in turn a version of Newell's Physical Symbol System Hypothesis.)[8] Whereas according to the second (connectionist) conception, intelligence depends on the fine-tuned behaviour of a dynamic physical system whose most accurate description is numerical rather than symbolic.[9] Symbol manipulation, on the connectionist (or more accurately, on the pure distributed Smolensky-style connectionist) conception is an 'emergent property' rather than a 'cause' of intelligent behaviour. A property is emergent in this sense if it has no *direct counterpart* in the local level processing details, but acts as a useful statistical and approximate guide to the system's behaviour. In other words, such systems (it is claimed) do not *really* operate on symbols (word-like entities) at all, but manage to look as if they do when viewed from a certain 'distance'.

The best way to grasp this contrast is by example. But the examples, I fear, would not make much sense in advance of some notion of the structure and operation of connectionist systems. So we need to pause and look at connectionist architecture and representation.

Connectionist architectures are made up of (often large) numbers of simple processing units. Often, all such units can do is *receive* inputs (electrical charges coding for positive or negative numbers like $-1, 1, 2, 3 \ldots$), sum them, and *if* the sum exceeds a certain threshold (5, for example) send out a signal to the units to which they themselves are connected (such connectivity being, in the simplest 'feed-forward' systems, entirely one way). If a unit's threshold is exceeded and it sends out a signal, the strength of this signal (whether it is -1, -2, $+1$, $+2$ or whatever) is determined by what is known as the weight (of -1, -2, $+1$, $+2$ or whatever) on the 'wires' connecting that unit to the subsequent ones. This is what is meant by speaking of networks of units connected by excitatory (positive number) or inhibitory (negative number) connections with specific weights (a value of the positive or negative number in any given case). In such a system (an 'architecture') information processing is carried out by the propagation of activity throughout the network. The very simplest example of such a system might thus involve three units, of which we designate two units (A and B) as input units and one unit (C) as output. Suppose we fix the weights, links and thresholds so that units A and B are each linked to unit C by connections with a positive weighting of $(+1)$. And suppose we give unit C an activation threshold of (0.5). The resulting system will compute inclusive-or. That is, if either unit A or unit B, or both units A and B are activated, then unit C will receive input which raises it above its (0.5) threshold and hence activates it. Unit C will thus be on if and only if at least one out of A and B is on.

A major sub-cluster of connectionist systems are what is known as constraint satisfaction networks. In a constraint satisfaction network each unit stands for a hypothesis and the positively or negatively weighted links reflect the relations of mutual support or incompatibility between the hypotheses. Thus consider a network whose task is to fix on a perceptual interpretation of an ambiguous picture such as a Necker Cube (which can look either as if the rectangle A, B, C, D picks out a front face of the cube or as if it picks out a back face – see below). Such a network can have a unit

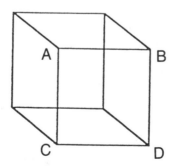

Figure 1 – A Necker Cube

which means that point A on the diagram should be interpreted as the front upper left corner of a cube, and another unit which means that that point should be interpreted as the back upper left corner of a (different) cube. These two units will be linked by a *negative* weight, hence mutually inhibitory (if one is active it sends a *negative* number hence decreasing the likelihood of the other being active). This makes sense, since a single spatial point cannot be *both* the front upper left *and* the back upper left corner of a real cube. A network which can achieve either interpretation (and flip between them) is detailed in Rumelhart, Smolensky and Hinton.[10] It can take as input a fixed representation of a few points, and will complete the pattern (courtesy of the positively and negatively weighted links) to one or the other of the two interpretations of the picture. Interestingly, it can also stabilize on a *mixed* interpretation (the 'impossible' cube) if we fix the inputs so as to suggest both views (i.e. give it inconsistent inputs).

The most interesting connectionist systems (at least from a purely conceptual point of view) are those in which the units represent very small (or sub-symbolic) features, or very soft constraints, and in which the system itself assigns some of the inter-unit weightings for itself.

The idea of a soft constraint is nicely illustrated by Paul Churchland's example of hearing the vowel sound 'a' (as in rain). We can hear that sound as an a under a surprising variety of conditions. We can hear it in the speech of a two-year old girl or a fifty-year old male. We can hear it through regional variations of accent and intonation, and so on. Yet there is no set of features which all these cases have in common and which we might unconsciously be looking out for. Instead, as Churchland points out, 'being an "a" seems to be a matter of being *close enough* to a *typical* "a" sound along a number of distinct *dimensions of relevance*'.[11]

What is quite amazing is that this kind of soft and intricately intertwined set of constraints can be learnt by connectionist systems using automatic procedures for the adjustment of inter-unit weightings. Here is an example, again drawn from Paul Churchland.

Sonar operators in US submarines need to tell, on the basis of reflected wave-forms, whether an object is a rock or a mine. This is a skilled art which is learnt only after an extended tour of duty. There are no simple rules which, verbally expressed, will enable new operators to make the right decisions. A connectionist network (set up in automatic learning mode) can, however, learn to do the job at least as well as the human operators. Such a network is trained as follows. It begins with random weight assignments, and is given an input which characterizes a reflected wave pattern. It has two output units, one designated as meaning 'rock' and one 'mine'. It has a layer of so-called hidden units which mediate between input and output. Using the random weights it will give a response (equally probably right or wrong) to the input wave-form. This response is automatically monitored and compared with the correct response. If the system gets it wrong, an automatic procedure minutely adjusts the weights which were most responsible for the mistake so that, were it given the same input again, it would be slightly less likely to make a mistake. This procedure (known as the back propagation of errors, or back propagation for short) is repeated many thousands of times for many hundreds of different inputs. Finally, the system will (in general) find an assignment of weights which enables it very successfully to negotiate the problem domain, that is, it becomes a 'rock/mine expert' and reliably diagnoses rocks as rocks and mines as mines. It seems to have been able to extract the rules or criteria by which rocks are differentiated from mines as a result of 'learning from experience' rather than relying upon those rules being embodied beforehand in the network.

A final example, which nicely illustrates the spirit of the connectionist approach, is Smolensky's network which solves problems concerning a simple electrical circuit. This network (detailed in Smolensky (1988) aims to solve *qualitative* problems about a given electrical circuit. These are problems like: what happens to the voltage if resistance is increased at point A? The network contains units which (if active) mean such things as 'voltage goes up', 'voltage goes down', 'current goes up' etc. It also contains a second set of units (which Smolensky calls 'knowledge atoms') which encode all *legal* combinations of feature units (for example, resistance up at A, voltage down at B etcetera). And there is two-way connectivity between the two sets of units. The system can then be given a partial set of values over feature units (e.g. 'resistance at A increased' and in virtue of the excitatory and inhibitory links between feature units and knowledge atoms, it will complete the pattern, i.e. assign values to the *other* feature units.

Contrast this with a system whose problem solving depends on a representation of the hard laws of circuitry, for example Ohm's law that Voltage = Current × Resistance ($V = C \times R$). The difference is that the network's 'knowledge of Ohm's law' 'is distributed over the many knowledge atoms whose sub-patterns encode the legal feature combinations for current, voltage and resistance' (Smolensky (1988), 19). This mode of encoding Ohm's law has its advantages. (It also has severe *disadvantages* – see section 4 below.) The advantages are eloquently expressed in the following (characteristic) passage from Smolensky;

> . . . the system, when given a well-posed problem and unlimited relaxation time, will always give the correct answer. So under that idealisation, the . . . system is described by *hard* constraints; Ohm's Law, Kirchoff's Law – the laws of simple circuits. It's as though the model has those laws written down inside it. However, as in all subsymbolic systems the *performance* of the system is achieved by satisfying a large set of *soft* constraints. What this means is that if we depart from the ideal conditions under which hard constraints seem to be obeyed, the illusion that the system has hard constraints inside is quickly dispelled. The system can violate Ohm's Law if it has to, but if it needn't violate the law it won't. Outside the idealised domain of well-posed problems and unlimited processing time, the system gives sensible performance. It isn't brittle the way that symbolic inference systems are.
>
> 'On the proper treatment of connectionism', 20

In other words the system learns a lot of small-scale facts about its domain (when resistance at x increases, voltage increases and so on) and comes to *look as if* it is producing its output by deploying general rules (e.g. $V = C \times R$). But it doesn't depend on such rules for its performance. So it can cope sensibly in situations where a rule-book is not enough, for instance where too little information is given to deploy a general rule, or inconsistent information is given.

3   *The relative inscrutability of networks*

I hope I have said just enough to give the flavour of connectionist artificial intelligence. The excitement and promise of such systems seems to be two-fold. First, it is conceptually interesting to see systems which *look* as if they are operating using conventional symbols and rules – (for example a symbol for 'current' (C) and a rule (Ohm's Law) $V = C \times R$) – but which in fact achieve their goals without the use of such coarse-grained symbols or hard and fast rules. Second, there is the apparent *practical* advantage of being able to train such systems by example. This seems to hold out the promise of *by-passing the knowledge engineer*. The knowledge engineer (in traditional expert systems work) is someone whose job is to find the *rules* which the expert follows and then incorporate them in a computational 'expert system'. But if we can train a network (like the rock/mine network) up to the level of expert performance by just giving it examples of questions and answers, there is no need to find any such set of rules. This has a pragmatic advantage, since experts are often unable to state the rules they (seem) to be following. And it is especially attractive to those philosophers who believe that *no* set of explicitly formulated rules can possibly capture the fluidity of the expert.[12]

The methodological hope, then, is in effect to *invert* the traditional investigative order. Traditionally, workers in AI began by trying to understand how to solve a class of problems, and then wrote algorithms to do so. On the connectionist approach, a detailed understanding of how to solve the class of problems is unnecessary (though some general intuitions are required in order to give the network a fighting chance in terms of the numbers of units, layers and so on). This is not, of course, to suggest that there is no comparable possibility in 'traditional' AI. For traditional AI too encompasses learning algorithms (such as Quinlan's ID3) which are likewise 'example driven'. What seems powerful about connectionism is the *combination* of network learning 'on the job' with the end product of flexible, generalizable, representations which can underpin a robust fluency in the target domain. It is the combination of learning and subsymbolic representation which is novel.

This combination, however, is by no means an unmixed blessing, for it brings with it an obvious drawback. The drawback is that when these systems learn to solve a class of problems, it is often far from clear how they are finally doing so. All we see, if we get a print-out of what the system has learnt, is a set of values (numbers) indicating the positive and negative connection weights between the units. If we had hoped for a better understanding of how such problems can be solved (for example as a clue to how the human brain might solve them), a set of numbers is of little use. What the theorist is interested in is not numbers so much as *function*. She needs to know what *subtasks* the units, or groups of units, are performing. Where symbolic content and rules are emergent properties of large numbers of tiny numerical relations, this functional understanding needs to be elucidated retrospectively by means of a variety of *post-hoc analyses* of the successful network.

There are various ways of performing such analyses. For example, it is possible to damage (or lesion) the networks and then, by observing the effects of the damage (that is, the destruction or impairment of various units and/or connections) to get some idea of the particular role they played in the problem solving. It is also possible to perform various kinds of statistical analysis which pick out the units most responsible for particular types of output. (Cluster analysis is one such technique.) All the forms of post-hoc analysis so far devised are, however, unreliable. It is seldom clear which, if any, of the techniques available will actually enhance our understanding of what exactly the network is doing. This is a serious drawback, since for many purposes (use in medicine, law, loans-assessment and so on) it is obviously essential that the network be in some way answerable to its human operators. Ideally, a network (like a human expert) should be able to offer a symbolic justification for its decisions. It is in this crucial respect that we may question the enthusiasm embodied in the thought that 'instead of struggling to equal human expertise in a specific domain, (networks) promise to exceed it in almost every respect' (Churchland, *The Neurocomputational Perspective*, 252). Human expertise is symbolically accountable, even if it is not fully replicable by purely symbolic means. The expertise of connectionist networks, so far, is not.

4   *The scope and power of the learning rules*

Connectionist systems are much admired for their ability to learn. But this ability is, in fact, seriously limited along a number of important dimensions. First, most of the successful algorithms depend on *answerbook* learning strategies (see below). Second, it is not clear that these strategies will scale up successfully when the learning task becomes very large and difficult. Third, there is a problem about how to successfully learn new knowledge without disrupting what the network already knows. Let's look at these in turn.

The point about answerbook learning is quite simple. It is that the most widely used connectionist learning procedures (that is, back-propagation of errors and Boltzmann machine learning) both require a teaching system which already knows the right answers. This system tells the network when it is going wrong and makes specific adjustments to it in the light of the correct answer. This means that the networks would be lost in domains where the right answers were not yet known.

The 'scaling-up' worry concerns the time-scale of learning for particularly large or complex problems. In back-propagation, for example, a weight adjustment is computed for each individual link in the network. Since the number of such links increases exponentially with the number of units, and since complex problems require large numbers of units, the time required to compute an individual adjustment for each unit can rapidly become unrealistic, especially since the whole procedure needs to be repeated thousands of times for each example of a correct input-output pairing in the training set. As a result Churchland calculates that the training of networks of about ten units is already straining our fastest machines.

Lastly, and perhaps most seriously of all, is what has come to be known as the problem of new knowledge. A connectionist network (of the distributed, subsymbolic kind) stores all its knowledge in one finely orchestrated set of connection strengths. This finely balanced system is the result, as we remarked above, of repeated training on thousands of examples. If we then decide we want to teach the system one new fact, there are two unpleasant hurdles. First, it cannot just learn the fact from a single exposure. Instead, it will need hundreds of repetitions of the new fact before it learns it. (Contrast human experts, who at least seem able to assimilate new facts about their domain from a single exposure – though of course what exactly the brain does with that single exposure is another question.) But second, and more importantly, the new knowledge, since it has to be stored by adjusting some of the very same weights which encode all that the system already knows, has a tendency to upset the old knowledge. That is, the network's performance when tested on the old knowledge will suffer until such time as, by further training on the entire set of examples, the network can again achieve the delicate balancing act of superpositional storage.

This is not, in general, a phenomenon which is visible in human experts. Human experts seem able to assimilate new knowledge without compromising what they already know. There are, it should be said, connectionist proposals for dealing with this problem (see for example. Hinton and Plaut (1987)). Any successful solution will probably herald the second generation of connectionist systems.

What, then, are the implications of connectionist learning for the very idea of programming? The radical vision would be the death of the programmer. The only algorithms which anyone would need to write would be learning algorithms. For the rest, we would just find the input-output examples and wind up the machine. This vision, however, is still far off. As things stand, connectionist learning rules are not powerful enough to solve complex problems without substantial task-specific intuitions being brought to bear by the programmer. For the existing learning rules are in essence tools for finding statistical associations in an input-output set. And such statistical methods, if they are to succeed in real time, need to explore a relatively small space of possibilities. The task of the programmer is thus to give the system a fighting chance by a good choice of (a) input and output representations, (b) system configuration (number of layers, number of units per layer etcetera) and (c) learning rule. In short, we are not seeing (despite the advertising) the death of domain specific knowledge as the key to successful programs: a fact which is nicely summed up in a famous slogan from Arbib and McCulloch: 'If you want a sweetheart in the spring, don't get an amoeba and wait for it to evolve'.[13]

5 CAMRA (*The Campaign for Real Abstractions*)

Many connectionists (a leading example is Paul Smolensky) reserve only a relatively minor role for genuine symbolic structures within their account of mind and mental activity. I believe that this is a mistake. It is, however, a deep and complex issue so I can only scratch the surface here.[19]

Let us invent a name – 'subsymbolists' – for anyone who holds that an expert's knowledge consists entirely in the example-driven storage of soft constraints. Thus in the Ohm's Law case, the subsymbolist holds that the expert does not rely on any in-the-head tokens which stand for the absolutely general concepts of Voltage, Current and Resistance. Instead she relies on the storage of a multitude of examples of legal relations which have, as an emergent but not explicitly represented lesson, the moral that, in general, $V = C \times R$.

Now the subsymbolist (at least if he is Paul Smolensky) can allow that a student, when initially learning about circuitry, may form an inner representation of the rule $V = C \times R$. But such representations, according to the subsymbolist, are at best only an aid to the novice. They are the ladder by which we achieve a slow, rough-and-ready competence; a ladder which is eventually to be kicked away once we have trained up an in-the-head network on a stock of examples. This picture (detailed in Smolensky (1988)), posits a special device (the 'conscious rule interpreter') which encodes genuinely symbolic knowledge as a short-term aid for the novice. The overall picture is endorsed by philosophers such as Dreyfus and Dreyfus, who picture, for example, the chess master as deploying a subsymbolic, example-driven competence in contrast to the novice who must recall the rules of thumb found in chess texts. In short, real expertise is pictured as independent of real abstractions.

Here I must pause to expand on the idea of a real abstraction. Why is the emergent knowledge of $V = C \times R$ not just a way of encoding real abstractions (symbols) for V, C and R? The answer, as repeatedly emphasized by Fodor and Pylyshn (1988), is that real abstractions are (a) transportable and (b) have their causal powers independently of one another. The upshot of this (which I shall try to make plain shortly) is that systems with real abstractions are capable of sustaining fully general concepts and are easily able to define new operations to apply to that concept. The idea is most easily understood by example.

Suppose that your understanding of Ohm's Law is purely subsymbolic and emergent (as in the toy network described earlier). And suppose further that one day, the rules of the circuitry game are altered. That is, suppose you find yourself required to do problem solving in a domain in which $V = C \times R$ is *false*, – a domain in which things are systematically altered such that $V = C + R$, with resultant changes to all the other laws of circuitry. (You are, in effect, required to solve problems in 'deviant circuitry', just as we sometimes choose to investigate a deviant logic.) In such a case, any purely subsymbolic/emergentist representation of $V = C \times R$ is of no use at all. For the subsymbolist's very *idea* of V, C and R is inextricably bound up with her idea of the particular relations specified in the training set. Where the rules of the game are systematically altered relative to a symbolic description ($V = C \times R$ going to $V = C + R$) a purely subsymbolic encoding is left at sea.

It should now be clearer what we mean by transportable constituents with individual causal powers. A symbolic encoding of $V = C \times R$ makes it easy to redefine the relation as $V = C + R$ or whatever. In that sense, the V, C and R are 'transportable'. And the symbols have individual causal powers in so far as their abilities (for example, V's ability to call up sets of values of V) are not defined with respect to their relation to the other knowledge of the system. This is obviously necessary if the system is to preserve most of its knowledge despite the re-jigging of relationships between entities.

One response to this kind of worry is to say that the circuitry expert, if forced to do 'deviant circuitry', is reduced to the position of a novice and must rely purely on the data stored in the conscious rule interpreter. But this seems implausible. An expert traditional logician will be much more intuitive and fluent if asked to investigate a system of deviant logic than any genuine novice logic student. So it looks as if there is carry-over between the two tasks. It is hard to see how much carry-over can be accounted for on the pure subsymbolist view. As things stand, I am therefore inclined to favour what have become known as *hybrid* models, in which connectionist and symbolic competences are deeply interwoven.

Ideally, we want a system in which, first, connectionist learning automatically gives rise to a symbolic expression of what has been learnt (thus meeting the answerability requirement raised in section 2) and second, such symbolic expressions are capable of acting as a high-level programming language which can alter the networks's stored knowledge in very specific and appropriate ways. This would enable a network which has learnt the rules of traditional circuitry to negotiate the systematically altered domain by making a copy of the original network and then using the re-formulated symbolic expression (say, $V = C + R$) to reach into the copy and make exactly the right adjustments, thus overcoming the lack of plasticity bemoaned above.

An alternative hypothesis, more congenial to the subsymbolist, would be that the expert is able to learn to negotiate the altered domain quickly because of the extent to which a copy of the old network may provide a particularly well set-up template upon which to do the new learning. It would be as if we were still training by example, but the network was 'innately' adapted (in terms of overall architecture at least) to that kind of domain.

So all we can really say, at this stage, is that it is too early to say. But let us at least register the suspicion that genuine abstractions have a role to play beyond that of bootstrapping the novice to a modest success in the domain.

6 *The Far Side: two faces of language*

The technical story being told, and the necessary cynicisms evinced, we are finally at liberty to ask the serious question: why care about connectionism? How, if at all, might the advent of connectionist models affect our conception of the real nature of human thought? In this closing section I want to pursue a particular, somewhat idiosyncratic, answer. The gist of this answer is that connectionism helps us understand two very different properties of public language. One is the property of *disciplining thought* – a property made central, in various ways, by a lot of work in traditional AI. The other is the property of *fluidity and layered meaning* – a property deeply implicated in fundamental aspects of human cognition, such as the ability to understand metaphors and to write poetry and creative prose.

To see what this all means we need to introduce one final fact about the connectionist representation of meaning. This is its deep and fundamental *context-sensitivity*. If you take a public language word such as 'coffee' (see Smolensky (1987) (1988)), it is natural to assume that that word (if it is not simply ambiguous) has a literal meaning. In many traditional AI systems, there would be an internal symbol which shares that literal meaning. Now it is an obvious fact that sometimes when we use the word coffee, we 'have in mind' a certain kind of situation, while at other times, although we use the same word, we imagine a different sort of situation. Thus if we say 'the coffee is in the jar' we imagine granules and glass. If we say 'the coffee is in the cup' we imagine a hot liquid and porcelain. In many traditional approaches these differences would be marked by having the same internal symbol (call it 'coffee**') tokened on each occasion, but associating it with a different set of other symbols in each case (ones meaning 'hot liquid', etcetera). In a pure connectionist approach, by contrast, there will be no recurrent 'coffee' symbol but just a set of 'subsymbolic' features which are different according to the context concerned. Thus 'coffee in the cup' may be tokened as one set of subsymbols (appropriate to hotness, liquidity and so on) and 'coffee in the jar' as another. As Smolensky puts it: 'In the symbolic paradigm, the context of a symbol is manifest around it and consists of other symbols; in the subsymbolic paradigm, the context of a symbol is manifest inside it and consists of subsymbols' ('On the Proper Treatment of Connectionism', 17).

How should we understand this difference? To many, it has just seemed to amount to the claim that connectionism can 'do' context sensitivity; a feature which can hardly be said to distinguish it in any way from classicism. But the important fact, I suggest, is rather this: that by having a real internal *symbol* meaning 'coffee', classicism can register (at a particular level of description) *sameness* of thought where connectionism (bereft of such symbols) cannot. Take the thought that the coffee is on the table. And imagine two cases, one in which it is spilt coffee granules, one in which it is a cup of hot liquid. For the classicist, there can still be a definable sameness of *internal* representation across the two cases. In each case we find a tokening of the symbols for 'coffee', 'on' and 'table'. The difference is just in the other *associated* symbols. For the pure connectionist, there is no sameness of internal representation here at all. This has important consequences for the very idea of a *thought*.

We can see this best by making the same point in a slightly different way. For the classicist, there can be thoughts which consist in perfect internal analogues to the thoughts we can define in public language. Thus there can be a perfect internal analogue to the thought that the coffee is on the table such that the internal analogue is robust across differences of nuance introduced by context (of which our case is a somewhat brutish example). The nuances get dealt with *independently* of the tokening of the symbols for 'coffee', 'on', and 'table'. In connectionism this is not so. The nuances are built into the tokenings which consitute the thought. Classicism thus has the resources to mirror the public language ascription of thoughts. Connectionism eschews such mirroring.

The upshot is that the idea of 'same thought' calls (on the connectionist model) for some further work. There is a notion of 'same thought' such that the sameness amounts to sameness of public language description. And there is another notion of 'same thought' which makes the sameness depend upon the internal character of the thought. In connectionism, these come wildly apart – there is a great deal of slack between public symbols and inner states.[15]

It is this slack which enables the connectionist, slightly paradoxically, to have a much richer and more interesting conception of the role of public language than that found in more traditional work. For public language, on the connectionist model, has properties which the internal 'language' simply lacks. One such property, as just mentioned, is the ability to fix *sameness* of thought in a way independent of the nuances of context. It is this ability which made possible the development of a logic of argument forms, for example the inference 'If P then Q; if Q then R; therefore if P then R' – an inference which is valid (correct) whatever the context set up by specifics P, Q, and R. For, as Fodor and Pylyshyn (1988) notice, such argument schemas are valid only if we assume that the sentences which express the premises do not change their meanings when they are re-used in the derivation of a conclusion! Likewise we can define a notion of sameness of thought such that the differences between individual's experiences of the world is papered over. If you (a seasoned traveller) say 'India is fascinating', I can share that thought even if my internal states (being largely ignorant of India) are vastly different from your own. Moreover, public language provides a kind of external machine by means of which deeply parallel systems (like human brains) can negotiate highly sequential domains. To plan a difficult sequence of events so as to maximize efficiency generally requires the manipulation of tokens of public language symbols by pen and paper.[16] In all these respects, then, public language may serve to impose a useful discipline and metric upon fluid, connectionist representations.

The other side of this coin, however, is where the greatest fascination lies. Can a fluid, connectionist internal code help us to understand the more mercurial properties of our symbolic (that is, public language expressed) thought? It is here, if anywhere, that connectionism has its most profound (but embryonic) promise.

Very often, we seem to think in words, in the gross symbols ('cat', 'mat', 'cyclotron') of our public language. And yet this linguistically couched thought displays properties which are notoriously hard to explain in the terms familiar to conventional 'symbolic' AI. This is odd. One would have imagined that it is here, if anywhere, that gross symbol manipulation should win the day. The trouble is that although the public language symbols are relatively coarse-grained, they seem to carry many levels of meaning and to be capable of the most subtle and intricate interactions. Consider in this context the power of poetry to use the shape and sound of symbols to carry meanings far beyond the 'literal' sense of the words. Or consider our ability, by juxtaposing gross symbols in a verbal metaphor ('the atom is a solar system') to reconceptualize a whole domain. Finally, consider the strange case (rightly made much of by D. Hofstadter[17]) of the semantics of novel words, for instance new brand names for products. We have a sense that 'Turbomatic' is dated, that 'Flimp' and 'Luggo' are not good choices and so on. (These examples are Hofstadter's own.) But in what is such a sense grounded?

The radical hope, the thing which (in my view) makes connectionism a genuinely exciting prospect, is that all these phenomena are somehow or other a direct result of what we might call the 'hidden semantics' of the subsymbolic constituents of the standard symbolic expressions. This is what I mean by the idea of connectionism helping us to understand the fluidity and multi-layered texture of the meanings of public language symbols.

Let me close, in highly speculative mode, with a nice suggestion which I first heard from Martin Davies. Davies suggests that it might be illuminating to consider whether the public language symbols might seep back down, as it were, to the subsymbolic level.

The idea would go something like this. When we learn the word 'cup', one effect is to come to associate it with (context-sensitive) bunches of microfeatural properties. The classicist, we saw, expects us to deploy an inner symbol for cup, while the Smolensky-style connectionist rejects the idea of a symbol meaning 'cup'. But this need not rule out such a system's coming to treat the word 'cup' as just another microfeature associated with certain other microfeatures. Thus if I am shown a picture of a cup, I may understand what I see by having active a whole set of microfeature units (or groups of units) which encode such items as 'liquid-carrying', 'smooth', 'handle' and 'called-"cup" '. The word 'cup' is not here acting as a symbol in the classical sense, since it is not any kind of atomic meaning-bearer: the 'symbol' is not an essential constituent of the thought – it has the status of a piece of collateral information encoded amongst the general bulk of the connectionist representation. None the less the word becomes a real feature of the contents in which it figures. I leave the reader to speculate further concerning the possible effects of such seepage.

Perhaps, then, connectionism may help give us a sense of the hidden semantics which oils the wheels of surface symbolic transitions: the bubbling up of words and phrases out of the cognitive soup, the power of a word to set up a context in which our inferences in one domain are immediately disciplined by the standard relations amongst entities in another domain (the crux of metaphorical understanding – see Churchland, Chapter 11) and as we saw, the sense of inappropriateness which can attend novel words such as 'Luggo'. The symbols may help discipline the connectionist soup, but they have a second face as fluid, subsymbolic complexes. This symbol-subsymbolic complementarity, I believe, could profoundly affect our thinking in domains far removed from the technical and the philosophical. It could affect psychiatry and literary studies, sociology and semiotics. The duality and complementarity of mind may yet prove as deep and as important as that of its quantum cousins.

* The historical introduction in Section 1 is drawn from A. Clark, *Microcognition: Philosophy, Cognitive Science and Parallel Distributed Processing* (MIT/Bradford Books, 1989), 84–8. My thanks to MIT Press for permission to reproduce that material here.

Selected Readings

Clark, A. (1989) *Microcognition* (Cambridge, Mass.: MIT/Bradford Books).

Fodor, J. & Pylyshyn, Z. (1988) 'Connectionism and Cognitive Architecture', *Cognition* 28, 3–71.

McClelland, J., Rumelhart, D. & the PDP Research Group (1986) *Parallel Distributed Processing: explorations in the microstructure of cognition* (Cambridge, Mass.: MIT/Bradford Books), Vols I and II.

Smolensky, P. (1988) 'On the Proper Treatment of Connectionism', *Behavioural and Brain Sciences* 11, 1–73.

Notes

1. See T. Durham, 'Neural brainwaves break new ground', *Computing* (9 April 1987); McClelland, Rumelhart & the PDP Research Group (1986), II, chs 20–23.

2. See W. Koehler, *Gestalt Psychology* (New York: Liveright, 1929); R. Baddeley, 'Connectionism and *Gestalt* theory' (University of Sussex: unpublished manuscript, 1987).

3. W. McCulloch & W. Pitts, 'A logical calculus of ideas immanent in nervous activity', *Bulletin of Mathematical Biophysics* 5 (1943), 115–33; D. Hebb, *The Organization of Behaviour* (New York: Wiley & Sons, 1949); F. Rosenblatt, *Principles of Neurodynamics* (New York: Spartan Books, 1962).

4. See McClelland et al (1986), I, 36 for a brief discussion.

5. Ibid, 154–6.

6. Landmarks in the rise of connectionism include McClelland et al (1986), and G. Hinton & J. Anderson (eds), *Parallel Models of Associative Memory* (New Jersey: Erlbaum, 1981).

7. P. Smolensky, 'The constituent structure of connectionist mental states', *Southern Journal of Philosophy* XXVI Supp. (1987), 137–62, at 137.

8. J. Haugeland, *Artificial Intelligence: the very idea* (Cambridge, Mass.: MIT/Bradford Books, 1985); A. Newell, 'Physical Symbol Systems', *Cognitive Science* 4:2 (1980), 135–83.

9. See for example Smolensky (1987), 149.

10. D. Rumelhart, P. Smolensky, J. McClelland & G. Hinton, 'Schemata and sequential thought processes in PDP models', in McClelland et al (1986), vol. II.

11. P. Churchland, *The Neurocomputational Perspective* (Cambridge, Mass.: MIT Press, forthcoming), p. 11.

12. For example, H. Dreyfus & S. Dreyfus, 'From Socrates to Expert Systems: the limits of calculative rationality', in C. Mitcham and A. Hung (eds), *Philosophy and Technology* 11 (1986), 111–130.

13. M. Arbib, *Notes from lectures on Brain Theory and Artificial Intelligence* (Centre for Cognitive Science, University of New South Wales, 1988). The notes are excerpted from Arbib, *The Metaphorical Brain 2: an Introduction to Schema Theory and Neural Networks* (Chichester: Wiley Interscience, forthcoming).

14. See also A. Clark, 'In Defence of Explicit Rules', probably to appear in W. Ramsey, D. Rumelhart and S. Stich (eds), *Philosophy and Connectionist Theory* (New York: Erlbaum, forthcoming); A. Clark and A. Karmiloff-Smith, 'The Cognizers' Innards' (in preparation).

15. See also D. Dennett, *The Intentional Stance* (Cambridge, Mass.: MIT/Bradford Books, 1987), p. 227–35.

16. For more on this kind of proposal, see Rumelhart, Smolensky, McClelland and Hinton (1986).

17. D. Hofstadter, *Metamagical Themas: questing for the essence of mind and pattern* (Harmondsworth: Penguin, 1985), chapter 23.

8

Explaining and Explaining Away Insanity

RICHARD P. BENTALL

There are many sources and varieties of human suffering: disease, accidents (natural and unnatural), violence and injustice all contribute to the great toll of unhappiness that led Camus to liken the burden of humankind to that of the mythical Sisyphus. Only the ingenuity of humankind in developing new ways and means of avoiding suffering appears to offer some measure of hope and sanctuary. And indeed it is true that much of human history, and many of humankind's most remarkable achievements, have involved the constant, endless struggle to defeat suffering in its many forms. As a consequence there are medicines, machines and political institutions all designed to guarantee comfort and security (sometimes for particular individuals, sometimes for sections of society).

Yet, of the many different kinds of suffering, insanity has proved particularly resistant to humankind's efforts. Contentiously, the problem seems to be not so much that the resources needed to defeat insanity are beyond our current means (although this may be so) but that we do not know how properly to proceed. There is, after all, something peculiarly mysterious about a form of suffering which often has no self-evident causes, which waxes and wanes unpredictably, and which, on passing, leaves no mark upon its victim. Whereas there is often a clear course of action to follow in the face of other forms of suffering (although there may be a lack of will to pursue it), in the case of insanity there is no such obvious course. Deep divisions can be found in the theoretical literature on such basic issues as: What kinds of mental and behavioural phenomena can be considered insane? Is insanity a form of disease? If so, what kinds of treatment are warranted? Ultimately, ordinary people wish to see an end to insanity, and they look to experts in the field of psychopathology to achieve this goal in much the same way that people have looked to experts in medicine for remedies for disease, or to engineers for remedies for physical discomforts. Yet the explanation of insanity poses serious conceptual as well as empirical problems. In this essay I want to outline some of these problems. In particular, I want to show that much traditional thinking about insanity is misconceived and likely to impede progress towards a less insane world.

The Standard Approach

It is widely assumed that insanity is at least analogous to physical illness in the sense that the concepts, explanations and technologies that have proved useful in the understanding and treatment of medical suffering (disorders of the body) are precisely those which are likely to yield progress in the case of insanity. It is not farfetched to call this the *standard approach*. This approach, which encompasses what have generally been described as medical models of psychopathology, is widely seen as having implications for the definition, detection, explanation and treatment of insanity in the following ways.

The definitions currently employed in the study of psychopathology are usually those of different *diagnostic categories*, which are said to describe different forms of *mental illness or disease*. The detection of mental disease requires, according to the standard approach, a diagnostic expert who applies the diagnostic criteria to the symptoms reported by the *patient*. These symptoms are said to be explained in terms of underlying disorders which, in turn, may be biological (genetic, biochemical, neurological) in nature. Accurate diagnosis is said to be important if the correct *treatment* is to be prescribed.

To take a particular example, we may consider the diagnostic concept of *schizophrenia*. First described by the German psychiatrist Emil Kraepelin (who used the term *dementia praecox*; the diagnosis was renamed schizophrenia some years later by the Swiss psychiatrist Eugen Bleuler), this syndrome was differentiated from *manic-depressive or major affective disorder* on the grounds of its poor outcome. Both schizophrenia and major affective disorder are said to belong to the class of *psychoses*, mental diseases in which the sufferer often loses insight into his condition. (The less severe class of psychiatric disorders is the *neuroses*, which includes phobias, anxieties and the milder forms of depression, in which the sufferer usually has some understanding of his predicament.) Most psychiatric textbooks describe the symptoms of schizophrenia as including auditory hallucinations (hearing voices of people who are not in fact present), delusions (manifestly false beliefs), thought disorder (a misnomer for disordered speech), anhedonia (inability to experience pleasure), flat affect (lack of emotion) and social withdrawal. Major affective disorder, on the other hand, may also be manifest in delusional ideas or hallucinations but its main feature is a severe disorder of mood, in which the sufferer experiences extreme depression, extreme elation, or swings between the two. Because it has been acknowledged that it is often difficult to discriminate between schizophrenia and other psychiatric disorders, psychiatrists have attempted to develop operational criteria for diagnosing schizophrenia which can be applied to data collected in the course of structured psychiatric interviews. The causes of schizophrenia have been a matter of some speculation for nearly one hundred years but most theories implicate biological factors such as genetic endowment, abnormalities of brain biochemistry or structural defects of the brain.

It is difficult to specify the origins of the standard approach with any exactness, but it clearly predates modern diagnostic concepts such as schizophrenia. There are in fact a number of competing historical accounts of the development of psychiatric ideas and it has even been suggested that historical accounts of insanity and its treatment themselves fall into distinct historical periods, accounts prior to 1960 describing the emergence of what is here called the standard approach, in terms of the steady development of scientific ideas, while more recent accounts have been more critical of the claims of medical science, and have emphasized the social and political determinants of mental health practice.[1] Despite these difficulties, the following facts seem certain.

First, it is clear that cultures have distinguished between sanity and insanity for as long as history has been recorded and that some but by no means all early civilizations (or at least some members of those civilizations) theorized about insanity using terms and concepts not dissimilar to those of the standard approach (that is, within a framework of beliefs about disease and illness). Whether different criteria have been used by different cultures to distinguish between the sane and the insane has been a matter of some dispute. As evidence that quite serious differences do exist in what counts for madness, some anthropologists have pointed to the irrational beliefs of other cultures and also to the apparent acceptance by some cultures of behaviour (for example, shamanism) which we would regard as insane. Other anthropologists have argued that, when insane people are studied objectively and cross-cultural differences in diagnostic concepts are allowed for, insanity described in purely behavioural terms is surprisingly constant from one end of the world to the other. An interesting proposal is that all cultures describe behaviour as insane when it can no longer be accounted for in terms of the prevailing folk psychology (the system of psychological beliefs held by ordinary members of a society), in other words, when motives are no longer obvious and when ordinary language explanations of behaviour are exhausted. On this view, cultural differences in criteria for insanity reflect cultural differences in folk psychology, so that the connotation of insanity (what it means) is universal whereas its denotation (what it is) is culturally relative.[2]

Second, within the recent history of Western civilization the institutionalization of psychiatric concepts and ideas (for example, in terms of the emergence of a recognized profession of experts in insanity, with a perceived specialist body of knowledge and legally recognized qualifications to practice) has been a comparatively late development. In Great Britain, for example, physicians took over the control of the asylums from lay managers in the late eighteenth century and a theory of psychiatric classification became widely accepted (mainly following the influence of Kraepelin) only in the late nineteenth century.

Given the long evolution of the standard approach and its continuing development, it might be objected that questioning it, at least in the form in which it has been described above, amounts to tilting at windmills. In particular, it might be claimed that there is not one medical model of insanity but many. For example, it might be argued that there is a genetic model, a biochemical model, a neurological model, and so on. This objection reveals a misunderstanding of what is at issue. The confusion is between a general conceptual framework (analogous, perhaps, to the philosophical framework that informed physics after Newton), loosely accepted in one form or another by perhaps the bulk of mental health professionals, and scientific models in the more specific sense (for which the correct analogy in physics might be a particular account of sub-molecular structure such as Bohr's water-drop model of the nucleus). The standard approach, as described here, amounts to not so much a clearly articulated scientific theory but a general way of speaking about insanity which is widely accepted by experts but which has also permeated ordinary language. From the perspective of the philosophy of science, the standard approach might be thought of as a paradigm or a research programme, relatively resistant to falsification because it forms the unspoken conceptual background against which most research into insane behaviour has been carried out. Historians of science have suggested that such paradigms form an important role within the development of a discipline, providing a common language in which scientists can frame and test ideas. (These arguments are beyond the scope of this essay although, interestingly, the emergence of the standard approach to classification following the work of Kraepelin and other nineteenth-century psychiatrists might be thought of as evidence in favour of this type of history of science.) Clearly, the assumptions of the standard approach are open to examination. In particular, it is worth asking whether the standard approach directs us to try and explain *the right kinds of objects*, and whether the explanations offered within the standard approach are *the right kinds of explanations*.

With respect to the first question, the standard approach suggests that the proper objects of psychopathology are the *diseases* described according to widely agreed *diagnostic criteria* (for example, 'schizophrenia', 'affective psychosis', 'anxiety' or 'agoraphobia'). However, it is not diagnostic categories which are observed in the psychiatric clinic but rather certain classes of *behaviour* or *complaints* (which may be regarded as experiences or verbal responses, depending on whether one wants to be strictly behaviouristic) made by insane people. I will later introduce some empirical considerations which have some bearing on this issue, but it will first do no harm to emphasize the obvious, namely that insane acts are psychological phenomena in the minimal sense that they are defined in terms of the behaviour and experiences of the insane person.

Let us pursue this point further. It might be claimed that although the principal manifestations of insanity are presently defined in psychological terms, it will one day be possible to redefine them in terms of strictly non-psychological constructs. Such a line might be taken, for example, by someone who believes that most kinds of insanity are caused by diseases of the brain. Ignoring philosophy of mind arguments for a moment, let us therefore suppose that some astute neuroscientist discovers a brain abnormality which correlates with a particular form of insanity, say a type of schizophrenia. Would such a scientist then be able to propose a non-psychological definition of this type of madness along the lines that the schizophrenia is the brain abnormality? It is hard to see why such a redefinition would be justified. Suppose that the abnormality that the neuroscientist observes is not a brain abnormality but a discolouration of the left big toe or even a particularly unusual choice of clothing (the fact that chronic schizophrenics, especially those who have been hospitalized for many years, tend to wear trousers that are too short was once humorously proposed as a diagnostic sign). Would the scientist then be comfortable with a redefinition of schizophrenia in terms of big toes or clothing? Almost certainly not. The scientist's readiness to make the definitional substitution in the case of the brain abnormality but not in the case of the other examples presumably rests on a causal hypothesis, namely that the brain abnormality *causes the behaviour and distressing experiences of the insane person.* It is clear, therefore, that the behaviour and distressing experiences of the insane person cannot easily be dispensed with when defining the insanity.

Consider two further possibilities. Suppose, following the redefinition, that the abnormality, neural or otherwise, is observed in the case of someone who appears perfectly composed in behaviour and attitudes or, alternatively, that the disturbed behaviour and experiences previously described as schizophrenia are found to occur in the case of someone without the required brain abnormality. The redefinition proposal implies that the former person is really schizophrenic but that the latter is not. Under these circumstances the concept of schizophrenia has undergone such radical revision that it no longer bears any connection to the concept of schizophrenia as previously understood. Indeed, we would be justified in saying that the neuroscientist is not interested in schizophrenia at all but in some disease of the brain. The fact that the disease might perhaps cause the schizophrenia has no implications for this issue. What these considerations show is that concepts of psychopathology can never be cut entirely adrift from psychological referents. This is not to say that discoveries in the biological or other sciences cannot lead to the elaboration of concepts of psychopathology but, rather, that they could never replace them entirely. In this respect, concepts of psychopathology do not differ from concepts in the physical and biological sciences, which may be extensively revised as the science progresses, but which none the less retain their links with their original referents.

Examination of the imaginary neuroscientist's proposal leads us to consider the second question I have raised about the standard approach, namely the question of what kinds of explanations should be offered for insane behaviour. I will be discussing this point in more detail shortly, but a feature of the standard approach that is worth noting immediately is its tendency to focus on internal causes of the insane person's conduct to the exclusion of external influences. Indeed, for most researchers at least, the standard approach involves little more than the search for brain abnormalities and scant attention is given to the interaction between the insane person and his environment. A second, related and somewhat unfortunate feature of the standard approach is a tendency to 'explain insane behaviour away' rather than genuinely explain it. Indeed, if it is true that the common thread that links different kinds of insanity is their unintelligibility from the perspective of ordinary language, it is not always obvious that the language of psychiatry marks much in the way of an advance. Technical terms which began their lives as descriptions of behaviour have, over the course of time, often taken on a pseudo-explanatory aspect. For example, in the course of informal discussions on psychiatric wards and even in the more formal atmosphere of the courtroom, it is not uncommon to hear it asserted that so-and-so does such-and-such *because* he has schizophrenia. At worst, such assertions put an end to the search for real explanations, and allow external influences on the individual's behaviour (the circumstances under which the behaviour occurs) to be completely ignored.

I have laboured these points because they carry the implication that it would be wrong to think about the study of insanity as somehow separate from the study of 'normal' pychological phenomena. In fact, the findings of psychologists about normal conduct scarcely merit a mention in most contemporary textbooks of psychopathology and those few advocates of the standard approach who have given any attention to the relationship between psychopathology and normal psychology have sometimes suggested that the latter is simply not relevant to the former. Thus:

> It would be absurd to maintain that psychology can be to psychiatry what physiology has been to medicine, not only because the claim would be exaggerated, but also because it implies that psychiatry and medicine are mere cousin-sciences. . . . The primary concern of the psychiatrist is the morbid mental states; and however much is known about the psychology of the normal individual, in the pathological field new laws will be found to operate.[3]

Insanity, Disease and the Brain

At this point I want to consider the most common objection made to the standard approach, an objection which has become the focus of a considerable amount of philosophical argument. This is the objection to the idea that insanity counts as disease. Much of the debate surrounding this issue has, I believe, been unhelpful in advancing our understanding of insanity. However, it will still be useful to examine some of the relevant arguments because these will inform my conclusions about the types of explanations that should be offered for insane behaviour.

In the history of medicine there have been two quite different ways of defining disease. One approach, advocated by Virchow in the nineteenth century, locates the disease in the body as altered physiology, an idea which corresponds to much lay and scientific thinking about the aetiology of insanity (for example, the idea that there must be a biological cause of schizophrenia). The second approach can be traced back to Hippocrates but was most creatively developed by Thomas Sydenham in the seventeenth century. Sydenham attempted to describe clinical phenomena as carefully as possible in the hope of identifying signs and symptoms that occurred together. Sydenham saw this strategy as directly analogous to the task facing natural historians in their attempts to describe species; like species, diseases were considered to be autonomous and discrete entities. This second approach perhaps lies behind the many technical debates concerning psychiatric diagnosis (for example, arguments about which criteria best distinguish between schizophrenia and the affective psychoses). Clearly, these two ways of defining disease are not entirely incompatible; medical researchers generally expect that symptoms that cluster together into syndromes will often prove to be the product of common, underlying physiological defects.

Most of the philosophical debate about the disease status of insanity has focused on the notion, following Virchow, that diseases must reflect altered physiology. Most infamously, the American psychiatrist Thomas Szasz has argued that mental disease is a myth precisely because, in the case of most kinds of insanity at least, no biological pathology has ever been identified.[4] Szasz went on to argue that, because insanity fails to meet accepted criteria for disease, the ascription of disease to undesirable behaviour amounts to nothing more than moral condemnation, a kind of moral condemnation which is made all the more sinister by virtue of being disguised as a scientific judgement. The benefit of this kind of dishonesty is, according to Szasz, that it allows society to appoint psychiatrists as covert agents of social control. This is an argument which has struck a deep chord with many sociologists who, for reasons of their own, have seen the function of psychiatry as mainly the control of deviance.

Not surprisingly, these kinds of ideas have been the subject of considerable debate. One unhelpful objection that has been made against Szasz and others of a similar mind (a version of which we have already heard from the lips of the imaginary neuroscientist who wished to redefine insanity in neurobiological terms) has been the bold assertion that biological pathology will eventually be proven in the case of most if not all forms of insanity, even where it is not demonstrable today. This argument (if 'argument' is not an overgenerous description) has been a surprisingly consistent position held by medical practitioners over the years, and the use to which it was put in the middle of the last century is one piece of evidence cited in those historical accounts which have described the medical takeover of the asylums as a phase of empire building. Thus, an editorial in the *Journal of Mental Science* (later the *British Journal of Psychiatry*) dated 1858 announced that: 'Insanity is purely a disease of the brain. The physician is now the responsible guardian of the lunatic and must ever remain so.'[5] Much more recently, Hunter and Macalpine made exactly the same claim: 'The lesson of the history of psychiatry is that progress is inevitable and irrevocable from psychology to neurology, from mind to brain, never the other way round. Every medical advance adds to the list of diseases which may cause mental derangement.'[6] Even ignoring the dubiously dualist philosophy of mind implicit in this statement, it can be dismissed in much the same way that Popper dismissed political historicism: as an attempt to sell a questionable programme on the grounds of its inevitability.

In fact, Szasz's argument rests on two implicit claims: first, that physical pathology is required as proof of disease, and second, that the diagnosis of disease and moral judgement are two mutually exclusive exercises. With respect to the first of these, a more satisfactory line of argument against Szasz and his followers involves the counter-claim that a coherent account of disease can be given without referring to bodily pathology. Authors who have followed this course have attempted to elucidate some nonreductionist definition of disease which is equally applicable to the phenomena observed in physical medicine and those described in textbooks of psychiatry. There have been many proposals of this sort, mostly made by psychiatrists unhappy at the prospect of being reclassified as members of a secret police force, but a variant of this approach which seems particularly promising has been suggested by the philosopher Christopher Boorse.[7]

Boorse defines disease as an internal state of the individual which (i) interferes with the performance of some natural function characteristic of the organism's age and (ii) is not simply in the nature of the species. The interesting implication of this position is that it allows disease to be defined in purely psychological terms so long as there is some clear understanding of the psychological functions of an organism. Boorse cites psychoanalytic theory as a good model of this sort, but modern cognitive psychology might fit his case even better. This is because in the past twenty years or so cognitive psychologists have made significant advances in understanding the mental processes involved in the brain's attempt to make sense of the world. If it can be shown, for example, that in cases of a particular type of schizophrenia there are abnormalities of the kinds of reasoning or information manipulation processes described by cognitive psychologists, then (assuming that reasoning and the manipulation of information are natural functions of the organism) it would follow that schizophrenia qualifies as disease, even in the absence of known abnormalities of neurophysiology.

Boorse's proposal therefore raises the following question: Is it possible to have an impairment of psychological function in the absence of an abnormality of physiological function? If this is possible then, following Boorse, it is reasonable to speak of mental or psychological disease in the absence of physical disease. This question in turn raises the wider issue of intertheoretic reduction: whether statements at the psychological level are always reducible to statements about neurophysiology.

The problem of intertheoretic reduction has taxed philosophers for many centuries, so there is obviously only so much that I can say about it in the present context. One widely cited argument from artificial intelligence is the claim of *multiple instantiability*, the observation that the same computer programme can be instantiated on physically quite different computing machines. Assuming a direct analogy between the human mind and a computing machine, it is argued that mental processes (programmes) cannot be reductively accounted for in terms of the machine that implements them (the brain) because the same mental states, with sufficient ingenuity on behalf of experts in artificial intelligence, might be supported by quite different kinds of devices. Countering this argument, some philosophers have taken issue with the idea that the symbol-manipulating computer is an appropriate model of the mind, whereas others who are broadly sympathetic with the findings from artificial intelligence have doubted whether the argument from multiple instantiability, once carefully considered, applies even to machines. Patricia Churchland, for example, does not see why reductionist accounts of cognitive processes should be expected to generalize from the domain of brains to the domain of machines, or even from one species of brain to another.[8]

None the less, and allowing for the arguments of Churchland and others, it seems unlikely that even the strongest of reductionist doctrines will pose a threat to Boorse's proposal. For, while psychological events might be theoretically reduced to events described at the level of neurobiology, it certainly does not follow that psychological functions are the same as the functions of neurobiological processes. Pursuing the computer analogy for a moment (and accepting its weaknesses), we might consider the case of an 'insane' machine which, although programmed for mulitiplication, insists that $2 \times 2 = 5$. However tempting it might be to examine the internal workings of such a machine, there is no guarantee that it would be found to be faulty at the level of its electronic functions. Of course, it is possible that something defective would be found within its circuits but it seems equally probable that inspection would reveal all to be in order. What might be defective is the programme, the rules the silicon circuits have been directed to follow in order to generate an arithmetical solution. Although the machine and its programme have been designed to derive correct conclusions to arithmetical problems, the functions of the circuit have to be described in terms appropriate to that level of description. More generally, as reductionists like Churchland have acknowledged, statements about functions are level-dependent and functions at one level are not necessarily functions at another.

It is important to note that there is nothing antibiological about this position. Indeed, if we accept Boorse's proposal, it makes sense to distinguish between three types of disease: psychological disease in the absence of brain disease (arguably the case in most forms of insanity), brain disease in the absence of psychological disease (for example, when certain kinds of hydrocephalus leave the brain damaged without any noticeable impairment of psychological function), and brain disease and psychological disease co-occurring (for example, when brain damage leads to psychological disturbance, in which case we can talk about the brain disease *causing* the psychological disease).

Returning to the arguments of Szasz, it will be recalled that the second claim implicit in his position is that diagnosis and moral judgement are two mutually exclusive activities. This claim can be dealt with much more briefly. As many authors have pointed out, moral judgement is implicit in the diagnosis of even physical disorder. Indeed, it is by virtue of the fact that some deviation from the physical norm is harmful to the individual that it is classified as disease. Far from being incompatible with diagnosis, moral judgement is an essential (if unobvious) component of it.

There is therefore nothing incoherent about calling insanity disease. However, for the most part at least, the kinds of arguments which we have so far considered do not seem to advance our understanding of insanity to any noticeable degree. It is worth remembering why the disease debate has attracted so much attention: because calling insanity disease has *seemed* to legitimize the role of the medical profession in managing the insane. Once the concept of disease is separated from the criterion of physical pathology, this becomes an illusion. A clinical psychologist, for example, could follow Boorse and argue that insanity involves psychological disease and at the same time quite consistently claim that psychological rather than medical skills are most appropriate for its treatment. Indeed, it is evident that attempts to define insanity as disease *a priori* cannot lead to conclusions about appropriate treatment skills, which can be reached only after a thoroughgoing analysis of the causes of insane conduct.

None the less, there is something to be gained from the above discussion; the fact that functions are level-dependent has an important implication for the explanation of insanity. For if the immediate causes of insanity are to be sought within the person (and bearing in mind that, in most cases of insanity, we would do well not to ignore the prevailing circumstances under which the insane behaviour occurs) they will be evident in some kind of psychological malfunctioning. This a further reason why psychological concepts cannot be dispensed with by psychopathologists. For example, to understand errors of perception such as hallucinations it seems necessary to understand the psychological functions normally involved in analysing perceptual information. Similarly, in order to understand how the irrational beliefs of the deluded person are acquired, it will be helpful to understand the cognitive processes implemented by the brain during the acquisition of the more mundane beliefs of ordinary persons. Put another way, it is difficult to see how, say, observations linking brain abnormalities to schizophrenic behaviour can make much sense unless there is some understanding of the cognitive tasks sustained by those parts of the brain which are found to be abnormal.

This point is particularly relevant when we recognize that, as a matter of fact, external circumstances inevitably play some role in the determination of insanity. Most forms of insanity are precipitated by periods of stress. Moreover, when we look at particular types of insane behaviour, interesting relationships can be observed between the behaviour and the environment. Hallucinations tend to be heard under noisy conditions, thought disorder tends to occur when the individual is forced to discuss emotionally difficult topics, and the delusions of the insane reflect troubling events in their lives. Indeed, as a general rule both the presentation of insanity and the forms in which it becomes manifest are context-dependent. It is therefore only by understanding the ways in which brains make sense of their environment – the task of cognitive psychology – that we in turn can make sense of the behaviour and experiences of the insane person.

RICHARD P. BENTALL

161

Empirical Considerations

At this point I want to return to the question first posed about the standard approach, the question of whether it directs us to look at the right kinds of objects in our quest for an explanation of insanity. I have so far said very little about this, apart from arguing that it would be a mistake to define insanity in terms too distant from its behavioural manifestations. In point of fact, psychopathologists have paid little attention to the behaviour of insane people, preferring instead to attempt explanatory statements about broad diagnostic categories. Thus, by far the bulk of research in psychopathology uses diagnosis as an independent variable (for example, when comparing a group of schizophrenics to a group of depressed patients or a group of 'normals'). This strategy only makes sense if the target group (schizophrenics in this case) have something in common which the comparison groups lack (some marker of the 'cause' of their schizophrenia). Empirical data pertaining to the validity or meaningfulness of the diagnostic categories commonly employed in psychiatric research is therefore of some relevance to my argument.

It is interesting to note that the most widely used diagnostic criteria, those of the American Psychiatric Association, were decided by small groups of clinicians rather than on the basis of empirical findings, and therefore represent nothing more impressive than post-Kraepelinian clinical folk-lore institutionalized by committee. Astonishingly, it turns out that there is an almost complete lack of evidence that these criteria are scientifically meaningful. Indeed, those relevant empirical investigations which have been carried out provide little comfort for psychopathologists schooled in the standard approach.

There is no one test of whether a diagnostic classification is meaningful. Rather, a whole series of tests have to be applied. The more that we find these tests are satisfied, the more comfortable we can be that a diagnostic system is scientifically useful. The first test concerns the *reliability* of the system, which amounts to whether or not the system diagnoses people consistently (today's schizophrenic, diagnosed by Dr Smith, should still be schizophrenic when diagnosed by Dr Jones in the morrow). Further tests concern the system's *validity*. These might include tests of whether symptoms cluster together in the way predicted by the method of classification (a person with one symptom of schizophrenia should have a high probability of experiencing other symptoms of the disorder), and whether the diagnosis is predictively valid (on the basis of the diagnosis we would like to be able to know how long the disease is likely to last and what kinds of treatments are likely to make a difference). Finally, of course, we would like to be able to link diagnoses to relatively concise statements about aetiology, although the relationship between disease and aetiology might be complex (in the case of some medical disorders, for example, the disease is a common end-state reached by several distinct causal pathways).

It is no accident that I have chosen the concept of schizophrenia to illustrate the points which I have made so far. Despite nearly one hundred years of research since the time of Kraepelin, and despite the assumption that there must be something biologically odd about schizophrenics, little progress has been made in understanding the causes of schizophrenia. Virtually every variable known to affect human conduct has, at one time or another, been implicated as a potential cause of the putative disease including life stresses, family environment, genetic endowment, diet, abnormalities of brain biochemistry or neural structure, and hypothesized viruses. While it is possible that schizophrenia is simply an extraordinarily difficult disease to explain, one possible reason for the inconclusive outcome of so much research is that schizophrenia is not a scientifically meaningful concept. If the term 'schizophrenia' does in fact refer to a rag-bag of unconnected phenomena then the result that has been achieved as a consequence of so much effort – many variables implicated, none firmly – is precisely that which would be expected. In order to address this possibility I recently conducted a detailed review of the relevant scientific findings,[9] the results of which can be summarized as follows.

Diagnostic manuals and structured psychiatric interviews were introduced in the 1970s in an attempt to improve the reliability of psychiatric diagnoses, which until that time were widely criticized for being very unreliable. There have since been many competing proposals for diagnostic criteria so that, although the use of any one set of criteria allows an acceptable degree of diagnostic agreement, the competing sets of criteria are largely nonconcordant. Consequently, the different criteria diagnose different persons as schizophrenic. Statistical findings provide no evidence that any of these criteria are scientifically valid as studies of the distribution of psychotic 'symptoms' (the behavioural manifestations of insanity such as hallucinations, delusions and thought disorder) do not support the idea that these cluster together into any meaningful syndromes. Rather, perhaps the majority of psychiatric patients show a mixed picture, exhibiting some symptoms of schizophrenia and, at the same time, some symptoms of other supposedly distinct diseases such as major affective disorder. Nor is the diagnosis of schizophrenia a good predictor of outcome: whichever criteria are applied, roughly one third of schizophrenics recover, one third have intermittent episodes of madness, and one third progressively deteriorate. With regard to treatment, powerful neuroleptic (phenothiazine) drugs are usually considered to be the therapy of choice for schizophrenics, but research shows that perhaps the majority of patients diagnosed as schizophrenic are 'neuroleptic nonresponders'. In fact, treatments which are usually given to patients with other diagnoses (such as the benzodiazapine drugs, usually prescribed for anxiety, or lithium carbonate, usually given to those diagnosed as suffering from major affective disorder) have sometimes been found to benefit patients diagnosed as schizophrenic. Taken together with the many and inconsistent research findings on the aetiology of schizophrenia (for example, the inconsistent findings about the contribution of heredity to schizophrenia), these observations suggest that schizophrenia is not a useful scientific concept, and that patients diagnosed as schizophrenic form a highly diverse and heterogeneous group.

It is worth noting that the kinds of criticisms which I have just outlined are equally applicable to psychiatric diagnoses other than schizophrenia. For example, although the psychoses and the neuroses supposedly form separate classes of disorder, it appears that many patients show both psychotic and neurotic features. Similar difficulties to those observed when attempting to differentially diagnose schizophrenia and major affective disorder are observed when attempts are made to distinguish between depression and anxiety. Finally, of course, the idea that there is a clear distinction between sanity and insanity cannot go unchallenged: for all forms of psychiatric disorder (including psychotic features such as hallucinations and thought disorder) 'subclinical' variants can be found in individuals living in the community who are regarded by themselves and others as relatively 'normal'.

These kinds of findings are frustrating to proponents of the standard approach because, to those proponents, the only alternative to a diagnostic system seems to be theoretical anarchy. Indeed, it is instructive to note the responses given by psychiatrists when I have given talks on this topic. Typical objections have included, 'Yes, but surely without diagnosis, decisions about treatment are impossible' and 'Future research is *bound* to lead to better diagnostic systems and then these kinds of problems will no longer exist.' These objections only indicate the strength with which the standard approach grips the minds of ordinary clinicians.

Of course there is no reason to believe that diagnostic systems analogous to those employed in physical medicine should prove to be useful to psychopathologists. Nor is there any reason to suppose that abandoning post-Kraepelinian diagnostic systems will lead to theoretical anarchy. There is, in fact, a very simple and coherent alternative to diagnosis in psychopathology. This alternative is to make the behavioural manifestations of insanity – what proponents of the standard approach call symptoms – the target of research and the basis for decisions about treatment.

Emphasizing the 'Psycho' in 'Psychopathology'
(or What Theories of Insanity Should Look Like)

At this point it is worth summarizing the main arguments of this essay. I have suggested on both philosophical and empirical grounds that psychopathologists should attempt to explain the behaviour and experiences of insane people (those phenomena commonly called 'symptoms') rather than the broad diagnostic categories studied by advocates of the standard approach. I have also argued that psychopathologists should attempt explanations of the behaviour and experiences of insane people by studying the interaction between psychological functions and the environmental context in which insane behaviour occurs. In a nutshell, I am suggesting that it is time to give emphasis to the 'psycho' in 'psychopathology'.

In as much as the standard approach has hindered progress along these lines, I believe that it has been a serious impediment to the understanding of insanity. I now want to briefly demonstrate that the programme for psychopathology which I have sketched out has real promise. Because space is very limited, I will focus my account on two particular symptoms: hallucinations and delusions. I have chosen these because I have conducted some research into them myself but they have the added advantage of being sufficiently bizarre to be regarded by many as beyond psychological explanation. (A more detailed account of the following research findings is given elsewhere.[10])

Most psychiatrists assume that anyone who experiences hallucinations is seriously disturbed; indeed, the psychiatrist Kurt Schneider argued that auditory hallucinations should be regarded as 'first-rank' symptoms of schizophrenia. However, a minority of individuals who are otherwise well-adjusted seem to experience hallucinatory voices or visions, which are sometimes attributed by them to supernatural causes (ghosts) or to divine intervention (God). Moreover, there are cultural differences in the prevalence of hallucinations and in the types of hallucinations experienced. Thus, visual hallucinations seem to be much more common in undeveloped countries than in the West, and in many societies hallucinatory experiences are regarded as either unremarkable or desirable. Because of the dominance of the standard approach there has only been a limited amount of psychological research into hallucinations, but three observations are worth noting. First, people are more likely to suffer from hallucinations when experiencing stress-induced arousal. Second, auditory hallucinations are more likely to occur when the individual is in conditions in which there is a lot of unpatterned background noise. Third, there is good evidence that auditory hallucinations are accompanied by subvocal movements of the speech muscles.

The most satisfactory psychological explanation of hallucinations currently available implicates what are known as 'metacognitive' processes – those psychological functions involved in the individual's knowledge of his own mental states. On this view, hallucinations result when internal, mental processes are mistakenly attributed to a source external to the person, that is, when a person mistakes his own thoughts or mental images for events in the world. This makes sense of the observations I have just outlined. As stress impairs cognitive functions in general, it is not surprising that an individual's ability to discriminate internal and external events is handicapped under stressful circumstances. It is also unsurprising that it is easier to mistake one's own thoughts for external voices when external stimulation is masked by noise. Finally, it is only to be expected that auditory hallucinations will be accompanied by subvocal movements of the speech muscles, as such movements have been shown to accompany the kind of normal verbal thinking which is mistaken by the hallucinator for an external voice.

In the past few years more direct evidence for this account of hallucinations has been obtained from a number of studies which are too complicated to relate here, although a number of questions remain to be answered. In particular, it would obviously be useful to know why some people are more prone to hallucinations than others. There is some evidence that hallucinators are highly suggestible, and that their hallucinations reflect what they expect to experience. Indeed, a general effect of expectation on a person's classification of a perceived event as 'real' (external) or 'imaginary' (internal) would help to account for the apparent cultural differences in people's willingness to hallucinate; on this view hallucinated dead ancestors are more likely to be seen in the context of a culture in which a belief in visitation by the dead is the norm. But differences in suggestibility are unlikely to be the whole story and it is probable that a complex range of factors contribute to a vulnerability to hallucinate. Clearly, in order to advance our understanding of hallucinations it will be necessary to achieve a better understanding of metacognitive process in normal individuals, how these processes develop during childhood, and how they are implemented by the brain.

Delusions have received rather less attention from psychologists, which is somewhat surprising given that social and cognitive psychologists have invested a considerable amount of effort into understanding the acquisition of normal beliefs. Part of the blame for this lamentable state of affairs must again be laid at the door of the standard approach, and the resulting assumption that delusions are qualitatively different from normal beliefs. There is in fact no evidence to support this assumption; although the delusional beliefs observed by psychiatrists are often bizarre and typically involve persecutory or grandiose themes (for example, the deluded person may believe that there is a conspiracy to do him harm, or that he has been given a divine mission by God), a moment's reflection will reveal that it is not unusual to meet otherwise normal people who have not wished to seek psychiatric help but who harbour quite odd beliefs. Moreover, although delusions are supposed to be distinguished by their resistance to counter-argument the same is true for most keenly held convictions, such as political or religious beliefs.

On one view, delusions are caused by perceptual abnormalities and reflect increasingly desperate attempts by the sufferer to account for his anomalous experiences. Consistent with this idea, there is evidence that progressive deafness makes people vulnerable to persecutory delusions; a person with hearing difficulties may be tempted to assume that some of the people he sees but cannot hear are talking about him. It is also reasonable to believe that some delusional beliefs are driven by hallucinations. It seems most unlikely, however, that perceptual defects and abnormalities of this sort are the only source of delusional beliefs; after all, most people with perceptual impairments do not develop unusually bizarre ideas and many deluded people show no evidence of impaired perception or hallucinations. It seems likely, therefore, that biases or abnormalities of reasoning contribute to delusional ideas.

There are in fact two main types of reasoning abnormalities which have been detected in deluded patients. Whether these abnormalities are related has yet to be established. First, a number of studies have shown that deluded patients require less evidence and are more certain than non-deluded subjects when making judgements of probability. In fact normal subjects, too, are generally reluctant to detect random relationships and therefore typically overestimate the significance of probabilistic relationships (which may be why so many people are willing to attribute significance to coincidences), but deluded people seem to be even more prone to this kind of error. Second, together with some colleagues I have been able to demonstrate that many deluded subjects show particular biases when reasoning about the causes of events that affect themselves. These biases are akin to biases known to be present in depressed people. Whereas depressives excessively attribute the causes of unpleasant events to themselves (ignoring other causes), subjects with persecutory delusions seem quite unwilling to look at their own role in such events; this observation suggests that both persecutory and grandiose delusions are often a defence against depression or low self-esteem. This might explain why delusional ideas often develop after periods of great stress or disappointment, when a person's self-esteem is threatened. Speculating for a moment, it is possible here to see some similarity between the delusions of allegedly schizophrenic patients and the experience of conversion to extreme religious or mystical ideas, which often seems to occur during a life-crisis.

It is unlikely that these kinds of biases are solely responsible for the bizarre beliefs observed in the psychiatric clinic but I hope that it is obvious how a person with a particular style of thinking about the world might be vulnerable, when under stress, to developing odd theories about what is happening to him. It is possible, even likely, that the influence of perceptual defects and reasoning biases on delusional beliefs will be additive, so that someone with both types of abnormality will be doubly at risk. Again, we must look to normal psychology for accounts of how biases in reasoning develop in order to advance our understanding of these phenomena. Further studies in social and developmental psychology may be helpful in this regard.

The accounts I have given of hallucinations and delusions have been all too brief, but I hope that they have demonstrated the value of the approach which I am advocating. It would have been possible to attempt similar accounts of other forms of insanity such as thought disorder, mania, depression or anxiety, but to do so would be a task beyond the scope of a short essay of this sort. I would like to conclude by pointing out several important characteristics of the programme for psychopathology which I have outlined.

(i) The importance of studying insanity and normal behaviour side by side should be evident. This is likely to be as beneficial to psychology as to psychopathology: indeed, insanity should prove to be a rich source of questions and information about normal psychological functions. In retrospect, the attempt by advocates of the standard approach to divorce psychopathology from normal psychology appears nonsensical.

(ii) There is no suggestion that there must be one cause of any one type of insanity. For both hallucinations and delusions it seems that a range of factors may contribute to their occurrence. All that can be specified is which sorts of psychological abnormalities add up to make a person vulnerable to which types of insanity under which sorts of conditions. Some types of abnormality (for example, a tendency to becoming overaroused under stress) no doubt influence more than one type of insanity whereas others (for example, certain metacognitive abnormalities) may be specific to a particular type of abnormal behaviour or experience. I have said very little about the environmental contributions to insanity, but these are clearly important in determining both the occurrence and the form of insane behaviour. For this reason it would probably be fruitful to explore the relationships that exist between the contents of delusions and hallucinations and the life circumstances of insane persons; this is an issue which has been completed neglected by advocates of the standard approach.

(iii) It is worth repeating that a psychological approach to insanity is not antibiological. Indeed, it is clear that psychological disease is sometimes caused by physical disease. The neurological and geriatric wards of hospitals are full of patients whose psychological functions have been impaired by various insults to their brains, and who exhibit confused and sometimes psychotic behaviour as a consequence. None the less, as I indicated in my discussion of Boorse's proposal, it is equally clear that disturbances of psychological functions can exist without abnormal brain functioning. It would be quite wrong to believe that, because a particular psychological function is sometimes influenced by physical disease, disturbance of that function is always caused by physical disease. For example, it is possible that a disorder of metacognitive functioning which results in hallucinations is sometimes caused by damage to the brain and sometimes caused by unfortunate learning experiences; in the latter case there is unlikely to be evidence of a brain abnormality. What hallucinations caused by brain disease and hallucinations caused by learning will almost certainly have in common is metacognitive impairment.

Even where psychological disease is clearly caused by brain disease, it will be vital to explain the abnormal behaviours and experiences of patients in terms of disordered psychological functions and the interaction between those functions and the environment. Of course, it will also be important to explain how brain diseases impair psychological functions, but in any case this is likely to require some understanding of how psychological functions are normally implemented by the brain.

(iv) The approach which I have outlined is neutral with respect to the question of whether or not universal criteria for insanity can be found. Whereas the discovery that insanity is culturally relative would seriously jeopardize the standard approach, it would have no implications for an approach which regards psychopathology and normal psychology as closely related enterprises. Indeed, I would argue that exactly the same approach that I have outlined here should be taken when attempting to explain types of behaviour and experience (such as joy or creativity) which are statistically abnormal but which are usually regarded as non-pathological or even desirable.

Finally, I hope that it is obvious that the most important goal of a psychological approach to psychopathology is the reduction of the insane to the comprehensible. The strategy which I am advocating does not allow bizarre behaviour to be explained away by a simple trick of labelling. Rather, if it is to succeed where ordinary folk psychology fails, the strategy must bring insanity into the range of psychological phenomena that can be readily understood. Making insanity comprehensible will help mental health professionals to understand the needs of their clients, and will also help the insane users of psychiatric services to achieve a better understanding of themselves. This is the real benefit to be gained from extracting the discipline of psychopathology from the domain of medicine and relocating it within the family of psychological sciences where, in reality, it has always belonged.

Notes

1. See D. Pilgrim, 'Competing histories of madness: Some implications for psychiatry', in R. P. Bentall (ed.) *Reconstructing Schizophrenia* (London: Methuen, 1990).
2. See A. Horwitz, *The social control of mental illness* (New York: Academic Press, 1982).
3. W. Mayer-Gross, E. Slater and M. Roth, *Clinical psychiatry* (London: Cassell, 1975).
4. T. Szasz, 'The myth of mental illness', *American Psychologist*, 15 (1960), 564–80. Note that in recent years it has become customary to distinguish between 'disease' and 'illness' where illness is regarded as the disease state as manifest to the individual through distressing

symptoms. On this terminology Szasz's argument is against mental disease rather than mental illness.

5. Quoted in D. Pilgrim, op. cit.

6. Hunter and Macalpine, *Three hundred years of psychiatry* (Oxford University Press, 1983).

7. C. Boorse, 'What a theory of mental health should be', *Journal of the Theory of Social Behaviour* 6 (1976), 61–84.

8. P. Churchland, *Neurophilosophy: Towards a unified science of mind/brain* (Cambridge, Mass.: MIT Press, 1986).

9. See R. P. Bentall, 'The symptoms and syndromes of psychosis: Or why you can't play twenty questions with the concept of schizophrenia and hope to win', in R. P. Bentall (ed.), *Reconstructing Schizophrenia* (London: Methuen, 1990).

10. See R. P. Bentall, ibid.

9

Paranormal Phenomena

PAMELA HUBY

The subject-matter of this chapter is vast and controversial. I have tried to select the most important topics, and to provide illustrative examples. But many topics have been omitted, theoretical arguments have been compressed, and the examples pared to the bone. Full accounts of the original material are mainly in scholarly journals, but there are some good popular books which give an idea of its richness.

I take paranormal phenomena to be those which cannot be explained by ordinary scientific means, or rather, those that cannot be explained by matter-based science. This does not mean that these phenomena, if genuine, are ones that fall under no natural laws and are incapable of treatment scientifically; if they did not show some regularities it would be impossible to study and classify them at all; rather, they are evidence that we need to recognize natural laws different from those which we accept already.

The serious study of these phenomena began in the nineteenth century, when scientists believed they had a full understanding of the world around us in terms of physics, and reports of telepathy and apparitions presented a challenge. Changes of detail have occurred since, but many scientists are still hostile to such reports precisely because they do not see how they can be accommodated in what they believe they know. Modern phenomena are very largely the same as those that were identified by the pioneers of psychical research in the late nineteenth century. This shows that we have at least an agreed body of phenomena. Sceptics deny that any of this is genuine, while others try to isolate and study such of it as is genuine.[1] Unfortunately the period of high standards set by the pioneers, and still maintained in some quarters, has been succeeded by one in which any fantastic idea may be given credence, and few people have the scrupulous regard for evidential value necessary for advances in understanding to be made. Apart from sensationalism and commercial greed, the main reason for this seems to be a widespread belief among non-scientists that the world of the scientists is not the only one; once

they have discarded the restraints of science they have no reason
for disbelieving anything, however bizarre it may seem. Some of the
material is bizarre, and one cannot apply common sense standards to
it. At the same time, I am convinced that it is subject to natural laws,
and that it can to some extent be classified and treated as so subject.

Traditionally the evidence has been classed as either spontaneous
or experimental. We may add a mixed group, where phenomena
are invited, as when mediums are studied. A traditional cross-
classification is into physical and mental phenomena. In the former,
there are effects on the material world: in the latter only minds
are affected. Over the years complications about definitions have
crept in, but the basic division still stands. In what follows I
shall use a few technical terms: psi is a general term covering
ESP and PK; ESP (extra-sensory perception) covers telepathy,
the paranormal awareness of other minds, and clairvoyance, the
awareness of external objects; PK (psychokinesis) is 'mind over
matter'.

Spontaneous Phenomena
The serious evidence comes primarily from first-hand witnesses, who
claim themselves to have experienced something unusual. But such
tales have to be evaluated, and there are two main sources of error:
a) deception, innocent or intentional, and b) coincidence.

(a) Many people, some even of the utmost probity in ordinary
matters, regard the psychical as a field in which to tell tall stories;
more important, however, is the honest witness, who like witnesses
to other matters, makes mistakes through faulty observation or
failure of memory. But these difficulties can be got round, because
sometimes people recorded their experiences before they knew
whether a fulfilling event had in fact occurred, either because it
had not yet happened or because it had happened at a distant place.
Cases of the latter kind were more common in the last century, when
what had happened in Australia, for example, could not be known
normally in Britain for several weeks.

(b) The Census of Hallucinations of the Society for Psychical
Research, started in 1889, accumulated a body of first-hand cases.
I shall discuss these at some length, to give an idea of the methods
and problems involved. Critics pointed out that some matchings
would occur by chance, and that what was involved was a series of
coincidences and nothing more. Since many cases were dreams, that
was not implausible. Millions of dreams occur every night, and by
chance some will resemble actual events. But there is other material
not from dreams but from apparitions and similar auditory and other

experiences, which are uncommon. Sane people do sometimes see figures that are not there, and hear voices when there is nobody speaking. And in a large number of cases the figure or the voice is recognized as belonging to someone known. Further, a large number of the latter group turn out to coincide closely in time with some crisis in the life of the person recognized, either actual death or grave danger. These are known as Crisis Apparitions. Here a fair proportion of a group of unusual events in the life of the percipient coincides with an unusual event in the life of another person.

Here is a short but typical case: Mrs C. saw the figure of a friend in front of her, 'ascending', that is, in the air and high up. She later heard that the friend had died suddenly, as the result of eating a pork chop. She had not been thinking of the friend at the time, and this was the only hallucination she had ever had. This occurred in 1852, but similar cases are still being reported. Further, a Mass Observation Census of Hallucinations of 1947 closely resembled that of 1889 in its statistical breakdown.

Similar to Crisis Apparitions is a small group of experimental cases, where people have tried successfully to 'appear' to someone at a distance.

Experimental Work

Difficulties like those discussed apply to all spontaneous phenomena. It became evident, therefore, that it would be useful if the underlying process, whatever it was, could be studied in a more systematic way by means of experiments. Two main approaches have been tried: to study groups of ordinary people, in the belief that in such groups a weak effect would still be detectable; and to study gifted individuals who could be expected to produce a stronger effect. The problems of ensuring the probity of the people concerned and the exclusion of coincidence remained, and experiments were tailored to those purposes. As a result, most experiments were very dull; few outstanding and, more important, repeatable, results were achieved. Further, whenever a successful result has been achieved, critics have done their best to discredit it by showing how it might have been achieved by normal means, and sometimes their criticisms have proved justified. It is my own belief that no single experiment will silence doubt, but that the views of the scientific community about what is possible could be changed by a series of repeatable and coherent experiments.

Experimental work has also been done with mediums, for example by ensuring that they cannot know who the sitter is, by developing techniques to evaluate the successes and failures of the

communications, and, in the case of the professional medium Mrs
Piper, by having her shadowed.

In the rest of this chapter I shall assume that final scepticism is not
justified, and look at the phenomena for which there is respectable
evidence, and some for which it is less respectable, but which should
not be ignored if we are to have a fair picture of the situation.

Apparitions

In a highly regarded study, G. N. M. Tyrrell studied genuine 'ghost'
stories and fictional ones, and found that the former had a basic
pattern which differed markedly from that of the latter.[2] Real ghosts
appear solid, or nearly so, but leave no physical traces and say little:
fictional ones, on the other hand, are frequently filmy in appearance,
but may be garrulous and often leave physical traces behind them.

We have already looked at Crisis Apparitions. Haunting ghosts are
similar, but recur in a particular location and are not connected with
a crisis, though it is often assumed that they are connected with a past
tragedy. Most stately homes and many pubs claim to have one, and
sometimes more than one. But houses of all kinds are reputed to be
haunted, some for long periods. Two cases that have been studied
in detail are a) the 'Cheltenham ghost', which was first noticed in
1880 and whose appearances were recorded for many years by a
young woman medical student: the figure was that of a woman in
widow's weeds, and a similar figure was perhaps seen later by a
variety of people; and b) the ghost, or perhaps ghosts, of Abbey
House, Cambridge, a building dating in part back to the sixteenth
century. Rumours that it was haunted go back to 1860, and there
are first hand records from the couple who lived there between 1903
and 1911. The haunters were an animal like a hare, and a nun-like
figure. Each was seen about thirty times, and the animal may have
been seen later, in 1920 and 1947, and the nun also in 1920.

Poltergeists

Many ghosts overlap with poltergeists, in that while figures are seen
there are many other phenomena, like sounds, voices, and the
movement of objects. A carefully observed case is reported by Gauld
and Cornell in *Poltergeists*.[3] It occurred in 1971–2 in a fairly modern
(1929) two-storey house, belonging to a family of two parents and
three children aged between nineteen and ten, and a new baby. Even
before they moved in there were odd incidents, such as a moving
column of hot air, and phenomena continued until November 1972.
They included the frequent sound of a trunk being moved when in
fact the trunk was still in its place, sightings of figures and hearings

of voices, and various sounds repeated at intervals. By my reckoning, at least eight people observed something or other.

Let us now turn to poltergeists proper, where there are many physical effects. Reported cases are astonishingly frequent, and I have investigated more of these than of any other kind. It is not easy to say how many, if any, are genuine. Many normal explanations have been suggested: naughty children and adolescents, geological disturbances, the desire to exchange council houses, and mere sensationalism account for a lot. It is difficult for investigators to catch such cases when they are active. But some have lasted over months and even years, and observers have reported events that cannot easily be explained. A frequent phenomenon is the movement of small objects in abnormal ways – though the movement of large and heavy objects is not uncommon – along with unusual sounds and sometimes smells. Adolescents are often thought to be at the centre of the disturbances, not only when trickery is involved. But older persons are not immune.

I give two examples from my own experience, both within walking distance of my house, which may indicate how common these phenomena are. In one, in 1973, a family of mother and two daughters aged seventeen and eleven were troubled for a few months by phenomena like lights being switched on and off; the high point was when a dish of fruit 'crashed up and down', and a spoon lying in it rose suddenly and shot across the floor. The second involved an old lady of eighty-six who had suffered such activities for some time, and I was present when a cabinet burst open with a bang and a shower of Christmas cards poured out. Both houses had a long history. The first had been converted into two flats, and a staircase had been removed. One occupant once saw the figure of a Victorian maidservant going up the vanished stairs, which again illustrates the overlap between ghosts and poltergeists.

The movement of the spoon is a typical example of a physical event that appears to be caused paranormally, for the movement is not a natural one. The object may drop suddenly but softly, may go round corners, and in many ways ignore the laws of physics. It has been argued that there is always a centre of the activity in some individual, and that the effects depend on the distance of the moved object from this person; but possibly we should think of two types of poltergeist, those where a human being is the centre, and those where an 'elemental' is involved. This is supposed to be a low kind of spirit, a being with emotions and some power of action, which is attached to a place and manifests itself by physical disturbances. Further, if there are two such types it is likely that some actual cases involve an interaction between an elemental or elementals and a human centre.

The cases I have described are comparatively mild, but many are on record where the scene must have been quite frightening. In the Miami case of 1966–7 breakable objects stored on shelves in a warehouse were moved in various ways. 'At times objects were falling from the shelves as fast as they could be picked up or swept up.' Two hundred and twenty-four separate incidents were actually recorded by investigators, and there must have been many more.[4]

Mediums

It is unlikely that either crisis apparitions or haunting ghosts are the actual spirits of people, living or dead. Their actions tend to be limited and stereotyped, and any connection with a person must be indirect. But elsewhere there is evidence that suggests a more direct contact with spirits. Spiritualism developed as a religion in the nineteenth century in the belief that it was possible to get in touch with the dead through mediums. Spiritism is a similar movement, which began in France but is now most prominent in South America. The subject has also interested many who are not Spiritualists. The initiative usually comes from the enquirer, who visits a medium, or has developed the art of automatic writing. But there are cases where the initiative seems to come from the spirits, as with the 'drop-in communicators'. A further set of cases appears to involve elementals or demons or other non-human spirits, which intervene in seances and are even sometimes thought to take possession of human beings.

The typical mediumistic seance involves a medium who has found himself to have certain powers, and has trained them in an already existing tradition. In that derived from Spiritualism the medium has a 'control', claiming more or less convincingly to be the spirit of a dead human being, often of exotic origin like 'White Cloud' or 'Silver Birch'. The control communicates when the medium has gone into trance, and introduces other spirits who claim to be dead relatives of the sitter. In the best seances, a great deal of information is provided which the medium cannot have obtained by normal means. But opinions differ over whether this information comes by telepathy from the sitter or further afield, or whether it comes from the actual spirit of the dead. We have here a kind of higher scepticism. Those who cannot accept spirit communication are forced to accept telepathy. Few who are thoroughly familiar with the evidence dismiss it all.

The communicators, whoever they are, have the characteristics of the dead persons, but usually in an attenuated form. A rare exception is when, through the Direct Voice, a spirit appears to control the medium's body to the extent that sitters recognize the voice as that of the deceased. Great thinkers do not, on the whole, produce great thoughts. But the evidence is that if there is any genuine communication, it is very difficult, partly because the communicator is bound by the limitations of the medium's mind, and sometimes because of the state of the spirit himself, whose memories may have been dislocated by the trauma of dying. This may explain why recent attempts to prove survival in which someone leaves a sealed message, to be communicated by him after his death, have so far had little success.

An alternative method of communication is by automatic writing, in which the writer produces communications from spirits, frequently very rapidly. Group methods, with table turning or the ouija board, are slower but similar. One prolific medium, Geraldine Cummins, has produced material of many kinds by writing, from communications from the recently dead to whole books about the life of Christ and the early Christians. Such works are puzzling for the speed at which they are produced and for the fact that much that they contain appears to be outside the writer's normal knowledge. Sceptics claim that they are based on the writer's past reading, and even those who believe that they contain more than this find weaknesses which make it very unlikely that they are what they claim to be.

To return to seances, they may be interrupted by the so-called 'drop-in communicator', a 'spirit' who intervenes in a seance and has no connection with the sitter. As Alan Gauld says, 'the impression not infrequently given is of persons trying, under circumstances of great difficulty, to "put through" information about themselves of a kind which will enable total strangers to identify them'.[5]

Thus at a sitting on 28 June 1943 the following message was given: *Can you place Max of Ditton Park?* Sitter: Fields? *Perhaps. Christian name. RAF. Now listen. His surname has some connection with cables or chains.* Any message? *He wants his love given to wife and babe.* On 2 August 1943: ('Peter' the control, is speaking) *That takes my thoughts back to Max. The name was Cheynes. Plural may be wrong.*

Investigations made years later showed that a Max Langdon Cheyne of Ditton Fields Cambridge, a member of the RAF, had been killed in October 1942, leaving a wife and young daughter. The oblique way in which his name was approached, via cables and chains, is common in mediumistic communications. Another common feature is the failure of the supposed communicator to achieve his purpose. The sitters failed to trace Max Cheyne at the time, and he was not identified until over twenty years later. In any case, if he had been identified the sitters would have been placed in a dilemma. It is not easy to approach a perfect stranger with a supposed message from a dead husband.

An outstanding example of co-operation between mediums and automatists is the Cross-correspondences, a collection of material produced by members of the Society for Psychical Research and others, in which it was claimed that deceased members of the Society were communicating in a new way in order to give evidence of their own survival. Part of a message was given through one member of the group, and other parts through others, and it was only when the material was put together by yet another person that the message was recognized. Many of the people involved on both sides were Classical scholars, and the material abounds in Classical allusions. It is extremely impressive, but very difficult to judge. Here again we find scepticism at a different level. It cannot be doubted that these correspondences occurred, and that fraud was not involved. But critics have asked whether they were initiated, as is claimed, by the spirit of F. W. H. Myers, and continued by his discarnate group, or whether they were initiated by living members of the group who exercised a kind of super-ESP. If even that is accepted, there is here abundant evidence for the paranormal, but not for survival.

I give a simplified sketch of part of a complex case, the 'Alexander's tomb' (the quotations are much abbreviated):

a) (26 February 1907, in London) Mrs Piper (the only professional medium involved): *Moorhead. I gave her that for laurel.*

b) (17 March 1907, in Cambridge (?)) Miss Verrall: *Alexander's Tomb. Laurel.*

c) (27 March 1907, in India) Mrs 'Holland' (Mrs Fleming, the sister of Rudyard Kipling): *Alexander moors head.*

These were written independently, and *laurel* connects the first two, but by themselves they were misinterpreted as referring to Alexander the Great. The third shows that the reference is to Alessandro de Medici, who was assassinated in 1537 and buried in the tomb of Lorenzo de Medici, Duke of Urbino, one of the famous Medici tombs by Michelangelo. Alessandro had a negro-like appearance. The laurel was the emblem of Lorenzo the Magnificent, and was a punning reference to his name and to that of the younger Lorenzo.

This is only part of a very complex case, which involved further reference to the Medici tombs, and also to Laura, one of the communicating team.

Reincarnation

This is a field that has only recently been taken seriously in the West. It is different from the discarnate survival of the Spiritualists. There seems to be a single continuing personality, linked by memory and habits with two or more bodies, succeeding one another in time. It has been brought to the forefront by the travels of Dr Ian Stevenson, who has collected material from cultures of many kinds.[6] In most of his cases the previous life was ended prematurely and violently, and often the new body has a birthmark similar to the wound that caused death. Perhaps such cases occur only when there is an incomplete normal life, or possibly reincarnation occurs generally, but only in cases of violent death does the new human being have memories of the old. In any case it is customary for memories of the past life to fade after childhood, and there seems to be little of value in the experience, except in cultures where such occurrences are looked for and welcomed. But welcomed or not, cases are reported from many cultures. If any are genuine they show that the personality is not completely dependent on a single body. Alternatively it has been suggested that what survives is not a personality, but only memories detached, as it were, from their original owner. There is still something paranormal, but it is more akin to telepathy than to reincarnation. I summarize a typical case: at the age of one-and-a-half, Sukla, a girl born in Kampa, West Bengal, used to cradle a pillow and call it Minu. When asked, she said Minu was her daughter. Over the next three years she referred to her husband, 'he', and his brothers Khetu and Karuna, and said they lived in Bhatpara, a village 11 miles away. Through an acquaintance her father heard of a man called Khetu living in Bhatpara, who had had a sister-in-law, Mana, who had died leaving a girl named Minu. Sukla was taken to see that family and recognized several people and objects. Mana had had pimples on her nose, and Sukla, alone of her family had pimples on her nose.

These children have tended to lose the memories of the old life as they grow up. That is not surprising, as the situation is seldom an easy one, and the child more often than not adjusts to the present life. What such an existence might be like if the adjustment does not occur can be learned from *Died 1513, Born 1927* (London: Macmillan, 1978), by A. J. Stewart, who had already claimed to be James IV of Scotland. In this later work she describes the position in her present life of her memories of a previous life. Whether genuine or not, the tale is worth reading.

Dr Stevenson found that the vast majority of his subjects remembered only one past life. But fashions come and go, and there has recently been a tendency to discover multiple past lives by hypnotic regression. Once the conventions had been established, a multitude of cases were reported, some of them very impressive. Subjects gave accounts of past lives the details of which can be verified, but only in extremely obscure sources, unlikely to have been known by the subjects. But even the best are sometimes wrong, and alternative explanations have been put forward, none of which is without its difficulties.

Possession

This has been another fashionable belief. The Christian tradition is that possession is by evil spirits, and even in the second half of this century many churchmen have taken an active part in the casting out of demons. But scandals developed, and much less is heard about it nowadays. A different form of possession is that by a discarnate human being. The body is taken over by a personality claiming to be different from the original personality, which is displaced for the time being. There are similarities with reincarnation, but in possession the take-over is complete though temporary. Possession in its turn shows some similarities with the phenonemon of Multiple Personality. Here a single body is controlled by two or more – sometimes many more – different personalities. Paranormal phenomena occur occasionally in such cases, and it has been suggested with some plausibility that the controls of mediums are secondary personalities and not genuine spirits.

Out of the Body and Near Death Experiences

I shall consider Out of the Body Experiences only in so far as they contain paranormal elements other than the change of position of the viewing subject. The subject finds himself detached from the body, frequently floating above it, and able to observe it and its surroundings. Some people have such experiences in normal life, and a few are able to initiate them voluntarily, but they occur very often also in serious illness or in accidents. The paranormal comes in when the subject becomes aware of events that could not be known by the body on the bed, or when he is able to affect someone at a distance. In one case a wife who nearly drowned in the bath was able to attract her husband's attention and so was saved. She said that she had watched all his actions.[7]

Similar to these are Near Death Experiences, which have been increasingly frequently reported as it has become possible to resuscitate someone whose heart has stopped beating. But they are not confined to such situations. George Gallup Jr., of the Gallup poll, and William Proctor's survey of American attitudes to life after death indicates that millions of Americans have had such experiences.[8] Sceptics argue that physiological conditions, like the cutting off of the supply of oxygen to the brain, account for everything, but there are features which suggest that that is not the whole story.

It is tempting to link these with the 'astral bodies' that have sometimes been observed to rise up from a body at the time of death. These mostly appear as a cloud which sometimes, but not always, takes on the form of the dying person.[9]

Recent Experiments

Experimental work has followed its own course. Techniques are highly sophisticated, and use the latest computer and statistical methods. Recently fifty-one unselected volunteers participated in a computer-based psi experiment in which hitting was accomplished through the correct timing of keypress responses. The volunteer was required unconsciously to select a rapidly changing clock value that would appropriately seed a pseudo-random algorithm to yield an integer that matched a similarly randomly generated target integer. Significant psi hitting was observed. The procedure involved an unconscious, effortless response, and was one that supported significant psi-hitting over an extended time period and for a large number of unselected subjects, with minimal experimenter involvement.[10]

Significant points here are: a) the use of unselected volunteers. This reflects the assumption that psi ability is widespread, and can be discovered by testing comparatively small groups. But it is a very weak ability in most people, and its presence in a group can be detected only by statistical methods. That such procedures are still to be found shows that few gifted subjects are available for study – though occasional ones have been found – and that there is no easy method of training ungifted subjects to do better. b) The effort required on the part of both the subjects and the experimenter has been reduced to a minimum, once the experiment has been devised and the computerware obtained. The subjects were unaware of the precise method by which hits were produced, and the successful completion of the task was beyond their conventional sensorimotor and cognitive capacities. Further, the experimenters themselves were aware of two possible interpretations of the results. In other words, neither the experimenters nor the subjects were sure of what was going on.

It is easy to be critical of a single experiment of this kind, for all that it appears to show is that something odd is going on. But at present it is that or nothing. There is reason to suppose that something strange does go on, but its nature is not understood and so far we have little knowledge of how to control it. A further factor which is absent from most, though not all, other areas of scientific experimentation is that there is still a pressing need to exclude the possibility of fraud on the part of both experimenters and subjects. This difficulty is unlikely to be overcome until experimental success is repeatable, if not by everyone, at least by many competent and reputable people.

But every little helps, and at intervals surveys of published material are carried out which find a few grains among the chaff.

One well-established finding is known as the Decline Effect. In many successful experiments the rate of scoring has fallen off over a psychologically definable period, that is over a set of experiments, during a single experiment, and even from the top left to the bottom right of a page. The obvious explanation is that the subject gets bored doing what is usually an unexciting task. The Sheep-Goat phenomenon, so named by Gertrude Schmeidler, also occurs. That is, 'sheep', who are inclined to believe in psi, tend to score better than might be expected, while 'goats', who reject the possibility, tend to score below chance level, which is itself also significant. Both these findings suggest that to some extent psi ability, even at a weak level, follows ordinary psychological laws.

Time Problems

At this point it is necessary to bring in Precognition. By definition, what is precognized is a future event or set of events that cannot be predicted by normal means, unlike an eclipse, for instance. It has been suggested that by knowing enough about the present situation by telepathy, and making deductions from that knowledge, a similar result might be obtained.

Alternatively the precognizing mind might affect events in such a way that the foreseen event occurs. Either of these ways would avoid the metaphysical complications of supposing either that one can foresee something that has not yet happened, or that the event cognized already in some sense exists. Both possibilities have given rise to much theorizing by philosophers, and there are also consequences for our theories of mind. In spite of theoretical difficulties, we tend to think that an individual has free will at least in the sense that he can at the present moment make a choice between two or more open possibilities. But if the future already exists, that seems impossible.

The evidence, however, cannot be ignored. And we should

recognize that recorded spontaneous cases have passed through a kind of net. Those where the outcome might have been predicted normally, like the illness of someone well known to the percipient, and those where the percipient might even unconsciously have had a hand in bringing about the event, are ignored, so that we do not necessarily have a fair selection of cases. It may be that precognition is far more widespread than appears. Against this it is also true that there have been many predictions which have not come off, and the field is a difficult one for the statistician. A final difficulty is that precognition is on the whole remarkably useless. It seldom helps people to avoid disaster, though it might be argued that when disaster has been avoided the predicted event has not happened and the evidence for precognition in such a case is ignored.

Spontaneous precognition varies between long and short-term, and covers everything from trivial events to global disasters. People who foresee disasters, particularly those that do not affect themselves, are in a difficult position. Some have tried to give warnings to people in high places, and have been ignored. That is not surprising. It would in the present state of our knowledge be irrational for the authorities to act in any other way.

I give an example of a useless piece of foreknowledge: on 17 January 1964, Juliet, Lady Rhys-Williams, turned on the Voice of America, and seemed to hear the end of a news bulletin about a disturbance in Atlanta, Georgia between Klu Klux Klan members and a large crowd of blacks, followed by casualties and arrests. She could find no reference to this elsewhere, but later discovered that there had been such an incident – the first for some time – on 18 January about twenty-four hours after she had 'heard' of it.[11]

The extensive experimental evidence may also be biased. There are constraints on all experimentation, and much of it is concerned with short-term and often unconscious prediction.

But precognition had a further effect, by producing chaos in theorizing about experimental work. For a long time that was concerned with card-guessing and dice-throwing, which had the advantages that the apparatus was cheap, and experiments capable of statistical analysis could easily be devised. Card-guessing was a matter of either telepathy or clairvoyance: if someone was looking at the cards it was supposed that the percipient read the agent's mind; but if no one was looking it was clairvoyance. Statistical success was achieved in both conditions. When dice were thrown, it was supposed that the agent affected the fall of the dice, and that was psychokinesis (PK).

These simple divisions were upset by the realization that pre-cognition seemed to occur in card-guessing experiments: sometimes a subject scored with hits on a series of cards which had not been looked at, or had not even been chosen, at the time of his guess. Or was it that by PK he somehow influenced the following choice of cards? Or again, when dice were thrown successfully, was their future fall foreseen and the targets set up to correspond with them?

Further complications have been introduced by the claims of Helmut Schmidt to show that it is possible to influence an event, or series of events, that has already happened. In a typical experiment, a series of numbers is produced by a random number generator, and used to provide a series of tones and silences through earphones. The subject is asked to keep the tone on while listening. If he succeeds, there will be more tones than silences. But their presence or absence has already been decided by the random number generator, and so it looks as if the subject has retroactively affected the generator. Schmidt's successes have been difficult to repeat, and there are still great theoretical difficulties involved.

Experimenter Effect

It has long been known that some experimenters seldom obtain successful results. Sceptics say that that is because they are better experimenters and exclude the normal means by which apparent successes are achieved, but others think that some aspect of their personalities inhibits genuine results. More work on this subject suggests that the experimenter influences not just the presence or absence, but the very nature, of the success.

Oddities

The matters considered so far make some kind of sense, but others are bizarre. One example is the 'thoughtography' of Ted Serios. He appeared to produce on photographic film distorted and unfocused pictures of distant buildings, often from apparently inaccessible viewpoints. The distortions suggested that something genuinely paranormal was involved. Similar results may have been achieved by the Japanese Masuaki Kyoto, though the evidence is less strong. Oddities like this – and there are many more – suggest trickery to the most unprejudiced mind, but to ignore them may be to discard important clues.

Cultural Differences

Paranormal phenomena occur all over the world, and have occurred in past centuries, in very much the same forms, but within the similarities there are puzzling differences. It may be easy to understand the connection of modern mediumistic phenomena with a Spiritualist tradition, and not surprising that when seances were held by the ancient Greeks the communicators tended to be gods and goddesses. But when we see that within Ian Stevenson's collection there are groups where reincarnation occurs only within the same sex, but in others some return into the opposite sex, that in some societies returns are within family groups, while in others there is no such restriction, and, finally, that the length of time between death and rebirth varies greatly between groups, this is puzzling. Again, poltergeists have been recorded in Europe from medieval times, but, as E. R. Dodds has noted, they seem to be absent from the ancient world, in which most other kinds of spontaneous phenomena are found. This difference is too great for simple cultural explanations.

We should also take account of other types of phenomena. Appearances of the Virgin Mary, for example, with inexplicable accompaniments, are still frequently recorded, sometimes in Islamic countries. The history of witchcraft cannot be ignored, and anthropologists have recounted much that does not fit into patterns familiar elsewhere.

Conclusions

I have already considered problems connected with Time and Causation, and will now turn to those more closely connected with mind.

a) Nothing will count as ESP unless it cannot be explained by some bodily mechanism. Recorded cases include many that are emotionally important, and support the view that human minds can connect with one another independently of the body. But there is evidence also that they can be aware of trivial facts, as if they have a general scanning mechanism. Apparitions are probably to be classed as striking forms of ESP, and not as spirits themselves.

b) Nothing will count as PK unless it cannot be explained by some bodily mechanism. But here the emotional factor seems more abnormal. Poltergeists are evidence of emotional disturbance, and there is little that corresponds to what one might call the day-to-day working of ESP. Instead there is the suggestion that sometimes low-grade spirits may be at work.

c) With regard to survival after death, the effect of cultural differences is great. The Christian doctrine of the resurrection of the body is out of favour, and instead there are two contenders, the survival of discarnate spirits, and reincarnation in another body. These have in common independence of a body and continuity of memory. It is natural to think that a soul-substance could survive without memory, but difficult to see what evidence one could have of this. But philosophers have argued that survival without any kind of body is inconceivable, certainly if it is more than a dream existence. To communicate with others, and to act, calls for a means of distinguishing between the subjective and the objective, a bill most easily filled by a body.

So we may, very tentatively, think of minds as entities independent of a single body, and aware of, and perhaps able to influence, people and things not only by physical senses and activities, but also more widely in a way still little understood.

Notes

1. A useful study of varying attitudes to the paranormal is H. M. Collins & T. J. Pinch, *Frames of Meaning* (London: Routledge and Kegan Paul, 1982)

2. G. N. M. Tyrrell, *Apparitions* (London: Duckworth, 1943).

3. Alan Gauld & A. D. Cornell, *Poltergeists* (London: Routledge & Kegan Paul, 1979), 284–94.

4. Ibid., 88–94.

5. *Proceedings of the Society for Psychical Research* 55 (1971), 332.

6. Dr Stevenson has surveyed his extensive material in *Children who Remember Previous Lives* (Virginia University Press, 1987).

7. Celia Green, *Out-of-the-Body Experiences* (Oxford Institute of Psychophysical Research, 1968), 132.

8. George Gallup Jr & William Proctor, *Adventures in Immortality* (London: Souvenir Press, 1983; Corgi Books, 1984).

9. For a collection of such cases, see S. Muldoon & H. Carrington, *The Phenomenon of Astral Projection* (London: Rider, 1951; 1969), 103–11.

10. A shortened abstract of the experiment by William G. Braud & Donna Shafer, *JSPR* 83 (1989), 205.

11. This is only one of several similar experiences, mostly concerning public events, reported by Lady Rhys-Williams in *JSPR* 42 (1964), 348–53.

Personal Identity and Unity of Consciousness

MARK SACKS

Philosophers (and non-philosophers) have long been puzzled by the question of what it is that constitutes a person, and in particular the identity of a person over time. In the course of our lives we have many different experiences and we ourselves change significantly, both physically and psychologically. Yet it seems that the baby out of which I developed is not a different person, but a different stage, in the development of the same person that I am today. In what follows I address the question of how we are to make sense of this identity of persons.

I shall begin by comparing different answers that have been proposed, and then evaluate the merits of these contenders when considered not only narrowly, as theories of the self, but also in relation to our broader theories of the mind's place in the world, and our ability to secure knowledge of that world.

In talking of 'persons' here the intention is to focus on persons in the psychological sense.[1] Put very weakly, a person in this sense is a whole, to which conscious states (experiences) pertain, such that that whole comprises just those experiences and no others, along with a degree of consciousness of that fact (that is, self-consciousness).

This much would seem to be agreed by most who address the subject. But the question is how we account for the consciousness involved, and how we account for the way in which it is unified into a whole that constitutes the person. The former problem is so acute, and so little progress has been made in accounting for it, that some have recently thought it better simply to deny that there is any such thing as consciousness. I do not mean to preclude the possibility of similar despair eventually leading the rest of us to a similar conclusion. But I want here to ask how, assuming that we are still committed to the idea that there are conscious experiences, we are to account for those states being united into wholes that constitute persons.[2]

The person can be viewed either as it is internally, in its subjective experience, or as it is publicly. Correspondingly, it would seem that in trying to explain what constitutes the required whole we might approach the matter in two ways. We might look either for (a) some internal feature, some subjective connecting element experienced by the person, which will therefore be psychologically characterized – which is not to say, of course, that it might not also be identical with a physical state; or we might look for (b) some external feature, that is, one that is not essentially first-personal. This external feature could in turn be either (b1) psychological, such as some externally characterized relation between various conscious states, or it might be (b2) non-psychological, such as an externally characterized substance. Obviously, various combinations and interpretations of these three approaches are possible. I wish however to start by setting out just three options regarding the nature of persons, in accordance with the simplest understanding of the above classification, since these options correspond to important views that have in fact been held by prominent thinkers.[3]

1. *The Substantial View* is that persons are substances, whether spiritual (souls) or material (human bodies). It is in virtue of this substance that the person's experiences are all held together in a unified whole; they all inhere somehow in that abiding substance. The identity of that substance then determines the identity of the person. Here the appeal is to an external non-psychological feature ((b2) above).

2. *The Lean View* is that, although there is something in virtue of which all my experiences are uniquely tied together as mine, as distinct from those which are not mine, that feature is non-substantial. A person is that which has the ability to be conscious of different experiences being united, both at a particular time and over time, by the fact that one and the same *thinking subject* has each of those experiences. To put the point differently, a person is that which is conscious of its identity *as the experiencing subject* across different experiences. On this view then the feature in question is internally described ((a) above).

3. *The Reductionist View* is that there is no *feature*, substantial or otherwise, that constitutes the identity of the person. There is nothing more to persons than a range or bundle of experiences more or less connected and continuous with one another. There is no fact over and above that to determine uniquely which experiences are rightly called mine, and which not. There is no characteristic that runs through all my experiences and thereby marks them out as mine. This is the reductive view of persons, and of personal identity: all that can be identified receives an external description, here in terms of psychological events (b1), and it is merely an illusion that there is anything more than that to identify, to be captured either by way of internal or external description.

All three of these views have had defenders. The Substantial option, for example, was held by Plato, Descartes, and more recently by various materialists. This view of the person – particularly the spiritual interpretation of the substance in question – is perhaps still the most deeply ingrained in our common outlook. The Lean option, at least in the respect identified below, accords well with the insights urged in recent years by functionalists, elements of which can in fact be traced back to Aristotle. Its classical version is, however, due to Kant, for whom it was an alternative to the other two theories. It can be seen as constituting a mid-course between them. The third, reductive, option has been held most recently, and most clearly, by Derek Parfit.

Let us turn first to consider the comparative merit of the first two approaches – the Substantial and the Lean options – taken narrowly, merely as accounts of the kind of things persons are.

Saying, as we have, that a person is that to which conscious states pertain, in such a way that those conscious states together constitute a whole to which each of those states and no other belongs, does not yet tell us what it is that makes that unification possible. The Substantial view identifies the bearer of the unity in question with a particular kind of object. The idea is that there is some kind of substance which anchors all the different experiences, binding them together thereby into a single whole, with a single owner. In opposition to this the Lean view contends that it simply does not matter what substance underlies the unity of the experiences in question. What matters is not the unity of the substance, but only of the consciousness it supports. This unity of consciousness requires the ability to be conscious of different experiences being united, both synchronically and diachronically, by the awareness that it is one and the same thinking subject that has each of these experiences.[4] It is the unity of consciousness that constitutes a sufficient and necessary feature of personal identity, of remaining the same person.

As long as that feature is preserved, the person remains identical, regardless of how much that which bears the feature has changed. And once that feature is lost, it matters not at all that the bearer of it persists otherwise unchanged. On this Lean view, although not anything will do as the substrate for the relevant feature – and it remains to establish what the range of viable substrates is – it nevertheless is relatively unimportant what the instantiating substrate of that feature is, just as long as the unity of consciousness is preserved.

This emphasis on unity of consciousness rather than on the unity of the substrate that preserves that feature, constitutes a shift of the sort that Locke offered away from Descartes. Locke agreed that we are human beings in virtue of having a soul. But although being a human being involves having a soul, maintaining one's identity as a person did not require, and indeed was not safeguarded by, the persistence in the body of one and the same soul. For him the crucial factor was continuity of memory.[5] If that continuity is terminated, and a new consciousness with new memories takes off where the former one ran out, the fact that the change takes place in one and the same soul is irrelevant. We then have two different persons, residing at different times in the same soul.[6] Equally, as long as this psychological unity is preserved, it does not matter whether it persists in one soul, or is passed on from one soul to another at every turn.

Locke, who defends both these points, expresses the latter particularly well, saying that

if the same consciousness . . . can be transferred from one thinking substance to another, it will be possible that two thinking substances may make but one person. For the same consciousness being preserved, whether in the same or different substances, the personal identity is preserved.[7]

The same thought is expressed by Kant, in the Third Paralogism:

Despite the logical identity of the 'I', such a change may have occurred in it as does not allow of the retention of its identity, and yet we may ascribe to it the same-sounding 'I', which in every different state, even in one involving change of the [thinking] subject, might still retain the thought of the preceding subject and so hand it over to the subsequent subject.[8]

Kant's footnote to this sentence brings out clearly the model underlying his and Locke's common insight:

An elastic ball which impinges on another similar ball in a straight line communicates to the latter its whole motion, and therefore its whole state . . . If, then, in analogy with such bodies, we postulate substances such that the one communicates to the other representations together with the consciousness of them, we can conceive a whole series of substances of which the first transmits its state together with its consciousness to the second, the second its own state with that of the preceding substance to the third, and this in turn the states of all the preceding substances together with its own consciousness and with their consciousness to another. The last substance would then be conscious of all the states of the previously changed substances, as being its own states, because they would have been transferred to it together with the consciousness of them.[9]

This captures well the way in which Locke and Kant, both reacting against the Cartesian philosophy of mind, introduce what is fundamentally the dualism characteristic of functionalism. The ontological dualism between different kinds of substance, traditionally advocated in philosophical work on the mind, is superseded in functionalism by the logical dualism between the instantiating substance, whatever its kind, and the function (software) instantiated by it.[10]

No one need be seriously perturbed by the fact that Locke holds that the viable instantiating substances for persons are souls.[11] After all, almost everyone would agree that not *any* substance could instantiate persons, that there is a limited range of viable instantiating substances.[12] At most it might be objected that Locke has identified that range incorrectly (perhaps even to the extent of inventing a non-existent range). The important point is the relation that both he and Kant recognize between the instantiating range – *whatever* it is – and the identity of the person. The identity of the person requires only the preservation of a certain instantiated feature, which itself does not entail, and is not entailed by, the identity of the instantiating substance over time.

It should be emphasized here that the intention is not to saddle either Locke or Kant, or indeed the reader, with a functionalist theory of mind more generally. The account given of mental particulars (whether qualitative states such as sensations or propositional attitudes such as beliefs and desires) is not the issue here. The point pertains only to explanation at a higher level, at which level mental states are taken as given, irrespective of whatever explanation of them has been assumed. At this higher level those states are unified across modalities and over time as belonging to individual persons. It is that *unification* that Locke and Kant (the latter in a way more sophisticated than the former) see as residing not in the unity of an underlying substance, but in a feature that is logically distinct from the substance in which it is instantiated. Whereas for Locke that feature is continuity of memory, for Kant it is the unity of consciousness. But both agree that the preservation of the relevant feature is independent of the preservation of the substance in which it is instantiated at any one time. So both identify a feature that offers precisely the sort of independence of the material in which it is instantiated that the functionalist dualism afforded.

So far we have set out salient differences between the Substantial and the Lean views; it is now time for more evaluative comparison. The emotional attraction of the Lean view will be apparent; for it suggests that the fate of the person can be independent of the fate and frailties of the particular substance to which it is harnessed at any one time. It offers thereby an idealized version of the prospect of immortality that traditional theories of the soul were after. Those theories offer persons freedom from the fetters of flesh and blood, but only by anchoring persons in some other substance. In contrast, the functionalist dualism of the Lean view avoids seeing persons as essentially tethered to, and so subject to the weaknesses of, *any* one kind of substance. Furthermore, the resulting form of immortality is then demystified and placed within the reach of simple technological progress; immortality being now dependent only upon the ability, when the need arises, to provide a different instantiating substance for the same person. Moreover, this immortality is possible in *this very world*, rather than in some postulated world to which the decay of the body was somehow supposed to give the person (in the form of an eternal soul-substance) access.

Leaving aside such utopian considerations, however, we need to see how well this non-substantial identification of persons fares in the philosophical arena in comparison with the Substantial view. There are well-known objections to the idea that the identity of persons consists solely in psychological unity, or even indeed that such unity is a necessary condition of personal identity. Bernard Williams for one has suggested that consideration of certain hypothetical circumstances shows that bodily continuity can over-ride the loss of psychological unity; the latter is not necessary for personal identity, physical continuity alone being sufficient.[13]

Certainly such cases as Williams describes bring out the peculiar attachment we have to our own bodies. But they perhaps do not show that what matters is the persistence of one and the same body. Our reaction to such cases might equally show only that what matters is the persistence of that which I am able to regard as being *my own* body. The two are not equivalent. The difference is between a *de re* and a *de dicto* reading of 'my identity with my own body'. It might be a matter not of remaining identical with that physical substance which is *now* the referent of the term 'my own body', that is with a particular physical body, but rather of continuing to identify with what *at any given time* I judge to be the referent of the term 'my own body'.

We can imagine that what I judge to be the referent of the term 'my body' can change over time. Indeed, it does, through natural decay and renewal of our cells. This natural change of course by and large happens behind our cognitive backs; nevertheless it is enough to show that what matters is not that we remain in the same body, *de re*, but that we remain at any given time in that body which satisfies the same description, as 'my body' – the same body *de dicto*. Furthermore, we can imagine ourselves to change in such a way that we are made more aware of the gradual changes of body constitution. Having one relatively small part of my body surgically replaced with another, whether organic or electronic, would not bother me, so long as the change was indeed confined to my material constitution, and was not of a sort that could have any further disruptive ramifications. The modified substance would still count as my body. And after a while it would not be my body only *despite* the novel element introduced; for the transplanted element would have become incorporated into the referent that I pick out by the description 'my body' in just the way, and indeed in part because of the way that the transplant had become part of my *psychological* history.[14] And it is easy to imagine that if the transplant procedure were then repeated on some other organ, and so on until all my original organs were replaced with silicon chips and the like, then that which I regard as *my body* would gradually and very naturally come to refer to an object quite different from the original in terms of substantial constitution. This gradual body transplant thus preserves 'my identity with my body', interpreted *de dicto*, without preserving it on the *de re* interpretation. And it seems from our response to the prospect of such gradual transplant that what matters to us might be only that I retain my body in this *de dicto*, rather than in the *de re*, sense.

On the other hand the radical (abrupt) body change envisaged by Williams, even if we assume that the two bodies involved are very similar, contravenes both the stronger *de re* reading of my identity with my body, and the weaker *de dicto* reading. I am asked to imagine my unity of consciousness being transplanted not only to another body, not identical with my own now, but indeed to one which at the moment of transplant, were I able to have thoughts, would not be the referent of what I then regarded as my own body. I would not have had time to grow accustomed to it, to come to regard it as 'my own'. For this to be possible the physical change must be such as to be integrated into my psychological history, so that I can come to associate certain experiences with, and anchor certain memories in, that body and indeed in its different appearance if necessary. (It thus begins to seem, not surprisingly, that there is a link between the unity of consciousness, and my special relationship with what

I call 'my body'. Once this is appreciated we begin to see that the radical transplant, in not allowing for bodily identity in either *de re* or *de dicto* senses, might thereby preclude preservation of unity of consciousness and psychological continuity as well. But let us leave aside this claim.)

It seems then as though cases of radical transplantation do conflate two senses in which the preservation of one's body might seem to matter to personhood. And it seems that it is the weaker – *de dicto* – sense that sustains our intuitive reaction to the body-swap thought experiment, while it is only the stronger – *de re* – sense that leads to the conclusion that strict substantial identity plays a central constitutive role. And to the extent that this line of argument is sustained, it seems that the non-substantial view of persons, based on the unity of consciousness in abstraction from the substance in which it is instantiated (except in so far as that substance affects the unity of consciousness), should be examined further for adequacy in its own right, holding off objections based simply on the apparent appeal of the substantial option.

It is at this point that we might feel the need to move from comparing theories narrowly with one another, merely as competing accounts of persons, to consider how well each view fits with our broader beliefs about the natural world in which persons reside.

Before proceeding along these lines, it is worth noticing that to the extent that unity of consciousness is taken to be constitutive of personhood, such that personal *identity* does not involve anything beyond such unity, it must be recognized that questions of personal identity may not in all cases be appropriate, since personal identity may not always be determinate. If, as Kant claimed, my unity of consciousness is not anchored in the unity of any given substance, it can be passed from one embodiment to the next; and it is therefore conceivable that, in being passed on from a given instantiation, it could be duplicated, so that it is passed on simultaneously and equally to two subsequent embodiments. Each of the two resulting persons will have qualitatively identical unities of consciousness. Although as persons they will differ from one another from that time on, each of them is equally the continuation of my unity of consciousness prior to the duplication. Each would have equal claim to being (a continuation of) me. There just would be no answer to the question which of the two resulting persons 'really' *is* me. (Of course, in the normal run of events, questions of personal identity do have determinate answers; the case being envisaged is, as far as we can tell, entirely imaginary at the present time.)

These sorts of cases, and the idea that personal identity should unproblematically be considered indeterminate in such cases, are most familiar from the writings of Derek Parfit.[15] However, his view is quite different, and more austere than the view being canvassed here. He does not hold that there is any special feature, substantial or non-substantial, which makes all my experiences particularly mine; there just is no question of ownership that needs to be settled. It is from this that he concludes that in cases of fission, such as the one just described, there should be no expectation of an answer to the question which person is *me* (that is, which has retained some special feature).[16]

The trouble with this Reductionist view is that when examined in the context of broader philosophical questions, it turns out that it gives rise to serious problems.[17] For the Reductionist there is nothing more than atoms of experience, unified not *internally* in virtue of some common owner, but merely *externally* in virtue of a degree of objective psychological continuity and connectedness. But if our experience were as Parfit envisages, then each experience, no matter how similar it might 'objectively' be to some other, would have no access to any other. There would be no common subjective owner ranging over both, to whom they both belong. The experience I have at any moment, in any modality, is then quite isolated, a self-contained moment of experience, just in so far as there is no common subject which then goes on to experience the next moment.

On this view, each moment of experience is a unity of consciousness unto itself, no matter how *similar* it is to later moments of experience. But on this view there then is no room to explain how it is that our experience can be of a single objective world that holds together in our experience over time. Without any continuous subject of consciousness, there can be no *experience of the endurance* of objects such as this table, or the universe in which it exists. Yet clearly there is experience of the world as an objective enduring domain. Parfit's psychological atomism, whereby moments of experience are without any common ownership linking them internally into a single unity of consciousness, cannot allow for this. It would seem then that if we are to account for our experience of an objective world, we cannot afford to be Reductionists to the extent of denying some unifying thread of consciousness.

In fact Parfitian Reductionists would respond to this by pointing out that while there is no unifying subject, substantial or not, which persists over time and is the one bearer of the various experiences, nevertheless the various experiences over time are not utterly disconnected as the above suggests. They do not just *happen* to manifest qualitative similarity such as can count as psychological continuity; they do this because of a certain *causal connectedness* which leads from one experience to the next. Instead of an internal link, by some direct access of a common subject, there is an external causal link between one experience and another. This causal link is construed differently on what Parfit calls the *narrow Reductionist* view, and the *wide Reductionist* view. On the narrow Reductionist view the causal link must be what it normally is; viz. the continued functioning of the human body. On the wide Reductionist view any causal link will do.[18]

The trouble with this is that on either narrow or wide reading the external causal links between experiences are not themselves experienced. They are provided from the outside, by a side-ways on description. Because of this there is insufficient material here to account for *subjective* unity of experience across time that is required to allow for experience of an objective domain persisting from one experience to the next. On this proposed view there would be two experiences, two momentary snapshots, one of which at best contained both (a) what was taken to be a trace of the other, and (b) a story of a causal connection between them. There would be no telling that the experience containing (a) and (b) genuinely reached back to some prior experience referenced in (a), to which this later experience really is causally linked in the way specified in (b). However, let us for the present leave this danger of losing our experience of an enduring objective world, since it will emerge more clearly later, when we return to discuss this kind of psychological atomism.

The immediately preceding considerations reveal that in deciding on the right philosophical treatment of the self, we cannot refrain from considering the bearing that the proffered treatment might have on broader philosophical questions. In particular, one constraint on any theory of the self is that it should not, in the course of proffering a solution to specific questions at hand, generate insoluble problems elsewhere.

It is precisely in the light of this constraint that the Lean option can seem most promising. The Substantial view, identifying the conscious self with a substance, raises thereby a variety of other problems. If we take the Cartesian version of the Substantial view, in which the mind is an immaterial substance, we are confronted with all the problems of the traditional mind-body problem; basically, that of how such sublime minds can get their hands dirty. But even other forms of the Substantial theory, that identify persons with material rather than spiritual substances, and so avoid the Cartesian mind-body problem, still face the problem that they open the door to scepticism about the external world.

If the thinking self is simply identical with a substance, of one sort or another, then as long as that substance is preserved, so is the thinking subject. That means that if the entire world were to be annihilated, but that substance somehow survived, the person could go on thinking and experiencing. It means that the existence of the person as an item in the world, is not dependent on that world. This opens up the possibility of solipsism, methodological or otherwise: We can start our philosophical inquiry by assuming an individual person taken on its own, going about the business of thinking thoughts, formulating desires, and generally living a coherent mental life. We can make sense of that individual without making any assumptions about the nature or indeed the existence of anything beyond that substance.[19]

But once that starting point is granted, we seem to have got hold of an impossible end of the stick. For given the independence of the individual, how can we ever know that that individual is not systematically wrong about the rest of the world? And so it is only a short step from methodological solipsism to the emergence of the sceptical question.[20] It is important to note that the move does not require the Cartesian commitment to dualism. It arises simply from the identification of the experiencing subject as a substance, whether it be material or spiritual.

Of course, not every non-substantial identification of persons will preclude such 'Cartesian' individualism and the problems that arise from it. We can imagine a functionalist account of consciousness, which appeals in the functional specification to nothing outside the individual's instantiating hardware. The point is that, while this confinement was compelling when the identification of persons was with substances, there is room to avoid it on the non-substantial (broadly functionalist) account. Indeed, this is precisely what Kant took advantage of.

In Kant's use of it, the Lean strategy was designed precisely to avoid this Cartesian individualism, which results from the substantial view, and so too to avoid the sceptical predicament which Kant thinks results from it. On the Kantian view, the substantialist (and in particular the Cartesian) makes the mistake of assuming that one can start with the autonomy of an experiencing agent, and then proceed to deal with the question of how that individual can know that the world 'out there' is as it seems to be, or indeed that there is a world at all, or that it will not look utterly different tomorrow. The Kantian contends that we are in fact never in a position to have that worry, since there is no possibility of having secured the conditions for the individual person's unity of consciousness, while still being unsure as to whether the conditions for experience of an objective domain have been satisfied. The mistake according to Kant is in not realizing that, by the time we have secured the subject end of the subject-object dichotomy, it is too late for doubts about the objective end, since the two are inextricably linked.[21] It is, essentially, because of the background assumption of the substantial view of the self that we fall prey to the illusion of methodological solipsism, and the related sense that, secure in our possession of our mental lives, we can ask sceptically about the rest of the world.

This latter claim perhaps requires some clarification. After all, David Hume is the philosopher who did more than any other to debunk the substantial theory of the self; and yet Hume is also the philosopher who more than any other raised this sceptical spectre before Kant's eyes. It seems odd then to suggest that it is because of adherence to the substantial view that scepticism about the external world arises. To resolve this apparent tension it is enough to note that the Substantial view is sufficient, but that is not to say that it is necessary, for those sceptical doubts to get off the ground. But in fact the Kantian might rather like to say that there are two different mistakes to which he can point. Substantialists like Descartes make one; Hume makes another. On the substantial view, the sceptical problem would indeed follow, but it is a mistake to take the substantial view. Hume avoids making that mistake, but makes the other mistake of thinking that the unity of consciousness – which alone, and somewhat mysteriously, binds all my thoughts together – is secured in such a way as to leave us still in a position to doubt the unity of the objective world.

Of course it might also be thought that Hume is being even more reductionist than this suggests, by not leaving any room even for that unity of consciousness as the binding of the bundle. But this is not the case. Hume accepts that there are more than just perceptions: there are *bundles* of perceptions. He accepts that I experience all my perceptions to be mine. He merely confesses to be baffled by what it is that makes them mine, what it is that unifies the consciousness of them, given that no substance, and no other real (that is, external) connection can be found.[22] And it is indeed precisely because Hume is baffled about what renders the Lean solution possible, that he makes the mistake of thinking that the unity of consciousness, the fact that all my thoughts are mine, could be retained in a way that still leaves room for sceptical doubt about the external world.

Kant can be seen as attempting to answer Hume's puzzle about how the unity of consciousness is possible. And his answer reveals Hume's mistake. Kant's contention is that once we understand *how* it is that a variety of experiences are all mine, on the non-substantial view, it turns out that there is no room for doubting the existence of an independent enduring external world. The realization that the unity of consciousness can be seen to be a functional feature dependent on certain experienced features of the environment, rather than on features of a substance, meant according to Kant that there was no room to worry that the individual might retain all his or her experiential capacities independently of what happens in the surrounding world.

In this way, the Kantian treatment of the mind is supposed to provide an answer to scepticism. This in itself makes it particularly valuable as a contender theory of mind. It *solves* the kind of problem that the substantial model of the mind *introduced*, as Kant himself was aware. What we have here is an extra constraint, a sort of prerequisite for anything that is to count as a model for the mind. The essential question is: What is the contribution of any proposed model to either the solution or creation of other philosophical problems? The underlying idea being that where two or more competing theories are available, both of which may do a job equally well, but one of which renders a sceptical result, we should reject it and opt for the other, on the assumption that scepticism is more likely a product of our incorrect thinking than the truth about the world.[23]

So far we have seen the promise in this respect of the Lean (non-substantial) alternative, and in particular of the Kantian version of it. Now the question is whether the Kantian model of mind is indeed to be preferred as correct on these grounds. Does it do a better job than the Substantial or the Reductionist models in clearing wider metaphysical tangles rather than creating them? If not, some alternative other than any we have canvassed will be needed.

Let us turn back to the Kantian model. Kant, as we have indicated, like Hume, assumes that we start with particular experiences – we might call this starting point psychological atomism – all of which are owned by one and the same subject of experience. I wish to point out two problems that result for Kant's anti-sceptical project, both of which have their origins in this psychological atomism.

The first results from the fact that Kant takes such atomism as a premiss, and from that argues that whatever is necessary to bind those psychological atoms together into a single consciousness – that they are so bound being a further premiss – is thereby shown to be as certain as that of unity of consciousness. Since we do not doubt that unity of consciousness, we cannot doubt the necessary conditions for it. And the experience of an objective world of middle-size objects emerges as just one such necessary condition. So there must be an objective world of middle size objects. But the question is whether the first premiss – that of psychological atomism – is right.

The argument does not require just the unity of consciousness, but also that that unity is not primitive; that it is the result of combining under one ownership a bundle of different experiences. The way Kant puts it is, that all my experiences are mine. This is where the assumption of atomism comes in. But what if that assumption is challenged? What I am suggesting might be called into doubt is not that we have unity of consciousness, but only that it is comprised of atoms of experience which require unification in a certain way.

If that doubt is even plausible, then the rest of the deduction, which shows ultimately that there must be experience of an enduring law-governed objective world for all those atoms of experience to be held together in that way, falls from certainty at the first step. For it is then open to the sceptic, say to a revised Hume, to suggest that if there just are after all no atoms of that sort, there is no need for the conditions required for the unification of such atoms to be met. The unity of consciousness does not then depend on unity of the objective world (as it would on the atomistic conception of the former unity). It follows then that such unity of consciousness could withstand the collapse of unity in the objective world. So it becomes conceivable again that there might well be no objective world tomorrow.

Kant's line is that such loss of objectivity tomorrow would render my own experience even less than a dream. But in claiming this he is of course not offering a counter-argument, he is simply putting the same argument differently (in *modus tollens*, rather than *modus ponens* form). If unity of consciousness implies experience of a well-ordered objective world,[24] then without the latter, all the atoms of experience would be unbound, they would lose their unifying string, they would be nothing *for me*; I would not be around. I would have been reduced to even less than the predicament of the Cartesian dreamer; the loss of the objective world would also be my death. Hence, on the Kantian view, there is no need to worry that I might be deceived about the objective world. If I am around, it is too; if it goes, I do too.

But the point remains that if my unity of consciousness is not a product of atomist combination after all, then the fact that the sudden absence of the world of enduring objects would render such combination impossible, would not matter to me. My unity of consciousness will be preserved on this view in so far as consciousness is simply given whole as, say, an organic stream. So on this conception

Kant's response to the sceptic does not work. The sceptic merely has to go 'Jamesian', giving up psychological atomism, and he has thereby unhooked us from the train of the Kantian deduction.

So much for the first problem. Now for the second problem that arises for the Kantian view of the unity of consciousness because of the presupposed psychological atomism. Let us say that such atomism *is* right. Does it help Kant any? The problem is as follows: If the plurality of atomistic experiences is presupposed as a premiss, and the argument is that to be united into a unity of consciousness what is needed is an empirically real object domain, then the following question arises: How do we know that those moments are genuinely so united into a unity of consciousness?[25] It might be the case that each moment belongs to a different unity of consciousness, it is just that the later experience, at time t_2, includes the content of the experience at t_1 – but that is *internal* to the content of t_2. There is in fact no joint owner of t_1 and t_2, no common thread that causally connects the two. The consequence is that t_2 would be as it is even if t_1 had been different. An embellishment of Parfit's teletransportation story would exemplify this situation. (It is here that we pick up the problems raised earlier in discussion of the Reductionist view; they apply as much to Parfit as they do to Kant.)

In the teletransportation story, the Teletransporter sends me to Mars at the speed of light: I simply enter a machine, press the right button, whereupon I lose consciousness and wake up what seems like a moment later.[26] I am now on Mars. The process has in fact taken an hour. It involved the machine destroying my body on earth, recording as it does so every structural feature of every cell. That information is then radioed at the speed of light to the Replicator on Mars. Once the information arrives, the Replicator creates a new body (and brain) in full conformity to the detailed blue-print. This is the body in which I wake up, on Mars.

The embellishment is this: it is possible to imagine that the radio signals enter a large magnetic field *en route* to Mars, which totally destroys the information. However, by some remarkable coincidence, a magnetic field somewhere else in the universe spontaneously gives rise to a sequence of signals which reach the Replicator on Mars at just the time that the information *about me* would have reached it. The coincidence is such that the information contained in the arriving signals is identical in content to the information about *me* that was destroyed. The replicator goes to work, and within less than an hour has produced a new body (and brain), along the precise lines of the information received. This is the body in which I wake up at what seems to me like t_2.

Now there is of course no genuine unity of consciousness here. The person that wakes up at t_2 would have been as he is, with all the memories that are in fact qualitatively identical with mine, even if I had never existed, either at t_1 or ever before that. And of course once this is considered, it becomes clear that we are in no position to answer the sceptic who suggests that for all we know, in the relevant respects this might be just the situation regarding any two temporal moments of our consciousness. Our consciousness at any given point could be the simulated product of deceiving Replicators; it could simply be created anew at every moment.

Of course it seems that what we need to insist on is some causal link that holds between me-at-t_1 and me-at-t_2. But here it must be noticed that to the person that wakes up on Mars in my story it will seem that there *is* a causal link of just this sort. And in this respect it is only the spatio-temporal distance, rather than any difference of principle, that distinguishes that bizarre case from the case of ordinary consciousness over time. The fact that there seems to us to be a link with a past self is no evidence that there is one. As Hume realized, we are in no position to discover a *real* (external) relation between the two temporal stages.

The unity of consciousness over time is, in such a scenario, mere illusion. Now since that unity of consciousness is a premiss of Kant's Transcendental Deduction, and it turns out that it might be an illusion, it follows that the rest of the deduction is no more secure than it is. The problem results from the possibility of carrying sceptical doubt back into the premisses. If there is no genuine unity of consciousness, there is no need for an abiding objective domain to sustain it either.

It might be said that what is being envisaged here is merely transcendental illusion, rather than illusion in the empirically real world. But this is not quite right, at least in the way Kant uses his terms. The illusion is much closer to home than Kant's use of the term 'transcendental illusion' would allow. Furthermore, it is real enough to undercut the conclusion of the transcendental deduction.[27] For we now do not even know that there is one abiding empirical substance in the world, and that the causal laws go on applying throughout. They might well not. We from the inside might not experience the change in substance, or the fact that causality does not hold uniformly; and that is where Kant is right. But that is not to say that we cannot, from the inside, conceive that we are being misled in a very specific way – indeed, even to the extent of conceiving, as we have done here, that *this* very empirical world, in space and time, with which we are in contact, might be created anew at every minute. We are then getting *it* (this world) systematically wrong. Now this must count for Kant as empirical idealism, and is precisely what he wanted to avoid. For scepticism has now broken into the spatio-temporal world of experience, as opposed to being confined to the thing-in-itself, which he is happy to concede is unknowable. There is then no room for complacency in the face of this problem. The distinction between the empirically real world of which we can have knowledge, and the transcendentally ideal world of which we are in principle totally ignorant, has broken down.

I said that the problem was with Kant's psychological atomism. He has left himself committed to the premiss that different moments (not merely in the temporal sense) of experience must be tied together. This leaves him with the problem that they might not be tied together, that instead there might be only the illusion from within any one of those moments that they are so tied together. That is, my sense of being a unified being within and across moments of time might be an illusion that is reconstituted at each moment of experience.

It might look, then, as though it is Kant's psychological atomism that is at the root of the problem. This might suggest that we would be better off if we discarded it. Unfortunately, done in any straightforward way, simply by giving up psychological atomism and opting for psychological holism, this would only make problems worse; it would lead to the first problem outlined above (pp. 199–201).

Moreover, these sorts of problems that would result for the Lean view from the resort to psychological holism are precisely the problems that faced the Substantial view. Whereas the problems that result for the Lean view if it adheres to psychological atomism are of the sort that faced the Reductionist view. Either way then, the Lean option seems not to fulfil the initial promise of offering a view of persons that avoids the traditional sceptical worries.

To the extent that we think an adequate view of persons should avoid creating such sceptical problems, it would seem that there is still work to be done. We do not yet have even a reasonable candidate theory.

Reading

Locke, J., *An Essay Concerning Human Understanding*, ed. P. H. Nidditch (Oxford: Clarendon Press, 1975).

Hume, D., *A Treatise of Human Nature*, ed. R. H. Nidditch (Oxford: Clarendon Press, 1978).

Kant, I., *Critique of Pure Reason*, trans. N. Kemp Smith (London: Macmillan, 1973).

Perry, J. (ed.), *Personal Identity* (University of California Press, 1975).

Putnam, H., *Mind, Language and Reality. Philosophical Papers*, *Volume 2* (Cambridge University Press, 1975).

Parfit, D., *Reasons and Persons* (Oxford: Clarendon Press, 1984).

Williams, B., 'The Self and the Future', in *Problems of the Self* (Cambridge University Press, 1973; also in Perry.)

James, W., *The Principles of Psychology* (London: Macmillan and Co., 1901).

Notes

1. Persons in the legal sense, for example, would obviously involve some essential reference to responsibility, which is not obviously relevant to the present concern.

2. We might of course recognize that to the extent that all such attempts founder, those who would have had us eliminate consciousness from the outset might see this failure as our just come-uppance.

3. In setting out these options I have adhered more or less to an historical ordering, which also represents a gradual shift from the most full-blooded and obvious account, to the more restricted and sophisticated alternatives to which philosophers were gradually forced to retreat. Consequently the order is different from that of the analytical classification of the options given above.

4. Or, more accurately, the unity of consciousness is the way in which a certain cluster of experiences (thoughts, sensations) is held together, as distinct from any other experiences, in virtue of the fact that all and only these experiences are linked by a common subjective indexical, both synchronically and diachronically, across the various sensory modalities and cognitive acts.

5. This is distinct from unity of consciousness. For one thing, unity of consciousness involves unity at a given time, which memory continuity leaves out. More importantly, continuity of memory can be taken to mean continuity of memory contents, rather than of the remembering agent. This is how it is taken on the Reductionist View, which Parfit adopts. Continuity of memory is then the sort of thing that is preserved when memories are passed from one generation to

the next; and clearly this does not preserve unity of consciousness, of the remembering agent. It is not clear that Locke shares this view with Parfit. At any rate I will be quoting here a 'Locke' who does not take that view, but rather sees continuity of memory as much closer to unity of consciousness.

6. Plato's theory of the eternality of souls, divorced from his doctrine of recollection, leaves room to think of Socrates and Saul being different persons despite sharing the same soul. Of course, the doctrine of recollection complicates this, precisely by asserting that there is something like continuity of memory that with due care can be regained. On this see Locke, Book II, ch.27, section 14.

7. Locke, op. cit., section 13.

8. Kant, *Critique of Pure Reason*, A363.

9. A363–4. I have omitted the concluding sentence of this footnote – 'And yet it would not have been one and the same person in all these states.' This is confusing. What he should have said is that it would not have been one and the same soul-substance that would have been identified as the same person in all these cases.

To clarify the issue, recall that Kant in this paralogism is not in fact denying its first premiss, that unity of self-consciousness constitutes personal identity; rather he is concerned to argue that such unity of consciousness does not prove that there is one underlying soul substance which can be identified as the person or self.

10. See H. Putnam, 'Philosophy and Our Mental Life', in Putnam, *Philosophical Papers*, II, 291–303. See also chapter 4 of this volume.

11. Obviously we ought to be more perturbed, as Hume was, by the fact that this commitment does not square with his empiricism.

12. The crucial factor being, presumably, that the substance must have the appropriate causal powers.

13. Bernard Williams, 'The Self and the Future', in *Problems of the Self*. Williams describes a hypothetical case of two people, A and B, who simultaneously undergo a process whereby A's total psychological set (character traits, beliefs, memories) is extracted from A's body and transferred via a machine to B's body; while at the same time the A-body receives the psychological software that has been similarly extracted from B's body. This impersonal description of the case might make it seem that it can be regarded – in accordance with the non-substantial view of persons – as two persons having exchanged bodies. But Williams argues convincingly that looked at from the perspective of one of the persons involved, say A's, upon entering the laboratory his self-regarding concern will be for the future well-being of the A-body, rather than of the B-body, despite the total psychological discontinuity that is about to

be induced in the A-body by the transfer of psychological contents. That its contents are transferred to B's body, which *will* then be psychologically continuous with A, is little comfort to A, whose anxiety over his pending psychological disruption is not reduced by the fact that an equally acute disruption is in store for B.

There are equally cases which bring out opposing reactions (see Parfit, pp. 234–36). It is in any event not clear how seriously we should take our intuitive responses to such fanciful hypotheses, insofar as it is difficult to identify what it is about a given case that gives rise to those responses in the first place.

14. I have a friend, who was involved in a traffic accident when he was a small boy. One of his legs had to be amputated. Yet it would surprise me if I heard people describe him as having one leg. For those who grew up with him, he has *two* legs, and the fact that they are not made of the same stuff seems wholly distant. I mention this here because of a further fact: he recently told me – in a discussion quite unrelated to this philosophical issue – that he regards the mechanical leg as part of 'his body'. When he takes it off at night, and looks at it from across the room, or the children refer to it as 'Daddy's leg', it feels to him that the item referred to is not so much a *possession* of his, but a part, albeit a separable part, of *his body*.

15. In particular, the reader might consult his *Reasons and Persons*, which brings together and develops threads first expounded in his earlier papers.

16. He does not bring out the point that even if there is some special feature that unifies the person, it might – as we have just seen – be such that there is still not always a determinate answer to questions of personal identity in those special cases.

17. Parfit characterizes views which reduce personal identity either to the continuous existence of a physical entity (e.g. enough of the brain so that it remains the brain of a living person) or to psychological continuity as 'Reductionist'. By this he means to emphasize the *reduction* of a person's identity over time to the holding of certain facts which can be described in an *impersonal* way. Parfit's goal is to give an impersonal description of what constitutes the unity of a person's life.

18. See Parfit, 204–17.

19. It might be argued that such individualism is wrong for reasons put forward in recent years by Hilary Putnam, Tyler Burge, and others, to the effect that meanings are not in the head, so that even if the person is identified with a substance of one sort or another, having thoughts requires the interaction of that substance with the environment. On these grounds it has been argued that

methodological solipsism is false. If those grounds are good, methodological solipsism is indeed false. But that has nothing to do with the commitment of the Substantial view to such methodological solipsism. If those grounds hold good then either thinking is not required for something to be an experiencing subject, which perhaps seems absurd, or the experiencing subject involves some other feature – a relational feature defined by its interaction with the environment – over and above the instantiating substance. We have then shifted away from the purely Substantial conception, towards the Lean functionalist one. (The result might be some sort of hybrid.)

20. What we then propose to do with the sceptical question – regard it as challenge or succumb to its force – is not of relevance here.

21. See Kant's 'Refutation of Idealism' in the *Critique of Pure Reason*, B274–B279.

22. See Hume, *A Treatism of Human Knowledge* (Oxford: Clarendon Press, 1978), Book I, Part IV, Section VI, 251–63; Appendix, 633–6.

23. Why we should in fact think this is an interesting question, which I leave aside here.

24. Kant in fact holds not only this conditional, but the stronger bi-conditional; not only that unity of consciousness implies unity of the experienced objective world, but also that the unity of the experienced objective world implies unity of consciousness. It is because of the latter conditional that loss of the unity of consciousness entails losing the experience of a unified objective world. This is the case we saw in discussing the unacceptable consequences of Parfit's reductionist account which seems to tolerate the loss of that unifying thread of common ownership.

25. That is, here we grant the first premiss and concentrate on the problem that then results regarding Kant's second premiss; see p. 199 above.

26. Parfit, *Reasons and Persons*, 199f.

27. Or at least the conclusions of the transcendental deduction taken in conjunction with the more specific yield on the far side of the Schematism chapter.

I wish to thank Nicholas Nathan, Lucy O'Brien and the editor, Ray Tallis, for helpful comments and suggestions.